Corporate Wellness

Spiritual and Secular Principles in Corporate Turnaround and Transformation

Dr Michael Teng

Published in 2009 by
Corporate Turnaround Centre Pte Ltd.

Printed in Singapore
by Markono Print Media Pte Ltd.

9   8   7   6   5   4   3   2   1
09

ISBN   978-981-08-2213-2

Table of Contents

Vision, feedback and action – three meals a day keeps the corporate doctor away (James 2:14-25 – "In the same way, faith by itself, if it is not accompanied by action, is dead.")

When you drive an ambulance, be sure you know where you are going (Romans 8:28 – "And we know that in all things God works for the good of those who love him, who have been called according to his purpose")

Planning

Companies without strategies are heading for tragedies (Genesis 11:6, Proverbs 21:5 – "The plans of the diligent lead to profit as surely as haste leads to poverty.")

If you want good health, plan for it. If you want great health, plan and do a post-mortem. (Isaiah 43:18 – "Forget the former things; do not dwell on the past.")

Clone your successes by planning your succession. (Exodus 4:1-14 – "Who gave man his mouth? Who makes him deaf or mute? Who gives him sight or makes him blind? Is it not I, the Lord? .. Now go; I will help you speak and will teach you what to say.")

Thinking rationally before you decide will help you to sleep well (Proverbs 23:23, Proverbs 18:15, Proverbs 20:18, Luke 14:31: What king, when he sets out to meet another king in battle, will not first sit down and take counsel.)

Financial

There is a strong parallel between physical and fiscal health (Matthew 6:21 for where your treasure is, there your heart will be also)

Inventory is the burial ground (Proverbs 21:5, Proverbs 12:24, Proverbs 10:4 Poor is he who works with diligent hand, but the hand of the diligent makes rich)

Casual with receivables, you may land up as a casualty (Romans 13:7, Matthew 18:21-34 – "Give everyone what you owe him: If you owe taxes, pay taxes; if revenue, then revenue; if respect, then respect; if honor, then honor")

By the time the financial numbers show red, the company is already bleeding profusely (Jeremiah 22:13 Woe to him who builds his house without righteousness and his upper rooms without justice.)

Control

The key to successful turnaround is early intervention. (Matthew 6:33, Psalm 139:13 – "But seek first his kingdom and his righteousness, and all these things will be given to you as well.")

Companies should go for regular health checks. (James 3:1, 1 Corinthians 3:12-15 – "If what he has built survives, he will receive his reward. If it is burned up, he will suffer loss; he himself will be saved, but only as one escaping through the flames.")

Knowing the type of viruses that are plaguing the company is half the cure. (Deuteronomy 29:1-18 – "Make sure there is no man or woman, clan or tribe among you today whose heart turns away from the Lord our God to go and worship the gods of those nations; make sure there is no root among you that produces such bitter poison")

Tradition and past business assumptions may be the root causes of the disease in the ailing company. (Micah 6 – "You have observed the statutes of Omri and all the practices of Ahab's house, and you have followed their traditions. Therefore I will give you over to ruin and your people to derision; you will bear the scorn of the nations.")

To treat the symptoms, know your competitors and customers. To eliminate the root cause, know the market. (Proverbs 24:17-18 – "Do not gloat when your enemy falls; when he stumbles, do not let your heart rejoice, or the Lord will see and disapprove and turn his wrath away from him.")

To understand the disease, learn to be the patient. (Hebrews 2:17-18 "Because he himself suffered when he was tempted, he is able to help those who are being tempted")

People tend to do what you inspect rather than what you expect (Matthew 26:36-45 -"Then he returned to his disciples and found them sleeping. "Could you men not keep watch with me for one hour?" Jesus asked Peter.")

Life is Simple. And in business, the simpler the better (Psalm 19: 7 The decrees of the Lord are trustworthy, making wise the simple)

The greatest lesson is to learn faster than your competitors. (Proverbs 24:30-37 – Solomon: "I applied my heart to what I observed and learned a lesson from what I saw: A little sleep, a little slumber, a little folding of the hands to rest- and poverty will come on you like a bandit and scarcity like an armed man.")

Do not suffer from competitive myopia. Have 20/20 vision. (Ephesians 6:11, 1 Peter 5:8 – "Be self-controlled and alert. Your enemy the devil prowls around like a roaring lion looking for someone to devour.")

Just as a heart ailment is a major killer, competition is the silent killer leading to corporate failures. (Ephesians 6:13 Therefore put on the full armor of God, so that when the day of evil comes, you may be able to stand your ground...)

You can have wealth and wisdom, but you better have health. Similarly, you can have performance and quality but you better have pricing.. (Matthew 26:6-13 – "The poor you will always have with you, but you will not always have me. When she poured this perfume on my body, she did it to prepare me for burial.")

Your low cost competitors are not after your crumbs, they want to eat your lunch. (Numbers 25:1-5 – "While Israel was staying in Shittim, the men began to indulge in sexual immorality with Moabite women, who invited them to the sacrifices to their gods.")

The tongue is the window of your health. (James 3:5-6, Psalm 52:2, Proverbs 18:21 – "The tongue has the power of life and death, and those who love it will eat its fruit.")

When you are thirsty and water is available, you are not going to argue over the temperature of the water. (Proverbs 17:14 – "Starting a quarrel is like breaching a dam; so drop the matter before a dispute breaks out.")

Rumour is like the SARS virus, it can spread by mouth, by phone and sometimes pop up in the most unusual places. (Proverbs 16:28, John 21:22-24 – "A perverse man stirs up dissension, and a gossip separates close friends.")

Dead bodies stink from the head. (Exodus 5-12 – "Then the LORD said to Moses, "Now you will see what I will do to Pharaoh: Because of my mighty hand he will let them go; because of my mighty hand he will drive them out of his country.")

Board of directors should act like 'T cells' in the body to protect shareholder interest. (1 Peter 4:3, Matthew 6:7 – "For you have spent enough time in the past doing what pagans choose to do—living in debauchery, lust, drunkenness, orgies, carousing and detestable idolatry.")

Many chief executives pursue the four Ps - pay, power, perks and prestige rather than profits for the company. (Ezekiel 28:1-19, 26:1-21 – To Hiram: "Your heart became proud on account of your beauty, and you corrupted your wisdom because of your splendor. So I threw you to the earth; I made a spectacle of you before kings.")

Stage 3: Treatment

If you need surgery, call in the surgeon. (Mark 5:21-34, Matthew 11:28-29 – "Come to me, all you who are weary and burdened, and I will give you rest. Take my yoke upon you and learn from me, for I am gentle and humble in heart, and you will find rest for your souls.")

Do not depend solely on the doctor in the house to do the surgery. (Genesis 32:1-21, Ephesians 2:8-9 – Jacob: "Save me, I pray, from the hand of my brother Esau, for I am afraid he will come and attack me, and also the mothers with their children.")

Accomplish your dream, have a good team. (Matthew 10 – "He called his twelve disciples to him and gave them authority to drive out evil spirits and to heal every disease and sickness.")

The surgeon operates on only one patient at a time. Similarly, a sick company needs to concentrate on its core competence. (Hebrews 12; 2 Let us fix our eyes on Jesus, the author and perfecter of our faith...)

In times of trouble, do not become schizophrenic but let your focus be emphatic. (Philippians 3:14 – "I press on toward the goal to win the prize for which God has called me heavenward in Christ Jesus.")

Page 13

Building up your cash reserves is like eating calcium-rich food. It fortifies your bones later in life. (Proverbs 21:20, 2 Corinthians 9:6 – "In the house of the wise are stores of choice food and oil, but a foolish man devours all he has.")

There are three certainties in life: deaths, taxes and changes. (Genesis 12:1-7 "The Lord had said to Abram, "Leave your country, your people and your father's household and go to the land I will show you.")

The business that considers itself immune to changes will soon find itself immune to business. (Romans 12:3 Do not think of yourself more highly than you ought.)

A healthy culture is the immunity of a healthy organisation. (1 Corinthians 16:15, Isaiah 7:9, Roman 10:9, Colossians 1:21-23 – "If you do not stand firm in your faith, you will not stand at all.")

Everybody wants to go to heaven, nobody wants to die. Everybody wants to succeed, nobody wants to fail. (Romans 5:3-5, Hebrews 10:36, James 1:12 – "Blessed is the man who perseveres under trial, because when he has stood the test, he will receive the crown of life that God has promised to those who love him.")

Egotism is the anaesthesia that dulls the business sense. (Proverbs 16:5, Isaiah 13:11, Psalm 25:9, Psalm 149:4 – "The Lord detests all the proud of heart. Be sure of this: They will not go unpunished.")

An information system is the backbone and the nervous system of the company. (Job 12:22 - "He reveals the deep things of darkness and brings deep shadows into the light.")

Be innovative or be in a coma. (Genesis 1:1-31, Isaiah 65:17 – "Behold, I will create new heavens and a new earth. The former things will not be remembered, nor will they come to mind.")

Background of the Author

Dr Mike Teng is the author of a best-selling book "*Corporate Turnaround: Nursing a sick company back to health*", in 2002 which is also translated into the Bahasa Indonesia. In 2006, he authored another book entitled, "*Corporate Wellness: 101 Principles in Turnaround and Transformation.* He also published in 2007/2008 seven management books, namely entitled: *Internet Turnaround: The Use of Internet Marketing to Turnaround Companies; Training Manual: Corporate Turnaround and Transformation Methodology; Link Baiting to Improve Your Page Ranking on Search Engines* and *Corporate Turnaround: Global Perspective, Fundamentals of Buying and Selling of Companies, What we can Learn from the Animals on Office Politics* and *Turnaround Yourself.*

Following from the success of the first edition, *Corporate Wellness: 101 Principles in Turnaround and Transformation* in 2006, Dr Teng decided to write the second edition of the book incorporating the Biblical principles and the global recessionary events in year 2008.

Dr Teng is currently the Managing Director of Corporate Turnaround Centre Pte Ltd which provides corporate training and management advisory services. He has 28 years of experience in corporate turnaround, strategic planning and operational management responsibilities in the Asia Pacific. Of these, he held Chief Executive Officer's positions for 18 years in multi-national and publicly listed companies.

Dr Teng served as the Executive Council member for fourteen years and the last four years as the President of the Marketing Institute of Singapore (2000 – 2004), the national marketing association. Dr Teng holds a Doctor in Business Administration (DBA) from the University of South Australia, Master in Business Administration (MBA) and Bachelor in Mechanical Engineering (BEng) from the National University of Singapore. He is also a Professional Engineer (P Eng, Singapore), Chartered Engineer (C Eng, UK) and Fellow Member of several prestigious professional institutes namely, Chartered Institute of Marketing (FCIM), Chartered Management Institute (FCMI), Institute of Mechanical Engineers (FIMechE), Marketing Institute of Singapore (FMIS), Institute of Electrical Engineers (FIEE) and Senior Member of Singapore Computer Society (SMSCS).

Praise for the book:

"God wants us to be successful in business and He has shown us the way through His Word. Dr Mike Teng has very cleverly shown us how."

> Boyd Au – Founder and former Executive Chairman, Enzer Corporation Ltd.

"Dr Mike Teng's 'Corporate Wellness' provides a powerful lens through which to view corporations and companies, whether large or small. He has skillfully addressed the integrated nature of life and business, in which the intellectual, financial, physical and spiritual aspects are intricately intertwined. This book will empower you to assess the health and vitality of your business, especially in these turbulent times. Definitely recommended reading for all business executives!"

> Dr. Naomi Dowdy – International Speaker and Author of 'Moving On & Moving Up in the Marketplace'

"Dr. Teng's writing is dynamite! His Business Principles 101 coupled with comparable uses of the same principles in the Bible show an in-depth understanding of the needs of today's management from the small guy selling hot-dogs all the way to the CEO on Wall Street."

> Greg Eck – Specialist in Automated Natural Language Processing

"In this global financial crisis corporations are convulsing. Cancerous corruption is being uncovered. And once thriving companies are now on life support. Dr. Michael Teng's Corporate Wellness is just what the doctor ordered.

The word "corporation" is from the Latin word that means "body." So Dr. Michael's Teng's "wellness" metaphor is certainly apt. A good corporation is not a "well-oiled machine"-- a metaphor borrowed from an antiquated industrial age. Corporations are not machines, but organisms.

They used to say in the computer industry, "junk in, junk out." In other words, the problem is not with the computer, it's with the computer programmer--the human factor. Mike Teng reminds us that a corporation is healthy only to the degree that the people who operate it are healthy. Corporate Wellness reminds us that without a healthy body of living, breathing, individuals you'll never have a growing, productive and profitable corporation."

> Wayne Hilsden – Senior Pastor, King of Kings Community, Jerusalem

"A very useful book from Dr. Mike Teng that will benefit many marketers and business executives in this ever changing business environment. Timely principles that are practical and relevant in helping many companies to identify and steer of pitfalls before they occur. A compelling read."

> KC Loh – President, Marketing Institute of Singapore

"God is very much interested in how we run our businesses - for profit and purpose (divine). You will find powerful principles for a corporate turnaround. Read it, engage it and be transformed."

> Bryan Tan – Founder, Life Compass Learning Technologies, Bryan Tan Ministries, Former Pastor Trinity Christian Centre, Singapore

Introduction

Medical and spiritual metaphors are used abundantly in this book as we believe that people can comprehend their financial conditions much better than corporate matters. Metaphor is a comparative figure of speech in which a term is transferred from the object it ordinarily designates to an object it may designate only by implicit comparison or analogy. It is a comparison of something familiar to something unfamiliar and used in this book to explain a common "corporate wellness" principle. It is an effective way for people to create meaning by using one element of experience to understand another. Or to use an analogy, metaphor is like a bridge, it spans the gap between what the turnaround manager wants the sick company to know and what the sick company already knows. Metaphor gives us the opportunity to stretch our imagination, create powerful insights and deepen our understanding, thereby allowing us to see and act in new ways. Such metaphors couched into principles serve to enable the executives to draw parallels to their corporate issues and facilitate their diagnosis and remedies.

There are many similarities between a company and a person. Just like a human being, a company can get ill. Many companies are falling sick due to a whole host of factors such as the economic slowdown, competition and incompetent management. Sickness is a big business but nobody wants to be the patient or remain as the patient. Corporate ill health is also a big business, as in a declining and stagnant economy like the economic conditions we are experiencing in late 2008; there are more sick companies than healthy ones. Every company and individual wants to be in the pink of health.

It is important to keep your body healthy and well. Doctors generally only treat the disease and do not treat wellness. Individuals are beginning to recognize the importance of corporate which is becoming a big business. The pharmaceutical industry understands this as the drugs consumed for surgery and treatment is only for temporary demand. Whereas, the drugs consumed for healing and wellness are for the longer term. This is why medicines such as cholesterol lowering drugs, anti-depressant drugs and health supplements are in great demand. It is small wonder that there is such enormous research material on the Internet on health matters. Hence the growing trend is for companies to target wellness as a business.

God's creation is a more perfect one than men's creation of companies. There are no such things as internal viruses in men. However, because of the fall of Adam, men fall sick through external viruses or attacks from external factors such as infectious diseases, heart diseases etc. Companies get attacked by both external and internal viruses. The internal viruses are mainly management problems and generated internally. These external viruses include competition, economic and financial turmoil, namely factors from the outside.

This is why apart from the medical metaphors that are intercalated in this book; you will also find guiding Biblical principles that supplement our understanding of the corporate turnaround principles further, this time parallel to the different scriptures and stories in the Bible. We will later find that the corporate world and the world in the time of Jesus are not all that different, though it may sound like it. It is explored in this book how we are to keep the company and its workforce in fine fettle, the Jesus way. We will get to experience the Almighty in relation to our world and how we live – expanding our horizons in view of spirituality as not something to be only kept in our homes or churches, but also in the corporate world, and basically, in our everyday lives.

The crux of this book is this: God created men and men created companies. There are spiritual laws or Biblical principles and medical principles for men to follow to attain good physical health. As we are creators of companies, the latter too have to abide by spiritual and medical laws to follow for corporate wellness. As it is written in 1 Kings 2:3, "…observe what the Lord your God requires: Walk in his ways, and keep his decrees and commands, his laws and requirements, as written in the Law of Moses, so that you may prosper in all you do and wherever you go"

Similarly, we will see an increased awareness for companies to target for corporate wellness. After many years of growth and change in the 2000's, companies have found that the state of health has not significantly improved. Morale and loyalty of the staff have deteriorated quickly in the destabilized economic market of late 2008 and companies are becoming caught in a vicious cycle of restructuring to stay afloat. And this pressure to stay competitive is increasing with the continued downward spiral of the economy. Companies have found that it is better for them to stay well and healthy, as one does not have to get sick to get better.

There are workable preventive, diagnostic and therapeutic steps to treat sick companies, and to restore as well as maintain their well being. Similar to handling of a person's health, a company needs to monitor the five stages to sustain long-term health and wellness, namely, prevention, early diagnosis, proper treatment, recovery or rehabilitation and strengthening or health-boosting.

The issues affecting the health of a corporate entity parallel those for a human being, they are the preliminary, hard and soft issues. Preliminary issues are those matters that have to be right in the first place. For example, one needs to plan for one's physical and corporate health to prevent an onset of an ailment. In addition, the patient also needs to deal with the hard issues such as undergoing a surgery to remove a tumour. These hard issues are related to the "science" of the corporate wellness. There are also "soft issues" that the patient must be attuned to. These include strengthening the corporate culture also known as the immune system of the body. The soft issues are like the "art" of the corporate wellness.

Studies show that the use of metaphors help people understand and retain information as it acts as a framework to organize new information. However, the metaphor as mentioned earlier is merely a bridge to understand the concept; the sick companies have to cross that bridge.

Prevention (Isaiah 8:11 - "The Lord spoke to me with his strong hand upon me, warning me not to follow the way of this people.")

As the adage goes: Prevention is better than cure. In medical practice, prevention of the disease before its onset is better than giving medication when it is already malignant or full-blown. Getting it right early is much better than subsequent expensive treatments. Furthermore, when you lose your health, the road to recovery gets longer and rougher.

Seeing how Samaria disobeyed God, he warned Isaiah to not be like them. "The Lord spoke to me with his strong hand upon me, warning me not to follow the way of this people." God prevented Isaiah from ever falling on the same trap as the Samarians. Because Isaiah heeded God's warning and obeyed him, he prevented for himself the wrath of the Lord coming on him and saved his life all together.

Prevention is the name of the game for individuals and companies.

Just like people, most companies get into trouble simply through sheer neglect. Neglect has become the way of some businesses within the latter 2000's, including Fannie Mae and Freddie Mac, companies which would have benefited greatly from preventive medicine earlier in the game to avoid their later downfalls. Through the lack of monitoring, the accumulation of toxins or disease causing pathogens are allowed to perpetuate into a full manifestation of the ailment before any action is taken to contain it. At the outset, a company should adopt prudent practices to prevent the onset of corporate ills or financial problems. The preliminary issue such as prevention requires the direction to be clear as well as good planning. Next, the hard issues need to be implemented which include diligent financial and other controls. Also, soft issues such as taking good care of your people and the wise management of the talent pool are also crucial.

Diagnosis (Exodus 5-12 – "On that same night I will pass through Egypt and strike down every firstborn—both men and animals—and I will bring judgment on all the gods of Egypt. I am the Lord.")

Diagnosis is the identification of the disease based on its symptoms. However, the symptoms can sometimes mask the real disease. Also, many diseases share similar symptoms. Thus further probing is required in order to ensure that the disease is not misdiagnosed.

Page 25

When Jesus instructed Moses to go to Egypt to free Israel, Pharaoh refused. So God sent out ten plagues one by one to Egypt, telling him to let the Israelites go. However, Pharaoh didn't see these as symptoms to a much bigger "disease" that God was prepared to send out. Because he wasn't able to "treat the symptoms," this resulted in the loss and destruction of his country. "On that same night I will pass through Egypt and strike down every firstborn — both men and animals — and I will bring judgment on all the gods of Egypt. I am the Lord."

Just as a sick person may manifest early symptoms of the ailment, such as cough, running nose, fever and body aches, likewise, there are usually ample warning signs for a company. High staff attrition rate and the loss of brand equity are perhaps some of the symptoms that all is not well with the company. However, they are merely the symptoms rather than the real disease or root cause. Treating the symptoms is tantamount to upgrading a cancer-stricken patient to another ward in the hospital, the condition of the patient does not improve. Prescription without diagnosis is malpractice, and likewise, implementing a corporate restructuring without knowing the root cause of the problems can be disastrous.

The key is early diagnosis as it increases the chances of curing most diseases. Therefore, a company should put in place a detection system to facilitate this early diagnosis. How does a company get out of trouble? A good way is to diagnose how it gets into trouble in the first place.

Diagnosis starts with acknowledgement of the problem, good detection system and identifying the root causes from the symptoms. Then one needs a comprehensive diagnosis of the "hard issues" such as its pricing, process and communication. The company also needs to review the "soft issues" such as communication and leadership functions which may have got the company into trouble.

Treatment (Mark 5:21-34 – "Immediately her bleeding stopped and she felt in her body that she was freed from her suffering.")

There are panaceas that can turn a critically ill organization into a healthy one; however, proper treatment is necessary as the remedies may be worse than the disease. For instance, some cancer patients are killed by the chemotherapy rather than the disease itself.

In the Bible, there are many instances where Jesus was the proper and only treatment. Sick people who have sought medical help just made their conditions worse. Once there was a sick woman who had been suffering from her illness for twelve years. Though she sought doctors to heal her, her condition just keeps getting worse. However, when she saw Jesus and grabbed his cloak from behind, she immediately got healed. This sick woman needed grave medication, and Jesus was the only one who helped her. A sick company must find the perfect treatment for themselves as well.

As they say, a stitch in time saves nine. Usually an ailing company needs critical attention probably in the form of 'surgery' with the primary focus of restructuring the organization and improving its cash flow. Most troubled companies need to engage outside help encouraging change and drastic action to steer them out of the woods. Efforts are also needed to restore the company's bottom line and profits.

Treatment starts with the execution in appointing the appropriate corporate doctor or turnaround manager or a team. Next, the distressed company needs to focus and understand some of the techniques to remedy its ailment. Hard issues take precedence during this stage with restructuring, right sizing and cost cutting. In some cases, the rescue endeavour may come in too late; however, if this is the case, then an exit strategy may be necessary. After dealing with the hard issues, the company needs to deal with the soft issues of dysfunctional personnel and bureaucracy.

Recovery (Job 33:28, Joshua 1:8, James 2:24, Exodus 9:16 – "He redeemed my soul from going down to the pit, and I will live to enjoy the light.")

Once a company has completed its surgical care and come out of the 'intensive care' stage, it is of paramount importance that it can continue to nurse itself to health. The pace of recovery and rehabilitation can vary from patients to patients, even though they maybe afflicted by the same disease. Certainly the solution for saving AIG will not be the same as the one necessary to save Morgan-Stanley. Maintaining flexibility regarding recovery may be the difference between a successful recovery and a continued downward-slide, especially in the current economically distressed environment of the late 2000's.

Similar to the recovery after a surgery, a physiotherapist will start you on an exercise and rehabilitation regime such as assisting you to walk with crutches. As you recuperate in the hospital, the physiotherapist and occupational therapist will re-teach you the ways to walk, eat, bathe, sit and dress. They will also advise on your diet and exercise programmes when you are discharged from hospital.

Likewise, when we are recovered by Jesus Christ, redeemed from death and suffering, we can't take the back seat and just start living how we used to live. We need to have an exercise programme as well, to keep our health in tip-top shape. Our training programme from God requires one, reading up on his word, that we may know how to live. "Do not let this Book of the Law depart from your mouth; meditate on it day and night, so that you may be careful to do everything written in it. Then you will be prosperous and successful." Secondly, we need to back up our faith in him by doing what pleases him. "You see that a person is justified by what he does and not by faith alone." Third, we must proclaim the Good News for our salvation. "But I have raised you up for this very purpose, that I might show you my power and that my name might be proclaimed in all the earth."

A company during this stage of the cycle needs to give itself time for healing and recovery. Then it needs to review and reflect on some of the hard issues relating to sales and marketing, customers and market positioning. Oftentimes, these basic issues are taken for granted and can get the company into trouble even after drastic surgical issues have solved the more immediate needs. The recovery period is a good time for the company to recharge and reenergize itself through re-visiting its ethical values, inspirational and renewal process.

Strengthening (Isaiah 41:10 – "So do not fear, for I am with you; do not be dismayed, for I am your God. I will strengthen you and help you; I will uphold you with my righteous right hand.")

After full recovery, the battle to stay in good health is not over yet. The company needs to continue to strengthen and have foresight to transform and innovate. It must also continue to build up its cash reserves.

Likewise, even after the recovery stages with Jesus, we still need him to strengthen us, to make sure that we don't go astray. Just like the disciples underwent strengthening throughout their journey, so must we. We need to learn to trust him in our journey of faith; to continually be transformed to the person he wants us to become. We can be sure that God will be willing to help us stay on track, as long as we trust him to do so. "So do not fear, for I am with you; do not be dismayed, for I am your God. I will strengthen you and help you; I will uphold you with my righteous right hand."

Some doctors believe that the immune system can defend the body against cancer and germs. The immunity is the defence system to combat diseases. During this phase, the strengthening of the immune system is the key to boosting health.

The immune system for the company is the corporate culture. A dysfunctional corporate culture is one which is arrogant and full of ego. A company needs to strengthen its immune system through healthy mindsets and vision. In medical science of psychosomatic, it is believed that the mental health can affect the physical health; similarly the mindset of the company can hurt the financial health. Oftentimes, in a sick company, the enemy is within.

An organization that has regained corporate wellness needs to implement a sustained programme to remain in the pink of health. The company needs to strengthen its heart through exercising, good diet and vitamin supplements. As these are long -term measures, their benefits are normally not visible immediately.

Stage 1: Prevention

Direction

Principle No. 1

Vision, feedback and action – three meals a day keeps the corporate doctor away (James 2:14-25 – "In the same way, faith by itself, if it is not accompanied by action, is dead.")

Someone said that feedback is the breakfast of a champion. However, in today's turbulent marketplace, surviving on breakfast alone is insufficient. You need three meals a day to keep the doctor away.

In the corporate dietary system, you need vision for breakfast, feedback for lunch and action for dinner. Vision is a clear and precise mental portrait of a preferred future. Feedback is the return of a portion of the output to the input. Action is to the take a decision and execute. Vision and feedback without action is dreaming. Action without vision and feedback is wasting time. But vision, feedback and action – feeding on the three meals a day will serve to keep the corporate doctor away.

However, you must ensure that all three meals are based on a regimen of information. Information is the building-block of solid vision, quality feedback and decisive action. Some people believe that information is power. However, information without action is useless. It is similar to the treatment of a sick patient. The doctor can have all the right information on how to cure the patient. However, if he does not take the appropriate and apply timely treatment to treat the patient, the outcome for the patient remains unchanged. But action must be complemented with the correct information as well as taking the action which the patient desires. Acting on the wrong information may kill the patient as the remedies may be worse than the disease. This is why all three – vision, feedback and action – are necessary. They are the meals required to provide the required daily nourishments to the company. It is the harnessing and application of the correct information that unleashes power.

Even Jesus believes that vision and feedback, or *faith*, in his terms, is useless without action, or *deeds*. We can find in the book of James how it was strongly emphasized that faith without deeds is considered dead. Chapter 2 verse 20 reads "You foolish man, do you want evidence that faith without deeds is useless?," thereby giving us an example, rather a proof of this in the likes of Abraham and how his faith in God worked perfectly with his actions when he offered his only son, Isaac, to the altar. He had the vision for God's plan for him, the information about God's character and perfected it with his action by completely trusting God and obeying his commands.

In the context of management theory, it is useful to apply the best blend of Eastern and Western practices. Developing Asia can learn much from the more established and intellectual Western managerial professionalism in the area of clear vision, proper research and feedback. The Asia financial crisis in 1997 has exposed the weakness of some mega corporation in the East. For instance a number of Chaebols in Korea, Keiretsu in Japan and SE Asian banks collapsed. They were lacking in focus, over extended and diversified. Their product lines had little connections with each other. On the other hand, the top blue chip companies in the West such as Microsoft, Coke, and IBM were mainly one-product companies with clear and focused corporate vision. During that era, companies like Apple displayed this unified vision through the underlying theme running throughout their products that is even evident today in the marketplace. But you can look to the more immediate economic downturn of 2007 and 2008 and see that vision is simply not enough. Certainly Microsoft had a great vision for the launch of Vista, but in the months since its release in the United States, many companies have begun pursuing share-ware and pushing Microsoft out. Vision alone is not enough.

It is the combination of all three elements that will lead to a successful company. Just having vision and feedback will not win the day. For example, in the early 1990s, IBM almost went under. IBM then had good vision and feedback. Many major companies were using IBM systems and certainly gave feedback to IBM regarding its products and services. The problem was that such reports and feedback processes stopped short at IBM's head offices. Decisions were not taken to correct the situation on a timely basis. In the 2008, this inability to act also affected the major US automotive manufacturers General Motors, Ford and Chrysler resulting in the Japanese being able to penetrate the market and whittle away their market shares for years. And the new economic downturn across the world market is partially due to the increase in oil prices in the past year. If the Big Three had enacted their vision based on the feedback of their consumers for alternative fuelled automobiles over the summer, Asian influence in the American auto market would have diminished greatly. As it is, Asian auto makers have a fantastic opportunity to grow in the American market and virtually destroy the failing US manufacturers. And because Japanese manufacturers have been building more economical cars for longer, it is no wonder that the American government is contemplating a bail-out of their automakers.

The West can learn from Asia's entrepreneurs' acumen and instincts to quickly act on the information available. The Japanese have taught the West about quick implementation of quality systems and products and concepts like Just-in-Time which is only just now reaching deeper into the US to penetrate markets in the south and Central American regions. Now the Chinese and the Indians are winning the fight against the Japanese corporations in the areas of low cost and good quality products and services.

Therefore, to compete effectively in today's global marketplace, it is vital to integrate the vision and feedback management system of the West with the entrepreneurial and intuitive action of the East.

Principle No. 2

When you drive an ambulance, be sure you know where you are going (Romans 8:28 – "And we know that in all things God works for the good of those who love him, who have been called according to his purpose")

If you do not know where you are going, all the strategic planning and goal setting will be futile. You will be barking up the wrong tree. One of the important things in the world is not so much where we stand, but in which direction we are going. Knowing the direction and purpose provides a motivation as well as a catalyst for decision-making and execution. In the current economically distressed period we are entering in late 2008, a direction and purpose will be critical for companies seeking to succeed in spite of the economic difficulties. Without clear direction, no motivation will exist for not only the company, but its investors and boards – and certainly no clear decision-making will be possible as funds will be less and less available as we progress through this recession. Conventional wisdom says: "If you have wealth, you have everything." However, there are still many very wealthy people who commit suicide because they lost purpose for living. Rather the wisdom should be: "If you have purpose, you have everything."

Rick Warren wrote the book, "*The purpose-Driven Church*" in 1995 in the field of the church. Warren in 1980 launched Saddleback Church in Orange County, Cali from scratch. It quickly became one of the fastest growing churches in US bringing an average of 15,000 worshippers. The success of Saddleback can be compared with Dell, Google or Starbucks.

"*The Purpose – Driven Church*" sold more than 1 million copies. Its sequel, "*The Purpose-Driven Life*" sold more than 12 million copies worldwide. Warren's success notwithstanding his religious beliefs stems from his uncanny discernment of a burning consumer need out there. Without purpose, people will perish.

To Warren, purpose defines not only what business you should engage in but also what you should not. Therefore, the secret to effectiveness is to know what really counts and then to act on this. Nothing else should override or take precedence over the purpose of your business. Plans, programmes and personalities of the founders do not last, only purpose lasts. Purpose can bring healing to your business too. A rediscovery of your purpose and destiny can spark off a miraculous revival of a discouraged church and a troubled organisation.

Warren also draws on the medical analogy. His fundamental advice is not to try to grow your business but to strive to make it healthy. When it is healthy, it will naturally grow. Furthermore, challenging people to a serious commitment to a purpose actually draws people to your cause rather than repels them. If you can succeed in obtaining greater commitment, you can be assured of generating greater response.

We see the great importance of purpose in the Bible – we always hear that God has a purpose for us. In the book of Romans, Paul writes "And we know that in all things God works for the good of those who love him, who have been called according to his purpose." But what is God's purpose for us anyway? Ultimately, this can be answered in one verse, which we can find as early as in the book of Exodus in the Old Testament; that God may show us His power and that His name may be proclaimed all over the earth – repeated and further emphasized in the book of Romans in the New Testament.

Probably the most important factor that makes leaders successful is their clear purpose or vision of what they want to do and where they want to go. Vision is important as it provides a blueprint of what you have conceived as a viable business plan. It is also a road map for the future, generates excitement, creates order out of chaos and offers criteria for success. But vision is worthless if it is not shared by all the members of an organisation. Branson, Chairman of Virgin, Bill Gates of Microsoft, Barnevik, former CEO of ABB Brown Boveri and David Simon, former CEO of British Petroleum all have something of the showman in them. Branson's style is almost exhibitionist, Bill Gates style is casual and "geeky", Barnevik's style is a sophisticated mix of rational and humanistic and Simon's style is low key and friendly. Steve Jobs of Apple and Larry Page, the founding CEO of Google are two which both have an inspirational kind of leading style. Although these leaders differ in style, all of them have kept their vision simple. They exude passion, enthusiasm and self-confidence when sharing about what they hope to accomplish, where they want to go and all these render their visions contagious.

Sir John Egan, the Chairman of Inchcape plc and Confederation of British Industry also emphasized the importance of direction. He reminded managers that strategic planning needed to go beyond just worrying about how to achieve business goals and maintain profitability. He says: "If we are going to have a sustainable future, we have got to come to grips with where we are going. We will have to create a future where the growth that is necessary to create wealth is not endangering the planet, and governments will expect organizations and companies to do this."

A research study from PA Consulting showed only a startling 17 % of companies understand who are their most valuable customers and a mere 13 % know what are their most valuable products. Discovering the most valuable customers and products is just the starting point to a more effective purpose. In tough markets, the paramount purpose should be on the products' economic value. Furthermore, your staff also needs to know the products or services backing them.

As the old saying goes: "If you do not know where you are going, any road will take you there." But when you are driving an ambulance to pick up the sick or injured person, if you lost your way or take too long to get to the destination, it may cost the life of the person.

Planning

Principle No. 3

Companies without strategies are heading for tragedies (Genesis 11:6, Proverbs 21:5 – "The plans of the diligent lead to profit as surely as haste leads to poverty.")

Many businesses are still focusing on yesterday's problems at the expense of forgoing future opportunities. The best chess players always have a strategy in place. But in businesses future planning seems to play second fiddle to analyzing of past performance. Architects would not build a house without the architectural plans because selecting the wrong layout or laying the wrong foundation or using the wrong building materials could result in disaster. The house can collapse on you after you move in. A strategic plan is the architectural blueprint for your business.

Executives always have the excuse for not doing strategic planning. They reckon that things are changing so rapidly. It does not make sense to do ten or even five year planning as events will change and it is not possible to pre-empt changes any more. It is true that nowadays environmental changes are very rapid and that makes long-term planning even more difficult. Non-strategic planning companies give the excuse that planning results in paralysis through too much analysis. It is also true that some companies cover their backs with expensive market research and spreadsheet analyses.

However, one should not throw out the baby with the bath water. As a matter of fact, it is even more critical to have strategic planning during turbulent and rapidly changing environment. With the recent downward trend in the world economy of the late 2000's, strategic planning will become a necessity for many firms simply to stay alive. In this type of economically distressed environment, without strategic plans, many companies will see their impending doom too late to save themselves. It is like the Titanic, which had the most modern technology in her time but did not plan for eventuality and disaster when it hit the iceberg.

People in the Bible loved to plan, although if these plans were selfish and destructive, their plans were destroyed by God, albeit usually with the goal of betterment of his people. We see a lot of instances in the Bible where God frustrates the plans of the people. However, this doesn't mean that God doesn't like it when we plan, he would just guide us to plan well.

God wants us to plan ahead and build solid plans. He knows very well the power of planning. In Genesis 11:6, when the people came together to build the Tower of Babel, the Lord said, "If as one people speaking the same language they have begun to do this, then nothing they plan to do will be impossible for them," which gave Him the need to go down and confuse their language that they may not understand each other, because God knows that the people can succeed with this.

Nonetheless, it is always wise to plan ahead. Proverbs 21:5 tells us that "the plans of the diligent lead to profit as surely as haste leads to poverty." Now, if that principle was true then, imagine how much more this makes sense now.

No matter the economic stability of the market, we will always be living in difficult times today and tomorrow things may be worse. With the possible threats such as global recession, terrorist attacks, tainted milk, infectious diseases like SARS, bird flu etc, it will be naïve for any CEOs to think that they are immune or protected.

One must not be fooled into thinking that a company is successful because it has a good strategic planning system in place. Your success may be coincidentally due to a buoyant market or weak competition. Also, one must not be mistaken that the use of processes such as the annual budget is tantamount to application of strategic planning. If the data is purely internal that is sales figures and product costs, it is not strategic planning. You need to factor in the external factors such as customer data, competition, economic trends, etc.

Also, studies of successful companies such as IBM, Procter and Gamble, 3M found that new innovations and great ideas do not originate from the centralized strategic planning department at the headquarters. Most of the good ideas and innovations were generated from outside the industry or the people who regularly interact with the customers. Strategic planning must not remain in its ivory tower but should incorporate the realities of the ground. That is why feedback is so important and is a much easier way to incorporate new ideas rather than fund an expensive idea-generating team. This is the reason why Apple products are so much more user-friendly than other electronic gadgets.

The former chairman of General Electric (US), Jack Welch drew on the strategies of the Prussian general and military writer Clausewitz, Karl von (1780 – 1831). One of Clausewitz's theories included an explanation of why a military leader could not devise a complete battle plan and then stick blindly to it: "Man could not reduce strategy to a formula. Detailed planning necessarily failed, due to the inevitable frictions encountered. Strategy was not a lengthy action plan. It was the evolution of a central idea through continually changing circumstances."

His own strategic thinking matched that of the general. He constantly reinvented GE over the years as circumstances and the competitive environment shifted. There was an evolution to Welch's strategic thinking and each major initiative built on the one that preceded it. He would wage one "battle" and then wait to see how the results panned out. In tracing the evolution of GE during his tenure, Welch has drawn a stair-step-like chart that depicts the stages of GE's culture change. Work-Out laid the foundation for Best Practices, which created a platform for Process Improvement such as Six Sigma, etc.

The need for strategic planning goes much farther than just within a company. Governments too need to perform strategic planning in order to avert disaster. Without a doubt, every country which has participated in the global economy of the 21st century will be adversely affected by the economic downturn which began in 2008. The impending recession is not going to be the garden type variety which impacts only regions and as it is going to be protracted. This downturn will affect all the major global economies – at the same time. Many countries will not be able to cope. This is because the individual national economies are very dependent on the health of the global economy and the individual markets such as financial services, international trade, tourism, and foreign investments. To mitigate the dramatic changes necessitated by the harsh economic situation ahead, national governments should take the opportunity to plan strategically. For all of these governments, the following measures should be considered when they do so:

> Firstly, co-ordination should be improved between the government sector, private sector and grassroots movements. In difficult times like those ahead, all the major stakeholders must work in harmony and coordinate efforts seamlessly. Prior to implementing major cost increases, government agencies should discuss with grassroots movements and private sector bodies so as not avoid further hardships and mitigate any increase in costs for affected parties. Unrest and instability must be prevented during tough economic times as the entire society can be disrupted, as it is already occurring in some countries around the world.

Secondly, governments must consider the need to pump-up their economies by releasing more projects. However, the governments should also be cautious to ensure these projects get filtered down to the appropriate consultants and contractors to maximize the benefit for each country's domestic market as much as possible.

Thirdly, as in the last Asian financial crisis, governments must implement fiscal stimulus and statutory charges reduction and other such measures to assist distressed companies and also households. Just as some individuals have done, some governments have saved up for a "rainy day" - and now the "rainy day" is here. Now is the time to utilize the savings to get us all through the looming hard patch ahead.

Preparation of a strategic plan may not guarantee success but failure to do so is certainly a recipe for disaster.

Principle No. 4

If you want good health, plan for it. If you want great health, plan and do a post-mortem. (Isaiah 43:18 – "Forget the former things; do not dwell on the past.")

Planning tells you what is going to happen; post-mortem tells you what has happened. Both planning and post-mortem are essential management tools needed to achieve corporate objectives, as well as to prevent the recurrence of the same mistakes. Planning for change must be the ever-present concern of every executive. At the same time, if events do not happen as planned, a post mortem is to be conducted so as not to repeat the same planning errors.

General Dwight D Eisenhower's famous quote, "Planning is nothing and planning is everything" was a response to his cynical colleagues, who believed that, because plans never survive first contact with the enemy, planning was a waste of time. In the corporate world, quite often, planning gets thrown out of the window because of mounting short-term pressures to perform and deliver the bottom line. This is likely why many American banks failed in the early days of the economic downturn of the late 2000's. The pressure to perform and deliver in a short-term manner was leading some banks to invest heavily in high-risk loans. Other banks were focused on the long-term and had planned based on the long-term principles. Clearly we will see in the long-run who planned well and who did not.

Those who fail to plan are ultimately planning for a post-mortem. It is not that post-mortem is unimportant but companies should always plan to succeed and minimize the occasions to do post-mortem on failed projects. Planning companies outperform those non-planning ones.

Crises and the unexpected changes are no longer a rare, random or abnormal part of our lives. They are built into the very fabric of society and modern-day corporations. While not all crises can be foreseen or even prevented, all of them can be managed if we plan strategically and tactically for what is humanly possible. The impacts of the crises can be minimised if one has a thorough understanding of the basics of crisis planning and management.

Tactical is short term planning whereas strategic is considered long term. Strategic plan looks at the forces in the external environment and responses to them. Tactical planning usually covers one year and is the stepping stone of the strategic plan, which normally covers three to five years.

Having post-implementation analysis or post-mortem is also critical. Just as a post-mortem reveals the cause of death, a corporate post-mortem can be extremely revealing. You learn from your past mistakes and get all the feedback. It functions much like a resurrection experience, enabling you to have a new lease of life or second chance. In physical term it is reflection. Without this, the same mistakes may be made all over again and lessons learnt earlier will come to waste. This is why there is a saying that history repeats itself. Two world wars were fought within a short span of less than 30 years. Empires and dynasties fall and rise because of a lack of reflection and committing the very same mistakes that ushered them into power in the first place. Post-mortem job is dull and boring particularly when it is preceded by overwhelming success. But it is also from reflecting upon your successes that one can avoid the pitfalls of failures in the future.

In the Bible, we see the perfect example of someone who used his past to learn and correct his ways. Peter messed up a lot of times. Peter exhibited faith as he left the boat to join Jesus walking on the water, but found his deficiency 5 seconds later, he denied Jesus, and he talked aimlessly. However, he used all that Jesus taught him and took it to heart – he implemented not just quick fixes, but serious changes on his character and behaviour.

John Maxwell wrote a book called "Failing Forward." In this book we can see how we can make use of our mistakes as stepping stones to get us back on the right track. This is what Peter did with his life. He got up, took Jesus' correction and moved forward. Similarly, the book of Isaiah tells us to "forget the former things" and "not dwell on the past (43 v.18)." This works perfectly if we would only reflect on what we have done wrong and use it to not commit the same mistakes twice, even three or four times. Furthermore, this teaches us to not dwell on our sins and just mope around. This is where Maxwell's idea of failing forward and Peter's example comes in. We have to do something about our mistakes, and instead of falling behind because of it, we should choose to fail forward so we can get back right up.

Good managers always find out what has gone awry not so much to apportion blame, but to ensure that the same problems do not surface again. This is why some companies conduct exit interviews with departing staff to ascertain if there are more issues than meet the eye.

Even chaos has its patterns. The post-mortem is the process to ascertain the patterns of things that have gone wrong so that these mistakes will not be repeated in the future. In the past, three strikes and you are out. Today, one strike and you are history. This is because today's world is highly competitive and you may not have a second chance. Through one mistake, miscalculation or strategic error, your competitors can steal away your customers very quickly. Your margins for errors are very thin as resources are scarce. This amplifies the importance of post-mortem to minimise repeating the mistakes.

This trend is evident from what has happened to the big 3 US car-makers in 2008 in this most recent great depression. Since they hadn't planned right for the long term, now it is essential that they do a post-mortem in order to identify their mistakes. The same could be said for the current credit crisis affecting the world in 2008-2009. This depression is a key example which, if we look back and identify the real issues, can be used to change the banking system and put in new rules and regulations and prevent the same mistakes from occurring in the future.

Principle No. 5

Clone your successes by planning your succession. (Exodus 4:1-14 – "Who gave man his mouth? Who makes him deaf or mute? Who gives him sight or makes him blind? Is it not I, the Lord? .. Now go; I will help you speak and will teach you what to say.")

The downfall of many countries and political leaders are attributable to poor leadership succession. Yugoslavia plunged into civil war with the demise of President Tito in 1980. Till then, he was all-powerful and had no intention of passing control to anybody. Former President Suharto tried to perpetuate his powers too by surrounding himself with weak subordinates. This brought about his downfall and the economic disaster in Indonesia when the Asian economic crisis hit in 1997. However, the opposite occurred in Cuba with Fidel Castro's illnesses throughout 2007 and 2008. There was no tumult or negative outcome when Fidel announced that his brother would be taking-on his role and the transition was smooth because the succession plan was executed in the open with a strong successor, thus averting potential war in that country.

Many once successful companies have failed because of poor succession planning. Many entrepreneurs want their children to succeed them and take over the reins in their businesses. However, their offspring may not be the best people to take over from them. In the long run, it is more beneficial to the company, the entrepreneur, and his children to employ the best professional manager or managers from outside to run the business. Hence, there is a saying: "The first generation builds the business, the second generation enjoys the prosperity and growth, the third generation brings about the downfall." There is a moral obligation to create a successful next generation of management. As the Chinese proverb says: "If you want happiness for a lifetime – help the next generation."

However, helping the next generation by choosing the best and strongest to surround oneself proves to be too difficult for some managers. There is a fear and spirit of insecurity among some managers if their subordinates are better than they are. Such subordinates are deemed as threats, capable of rendering them redundant and eventually taking over their jobs in time to come. As a result, we often see managers stifling good subordinates and bringing in incompetent ones instead. To encourage succession planning, companies should introduce the policy that one is not promotable if one does not have a capable successor to take over one's existing portfolio. Succession planning should also become an important part of the company's performance appraisal measurement.

Page 43

We would like to think that God himself is good in succession planning – that is, finding the right people to carry out missions for him. Moses, however, seems to not trust God's ability to select the perfect person for the job.

In the fourth chapter of Exodus, we see that God had already selected Moses to be the one to save the Israelites from the hands of the pharaoh. God had already revealed himself to Moses in the previous chapter through the burning bush, and now God is actually relaying details to Moses on how to do about the job he had assigned him to. Scared and lacking of faith, Moses kept questioning God about his decision and believed that someone else should carry out this mission instead of him. God let Moses' brother, Aaron go with him to do what he had been told. In the end, they were successful: the people listened to them and after many battles with Pharaoh, he finally sets free the Israelites from Egypt.

The late Roberto Goizuetta of Coca-Cola had very good succession planning too. He established at least four people who could run the company after he decided not to run it any more, and behind them were ten people who could fill their jobs. The Economist, in October 25, 1997 reported: " Roberto Goizueta will clearly be mourned at Coca-cola, the company he headed, but he might not be missed. Strangely enough, that would be one of the greatest compliments a departed chief executive could receive."

One of the driving factors behind GE's success is succession planning. If it were not for GE's rigorous succession planning, Jack Welch might have never become GE's eighth CEO. Both Reg Jones (GE's seventh CEO) and Jack Welch started searching for their successors six years prior to their retirement and the board played an important role in the process. In November 2000, Welch finally named his successor, Jeff Immelt, the head of GE Medical Systems, who took over in September 2001.

As a corollary to cloning your successes, one should not create clones of yourself. The problem with some companies is that the CEO insists that somebody who is like himself or herself take over. However, this method is a sure sign of failure to come. If it is more of the same, then there is no renewal and transformation.

Welch said that Immelt should not do what he did but take the opportunity to reinvent the company, as Welch did when he became CEO. Months before his retirement, Welch suggested that the role of his successors would not be to blindly follow in his footsteps but to launch new initiatives and take GE to the next level: "My successor knows that his job is not to do what I did, but to take what I did as a launch pad to whole new ideas, new things...it is his game."

Therefore, always remind your staff and yourself not to be fearful of working yourselves out of a job. There is always a better job waiting for you once you have done your present job well. This was exactly the case with former Toyota America President, Jim Press, who moved to Chrysler when he saw he could not move further quickly enough at Toyota.

Principle No. 6

Thinking rationally before you decide will help you to sleep well (Proverbs 23:23, Proverbs 18:15, Proverbs 20:18, Luke 14:31: What king, when he sets out to meet another king in battle, will not first sit down and take counsel.)

Many companies often let their success and euphoria gloat over their heads and forget to do their homework. Expansion is done without proper evaluation or support from adequate market research and survey. Decisions are often overridden by the desire to accomplish business expansion as part of the company's objectives and the risk factors are ignored. If the companies have done rational thinking, simple homework and some reflection, they would have been spared massive headaches and avoided some of these projects. Rational thinking is going back to the basic and not allowing emotions, egos and euphoria to get the better of you when making decisions.

Even the Bible explicitly encourages clear thinking before deciding. For example, Luke 14:31 said: Or, what king, when he sets out to meet another king in battle, will not first sit down and take counsel whether he is strong enough with ten thousand men to encounter the one coming against him with twenty thousand?

There are many instances of poor rational thinking in business failures. For instance, many pioneering investors in China in the late 1990's and early 2000's lost money because their investments were based upon "China statistics". These statistics were based on the assumption that China has a population of 1.0 billion people at that time. So, the investors would say: "If we are able to capture one percent of the market, which though minuscule, translates into 10 million of captured customers." This is indeed an impressive captive market. Unfortunately, these investors learned to their dismay that China was still a third world country. The bulk of the population was unable to pay for their products and services. The immutable law in marketing that "You cannot make money from people who do not have money" is applicable here.

History reminds us that there are many companies that embarked upon major mergers and acquisitions but failed miserably. Sometimes, proper homework, reflection as well as rational thinking will reveal that it is better to buy over the key people and grow the business than buy another company lock, stock and barrel. Apart from the strategic synergies of a merger and acquisition (M&A), one also has to be mindful of the cultural fit. An example was the teething problems encountered by both the Chinese and Singaporean partners in the Singapore-China Suzhou Industrial Park project in China in the mid 1990s. Though the project had the support and endorsement of both the Chinese and Singaporean governments, there were many events of misunderstanding and conflict. These arose because of cultural differences even though both parties involved were of ethnic Chinese origin. The Singapore government eventually ceded the management of the industrial park in September 1999. If both the parties could have tried on a smaller scale project to understand each other first, many headaches might have been averted. Instead, the whole project went full scale without testing the waters first, ultimately leading the partnership to failure.

In Singapore in the early 2000's, many contractors in the construction industry landed up with projects' cost overrun because they did not estimate the projects' costs properly before the tendering stage. It is very critical to estimate the contract price correctly as during the project execution stage there is very little margin for error. Some contractors did not cater for contingencies in raw material price escalation such as the stainless steel, foreign exchange fluctuations, country risks and interest rates etc. Not preparing good cost estimates ahead of time is the same as ignoring the task of doing homework before an acquisition – a path that can only lead to failure as well.

Throughout history, we can see that there were problems with this same issue. The Sydney Opera House may be most prominent landmark building in Australia. However, it was apparent that the project cost was overrun by 15 times to over 100 million Australian dollars in the 1950s when it was built. The building was designed by a Danish architect, Joern Utzon, beating 200 other international competitors. Its design was not backed by realism and practicality in the actual construction. If the judges had thought rationally and logically that it would be an uphill task translating the dreamed design into reality, it would have saved them millions of dollars.

Another project that blew the budget was the Euro tunnel. It was constructed amidst much fanfare. It expected to capture a third of the commuters' market. However, when the tunnel was completed after much delays and cost overrun, it ran into a snag regarding competition - the ferry and air transportation services simply lowered their prices. By then, billions of dollars were already sunk into the project and it was too late to justify lowering the cost to commuters by setting a lower construction cost.

More recent examples abound. Already in late 2008, there are significant cost overruns on the 2010 Olympics Village in Canada. An approximate $60 million will be necessary in excess of the original construction estimates, quite a significant amount for any development project. And this is not an isolated event. With the increase in fuel and construction materials related to the economic downturn, cost overruns are rampant in recent memory. The only way to solve these overruns in the future is to plan well ahead of the market and understand consumers and the situation better than the competition through rational thinking.

To optimize success, rational thinking should be coupled with detailed planning, market feasibility studies and survey as well studying the mistakes made by competitors. All these efforts expended up front will pay great dividends in the long run. You avoid making many mistakes and tons of headaches and nightmares. It will help you to sleep well.

Financial

Principle No. 7

There is a strong parallel between physical and fiscal health (Matthew 6:21 for where your treasure is, there your heart will be also)

There is a strong parallel between corporations and medical science. Companies fall sick just as people do. Contrary to the common view, a company is not an inanimate object. Rather, it is a community of people, a living organism and an entity with its own distinctive personality and attitudes. Therefore, without proper care, a company, which has a life of its own, will perish.

The Bible understands this linkage between finances and the physical body and mind. In Matthew 6:21, it stated that "where your treasure is, there your heart will be also." If you value money, your heart will always be thinking of making money.

Rather than understanding businesses by using some mechanical or industrial models, it is useful to understand them from the perspective of ecology of organisms. Like all organisms, the companies exist primarily for their own survival and improvement as well as fulfil their full potential. Similarly, as human beings we exist to survive and thrive.

At the antenatal stage, just as in the case of the impregnation of the human embryo, a company is incorporated through a concept wherein the founder explores or brainstorms the initial idea. In the case of the person, the foetus will be nurtured through antenatal care till birth. For the company it is conceptualized from a feasibility report on its commercial viability followed by incubation and culminating in its start up. The company may have been born out of a merger or acquisition, the social marriage for corporations. At birth, the start up company is a baby. Some babies are stillborn and aborted due to various congenital defects. Similarly, some start-up companies are aborted due to lack of funds or breakup in the partnerships.

A healthy person is like a profitable company, full of vitality and energy, whereas a patient is akin to a troubled company plagued by problems. The trouble is often financial in nature. When the company is sick, it needs a corporate doctor for healing or turnaround. In many cases, the sick company requires fresh injection of funds to resuscitate it. This is where the company needs to turn to hospital.

The hospital is the bank, private investor or venture capitalist which provides vital financing and cash flow for the sick company to sustain itself. The surgery is known by a host of corporate euphemisms such as restructuring, rationalizing, downsizing and re-engineering. They all mean the same thing. If you have been a victim of re-engineering, it basically means that you have been fired.

Companies get attacked by viruses too. These viruses can include incompetent management, low cost competition, economic recession etc. The mindset also affects the company's financial health, just as psychosomatic problems can affect the physical health. Mindsets problems include the negative attitude, lack of enthusiasm and a general dysfunctional corporate culture that is resistant to changes in the marketplace.

When a company falls critically ill with a major disease such as loss of competitiveness, it needs to be admitted into the intensive care unit where it can receive turnaround treatments. When the company is healed, it is successfully turned around; otherwise, death in the form of financial collapse or bankruptcy ensues. Company also has its own undertaker, it is known as the liquidator, spelling its demise or death.

Thus, there are many similarities between fiscal and physical health.

Principle No. 8

Inventory is the burial ground (Proverbs 21:5, Proverbs 12:24, Proverbs 10:4 Poor is he who works with diligent hand, but the hand of the diligent makes rich)

Inventory is the burial ground for most sick companies. It buries all the slow-moving and dead stocks. Most of these stocks are probably going to be written off. Proper control of inventory is important as stocks tie up much needed funds and add to carrying costs. Inventory also robs the company of other investments or earning opportunities.

By shortening the inventory turnover cycle, the company can also yield remarkable improvements in its financial performance. At the same time, the company can also realise substantial savings on storage and carrying costs.

The problem of high slow-moving stocks frequently hit the trading and agency business as well as franchise business. The principals and the franchisers often insist on their agents, dealers and franchisees to carry more of their stocks. It is very important for these agents and franchisees to evaluate very carefully the commercial viability of these stocks. If they are not fast moving and have short shelf lives, the danger is that these stocks may end up as dead stocks and will be written off one day eventually. It is prudent that you seek reciprocal arrangement if your principals and franchisers require you to carry stocks as pre-condition in order for you to start agency business with them. Then you must ensure that they too are committed to taking back any unsold or slow-moving stocks.

Also, when a company has multiple products or stock-keeping units (SKUs), it is imperative that it can accurately forecast the rate of sale at the retail level and continually update the production to avoid over production. Unfortunately, many of these companies find themselves with high inventory position, holding stocks that are not in line with the retail rate of sale. For manufacturing companies, the production mix problems create obsolete products, which ultimately lead to costly write-downs and write-offs. The problem is further accentuated by the storage and warehousing costs. Usually, these companies are forced to dispose off their obsolete stocks for a song in order to cut future losses.

One of the major causes of poor inventory is due to negligence, slackness and hastiness as mentioned in the Bible in Proverbs 10:4, 21:5 and

Proverbs 12:24. As a result of such sloppiness and carelessness, the stocks are forgotten and soon become dead stocks fit for burial.

On the other hand, the turnaround CEO needs to monitor the inventory carefully to ensure that the stock-out situation does not arise. Such cases will result in loss of sales and may adversely affect the company's reputation. Therefore, in-depth analysis is necessary to verify that the stock situation is at the optimal level.

The CEO also needs to conduct a broad-based review of the company's stock or inventory items. This will help to reduce the amount of slow-moving and obsolete stocks. As mentioned earlier to ease the cash flow, the company should consider getting rid of passe goods at a discount. Sometimes auctions do provide a platform do provide a platform for disposal of such goods. However, it is not advisable to sell all slow-moving items in a panic. Such over-reaction may even jeopardise and hamper the recovery of the sick firm as it can degenerate into internal liquidation if it is not well administered.

One has not only to be careful with inventory but work-in-progress (WIP) items as well. Work-in-progress items are half completed work and products in the system. In the construction industry, sometimes the WIPS are left in the limbo because of contractual disputes. Therefore it is crucial to ensure that money is promptly collected when each progress payment becomes due. This is to avoid landing in a situation where you may need to write off the WIPs because of obsolescence.

In the manufacturing industry, it is common for WIPs to be left on hold because of in-process quality rejects or customer's rejects. The WIPs can sit in the production shop for months and years, tying up valuable cash and choking up the factory space.

Therefore it is important not to bury your company's cash unnecessarily in the inventory and WIPs.

This is the reason successful companies avoid WIP and prefer JIT concepts. This is the reason behind the success of Dell and Toyota in the early 2000's and is slowly being adopted throughout out the industry. However, there are some in the industry that were too slow to respond to these new concepts. For example, GM and Ford now have so much money tied in completed cars that they have ceased production of these models and thus are losing money in this way too.

Holding inventory can kill a company through many means, not the least of which is exhibited by the Big Three automakers being hammered by the economic change. In having too much inventory, all three manufacturers have too much of the old stock on hand – and too little capability to switch production to the more in-demand hybrid and alternative fuel automobiles. The consumers are speaking and because they were too slow to listen, the US automakers may be closing their doors during this economic crisis.

Principle No. 9

Casual with receivables, you may land up as a casualty (Romans 13:7, Matthew 18:21-34 – "Give everyone what you owe him: If you owe taxes, pay taxes; if revenue, then revenue; if respect, then respect; if honor, then honor")

Some companies' Achilles' heels are their accounts receivables, poor credit control or weak administration of credit policy. These weaknesses can smoulder the companies of their vital lifeline – cash flow causing them to asphyxiate.

In the construction industry, it is common for many contractors to run into problems with the receivables. Although the accounting practices allow for recognition of the profits from the receivables before the money is collected as the progressive payment is due, these receivables do not constitute cash flow. When the construction industry encountered doldrums a few years ago, many small contractors folded up even though they had substantial amounts of receivables. The problem arose out of non-payments by the main contractors, owners and developers.

In Singapore, the construction industry went through a bad patch in the 1990's. Projects were often clinched at a loss and quite often the receivables were not collectible. As with all construction, but especially so in the 1990's, there are typical monetary constraints that rule the market. For example, in some construction contracts, the last retention amount or progressive payment is not collectible as the owner will give excuses for non-payments due to disputes. It ends up with protracted litigations which further drain the cash flow of these contractors. In the early 2000's, the Singapore government tried to improve the situation by enforcing laws that government agencies and owners must promptly pay up the dues and not delay or drag payments unnecessarily.

Many private educational providers in Singapore are also financially in trouble. They bring in foreign students and allow them to pay on credit for their duration of studies in Singapore. With the economic slump, many of these students are going to be unable to service the credit and finish their course of studies. Some may have to disrupt their studies and return home. However, the private schools who take these students have to continue to teach out the remaining students albeit the class student numbers may have dwindled and become commercially not viable to continue. There is also a social obligation for these schools not to close the classes as they owe it to allow the remaining students to finish their programs.

Oftentimes, debtors who are unable to pay may give the ruse that it is a principle over some disagreements that cause them not to pay and not the money issue. However, you can be sure that in most cases, the reason for not paying is always the money and not the principle. And the principle for you to note is to collect the money first.

Even God is particular about debts. For debtors, Paul writes in the book of Romans to remind them to always pay their debts. "Give everyone what you owe him: If you owe taxes, pay taxes; if revenue, then revenue; if respect, then respect; if honor, then honor (13 v. 7)."

However, as creditors, we have to be reminded also to give at least a leeway for those who owe us. We learn in the parable of the unmerciful servant how the master cancelled the debt of his servant because he begged of him to. Yet when someone owed the servant, he wouldn't even give the slightest consideration. Now, this doesn't necessarily mean that we just cancel all the debts of our debtors. God has nothing against collecting debts; what counts is how we collect from our debtors the money or any payable they owe us. We cannot be casual or we'll lose it, neither do we need to shake what our debtor owes off out of his pockets.

Therefore, making a sale is not enough. The seller has to make sure that the money can be collected. You cannot pay your staff with receivables, you can only pay your staff with cash

The world economic crisis occurring presently in late 2008 is extremely similar in this same respect. Simply, the main reason for the current global credit crisis is that banks are unwilling to lend to each other as they are not sure if they are going to receive the money back due to the fact that large amounts of receivables have been tied down in sub prime mortgages. This has led to collapse of banks like Northern Rock, Bear Sterns and Freddie Mac. However, this problem would not have led to such a global catastrophe if in the late 1990's the banks had instead given loans to only those people which were proven to be able to service their debts – that the banks freely handed-out loans to unworthy borrowers was the path to the global economic crisis.

Principle No. 10

By the time the financial numbers show red, the company is already bleeding profusely (Jeremiah 22:13 Woe to him who builds his house without righteousness and his upper rooms without justice.)

There are many important imperatives and factors which are not quantified or measurable by the traditional accounting system.

Human capital is perhaps the single most critical success factor for companies. But its importance cannot be captured or measured by the financial numbers. One can anticipate the failure of companies by observing the high defections within their middle and senior management ranks. The exodus of these key managers is the precursor to a much more severe problem, which can impact the continuity of execution and administration of the company.

Another intangible factor of the financial health is the morale of the staff. Although good morale of the staff does not always equate to good productivity, poor morale certainly spells trouble for the company. A reduction in the staff morale will result in reduction of the flow of constructive ideas and effective operation of the company. In turn, poor morale can cause the exodus of good staff and eventually a decline in the profitability and market share of the company.

On another note, unfortunately, the traditional accounting statements also do not measure the brand equity. Brand equity is actually the amount of good will resident in the brand. It is the added value endowed upon the product or service as a result of past investments and marketing of the brand. It is also an asset that the company must ensure that its value does not depreciate. Unfortunately, the brand equity is not captured in the balance sheet because of its arbitrary nature.

Another significant root cause of corporate failures is the quality of the CEO. Most turnaround situations arise because of incompetent CEO. Weak board of directors and the financial controllers are also a possible cause. Yet, the current accounting system in place does not measure the quality of these key management staff and board members.

Other causes of failures include poor quality staff and dysfunctional corporate culture that are ill equipped to handle changes in the marketplace. The damage caused by such factors is often only manifested just prior to the financial numbers displaying the red flags.

The profitability barometer of a vulnerable company usually takes the form of negative or declining profitability. It may have been slipping for several years, consistently below the industry's average and compares unfavourably with the competitors. However, the declining trend is sometimes confused with many other factors such as poor economic conditions, shocks in the marketplace etc. An experienced manager needs to be able to identify the problems long before the financial numbers turn red.

At the end of the day it is going back to basics and many of these are not quantifiable. The financial numbers may not be able to detect the flaws early enough. This is why in the Bible, Jeremiah 22:13 said: Woe to him who builds his house without righteousness and his upper rooms without justice, who uses his neighbour's services without pay and does not give him his wages. There is so much the financial numbers can tell but the best indication is to building a strong foundation based on the correct values.

This is precisely what Barak Obama must do to nurse the US economy back to health, during the first months of his term in office. It should be his top priority to benefit both the American people and the global economic partnership. The global economy cannot recover if the US continues to languish in recession. An economically weak US only serves to further weaken the US stance politically – especially in the continuing Iraqi conflict. The US must regain its economic leadership role to continue to have respect and for other countries to support it in its role as the world's policeman.

Because the US government is now operating in the red, the Obama administration must immediately address the economic situation. Obama must start by shoring-up the US financial system's confidence and begin facilitating credit flow, getting business matters flowing back to normalcy. He must act quickly so banks can re-learn to trust lending to one another, allowing credit to filter to the rest of the economy.

Control

Principle 11

Acquisition binge can cause indigestion (Luke 15:11-16 – "After he had spent everything, there was a severe famine in that whole country, and he began to be in need.")

Over-eating or bingeing is detrimental to one's health. Similarly, over-acquisition can cause corporate indigestion such as over-leveraging, integration difficulties, cultural misfits etc. You are what you eat.

While fast growth through acquisition is a thrilling experience in running businesses, it also holds much more risks than meets the eye. When the company is in trouble, some CEOs also go on a shopping spree – acquisition. It is more glamorous and exciting than trying to fix mundane turnaround issues back in the office. It takes shareholders' attention away from the domestic problems and impresses them with expansionary programs. Rapid acquisition done in haste with inadequate homework, wrong timing, egoistic reasons and impatience for success can result in calamity.

In the book of Luke, Jesus tells us about the parable of the prodigal son. This story very much teaches us the basics of the dangers of over-acquisition. In his eagerness and impatience to inherit his share of his father's wealth, the son asks his father of what is due to him. The father then divides his property to give his son his rightful share. The son goes off to another country and squanders all the wealth he had acquired. Because of this thrill and pride he had of having money in his hands, he had not thought ahead of what to do with the money; thereby using every cent he had on useless, meaningless things, until all of it was gone.

Harvard don Michael Porter studied the success rate of 33 highly regarded companies over a 36-year period of acquisition. His data revealed that over half of the 'unrelated' acquisitions were later divested. Research by McKinsey & Company found a failure rate of 61% in acquisition programmes, with failure defined as not earning a sufficient return on the funds invested. Sometimes these failures are due to the fact that the acquisition was a mismatch in the first place, with small odds for success. A high percentage of merger difficulties and failures are the result of defective management. Target companies are strategically sought and stalked, but then the follow-up acts are poorly orchestrated.

Often people in both firms will be seriously troubled about how the acquisition may affect their personal careers. A good part of the merger/acquisition planning should be aimed at deciding how these concerns will be addressed. For instance, Novell's 1994 merger with WordPerfect caused people in both organizations to experience dismay and the combined company teetered subsequently on the brink of disaster. After buying WordPerfect for US$855 million, Novell sold it to Corel less than two years later for only US$115 million.

A more recent example would be the merger of AOL and Time Warner. This 2002 merger was rife with heated stockholder's emotions on both sides of the table and a poor reconciliation of cultures. Quickly, both companies saw a downturn in their stocks, followed by a downturn in their basic market. However, if they had been separate, perhaps their fortunes would have been for the better.

Media companies faced similar problems of acquisition binge. The conventional wisdom in the industry that spurs such manoeuvre was to grow the business by acquisition. Sony Corporation (Japan) was a case in point of being one of the first to venture aggressively into music and films. The same course of action was adopted by Vivendi Universal (French), Bertelsmann (German) and AOL Time Warner (US). It was believed that a product could be developed, and then marketed through a wide range of in-house channels, from compact disks, DVDs, Web sites and even theme parks. This led to a proliferation of businesses requiring different skills and expertise, resulting in the failures of these acquisition ventures.

In their haste to capitalize on the boom years of the late 1990's, many companies reckoned that the fastest way to beat the competition was to join in. After all the saying goes: if you cannot beat it, join it. Thus goes the acquisition spiral. With each new acquisition, it is assumed that revenues automatically jumped up, while margins presumably stayed within acceptable ranges, especially if the deal is accomplished through stock swaps. The growing company acquires not just the market share but the expertise as well. Everything seems to augur well especially from the stock market as long as the company grows and numbers are good. However, therein lies the fundamental flaw with the growth-by-acquisition strategy. This is what Herb Greenberg of Fortune magazine commented of the US corporate scene: "As with any addiction, the growth-by-bulk acquisition approach necessitates increasing doses of the drug to preserve the high. The only way to keep revenues growing fast enough for Wall Street is to buy ever more companies."

Once the growth curve halts the stock price plummets to an extent that initiates a vicious downward spiral. The company loses its leveraging ability when capitalization decreases and interest expense increases to service the loan financing for acquisition. In the bid to reduce costs, the company starts trimming corners at the expense of quality, customers, and employees.

Therefore, the adage still holds true, "Do not bite more than you can chew". It can become toxic for the company if they go into acquisition binge.

Principle No. 12

Litigation can put you out of business in a heartbeat (Romans 13:1-7 – "Everyone must submit himself to the governing authorities, for there is no authority except that which God has established.")

Many companies underestimate the potential gravity of getting into litigious situations. Lawsuits, especially in cases where one does not have strong legal legs to stand on, are potential minefields for disaster. Many organisations work hard to grow the top line only to have a lawsuit siphon off the money. It is like having a purse with holes in it. Regardless of whether you win or lose the lawsuit, the ultimate winner is the lawyer. Unfortunately if your company happens to be the loser, the magnitude of the costs and damages could possibly derail your business overnight.

In the late 1990's and early 2000's, many contractors in Singapore also got themselves into trouble by taking on contracts indiscriminately despite poor margins, unrealistic deadlines and liabilities. Eventually, they were held liable for massive liquidated damages for delays in completion and consequential damages resulting from their work. The risks involved were disproportionate to the returns from such jobs. Some of these sub-contractors were hopeful that they could make money from variation orders or additional scope of work not stipulated in the original contract. However, these variation orders were not properly signed off before the additional work was executed and as a result some main contractors took advantage not to pay in times of contractual disputes. Also, projects often became delayed for many uncontrollable reasons and these sub-contractors had to contend with counter claims and back charges from the main contractors. In many cases, these sub-contractors could not afford a protracted litigation battle and had to settle out of court with the main contractors for an unfavourable settlement. Many of these sub-contractors would have been spared the headaches if they had avoided taking on such onerous contracts.

Be wary of the ramifications of litigation especially in the case of China. An effective strategy in China means understanding the myriads of legal and regulatory issues at the state and provincial level, the city or even local level. Conflict and contract dispute resolution, remedies and legal recourse significantly differ from region to region. This can be a minefield through which to navigate. However, much of the headaches can be minimised if one clearly understands the legal issues involved at the outset. It is important to understand these issues at the start. In China, the government has great involvement with the business sector. For example for state-owned enterprises (SOEs), it is difficult to delineate

Page 61

between public and private business ownership. Therefore, it is important to understand the legalities before entering into partnership with the SOE.

With the entry into World Trade Organisation, China has progressively removed many artificial barriers in the business sector. However, China remains basically a closed market and tightly managed by the government. It is a prerequisite to understand the rules and regulations of your industry. The law will always catch up with you if there is any non-compliance whether deliberate or through sheer ignorance. Your disgruntled staff or competitors will report to the authority on your non-compliance as reporting against one another is a common communist trait.

Litigation once nearly destroyed America's small aircraft industry. It also threatened to topple powerful brokerage firms because of the conduct of their analysts. The Catholic Church is also vulnerable to an onslaught of litigation due to the spates of alleged abuses by its priesthood. The other classic example is Arthur Anderson. The suspicion of improprieties and litigations caused massive customer defections in the early 2000's.

During hard times when you cannot repay your creditors, try convincing them to extend the payment period rather than sue you in court. Most creditors such as the banks would prefer that the matter be settled amicably as it is bad publicity for all parties concerned, both the plaintiff and the defendant.

But many times, although there isn't even any litigation, the insinuation that there should be from the public perception can also take-down a company. Currently, the economic slow-down of China is being exacerbated by the large number of toy companies closing down because of downturn in US in Chinese-made toys. This downturn in both the US economy certainly would have affected China without this toy-company falter, however, the Chinese economy is feeling the affects of this downturn more acutely because of the of the toy company losses. US consumers have become extremely discriminating in toy purchases from China in the later part of 2006 through 2008. This is due to the safety regulations being dissimilar in China and the US. Many US consumers assumed that because they were purchasing a toy in the US that the toy would meet US standards. That was not the case. And when the consumers realized that there were dramatic differences, the US market rejected the toys which did not meet US standards and recalled many of the toys that were already on the market. Although the Chinese had done nothing illegal, certainly there was a mis-communication with their US consumers and the loss of public good-will with their consumers meant that many companies would have to shut their doors.

If you reckon that your company can benefit economically by ignoring a law or even skirting around standards in another country, you may be kidding yourself. Be extra careful. If non-compliance results in safety hazards for employees or the public in general, do not break the law, it is not worth it.

Obeying the law in the "real world" is as crucial now as it was in Jesus' time. In Romans 13, Paul tells us that we must submit ourselves to governing authorities, because these authorities are established by God himself. Rebelling against authority means rebelling against what God had established. Romans 13:5-6 reads "Therefore, it is necessary to submit to the authorities, not only because of possible punishment but also because of conscience. This is also why you pay taxes, for the authorities are God's servants, who give their full time to governing." So if it is taxes you owe, then it is taxes you must pay. If it is honor, then honor shall you give back.

Therefore it always pays to play by the law in the long term. If you are a boxer, you do not chew up the ears of your opponents. You will be barred from future matches or worse still be put in jail like Mike Tyson. Your reputation will also go down the tubes.

Principle No. 13

Corruption is short-term gain, long-term pain. (Deuteronomy 16:19, Hosea 9:1-17 – "Do not accept a bribe, for a bribe blinds the eyes of the wise and twists the words of the righteous.")

There is a misconception that Asia is corrupt and corruption is unique to Asia. The truth is corruption is bad and not an acceptable business practice in Asia. Neither is it an intrinsic part of Asia's culture. With the opening up and rapid growth of the Chinese and Indian economies, there is a perception that corruption is mounting in Asian countries. The US accused China of selling tainted milk. But the US sells an even more toxic asset – tainted Collaterals Debt Obligations that have brought several of its own major banks on their knees.

Offering of gifts and entertainment are a part and parcel of many Asian cultures. What then constitutes corruption? It is a difficult question to answer. Much of it boils down to motives and whether it is excessive. What should you do when you are asked to give a bribe? Remember that a bribe once given is always there to be unearthed by investigators, competitors and the media. Therefore, it is better to explain that the laws prevent you from giving to the company. You can explain that it is a criminal offence and that the company could receive a massive fine, your government could jail and fine you and you would almost certainly lose your job.

Bribery, even in the Bible, is very rampant. People do away by bribing others just to attain their self-serving goals and suffice their selfish desires. However, God doesn't tolerate this act. Several books on the Bible talk about how we shouldn't give or accept bribe. One of the best examples about this can be found in the book of Deuteronomy - "Do not pervert justice or show partiality. Do not accept a bribe, for a bribe blinds the eyes of the wise and twists the words of the righteous."

Corruption is no different story. It too is commonly practiced in Jesus' time, and is very much punishable as well. Hosea tells us about how Israel is punished by God because of their practices, and yes, corruption is very much part of it. "Do not rejoice, O Israel; do not be jubilant like the other nations. For you have been unfaithful to your God; you love the wages of a prostitute at every threshing floor." They have sunk deep into corruption, as in the days of Gibeah. God will remember their wickedness and punish them for their sins."

In Asia, purchasing and supply are huge areas for potential corruption. Kick-backs are becoming routine and commonplace in many countries. Companies doing business in Asia must protect themselves against corrupt practices when they buy their own supplies and scrutinise all their purchasing officers in Asia carefully. They need to be on a constant lookout for unnecessary or unscrupulous purchases, family connections between purchasing staff and suppliers, unexplained wealth of purchasing staff and doubtful practices such as the absence of alternative quotes for the same supply, etc. It is wise to rotate the staff responsible for purchasing on a regular basis. This will deter the formation of cosy relationship between the staff and suppliers.

Anwar Ibrahim's election saga in Malaysia is a good example of the short-term/long term conflict that is generated. In Malaysia, the Barisan Nasional (BN) party led by Dr Mahathir had accused Anwar Ibrahim, the opposition party candidate, of sodomy, had him arrested and attempted to paint him as the immoral villain. However, the voters saw through the corrupt play of the BN party and voted almost unanimously for Anwar and the opposition party.

Another Asian example is ousted Thai Prime Minister Thaksin Shinawatra. Thaksin was accused of corruption, specifically related to his wife's purchase of some Bangkok property from a government agency in 2003. She purchased this property despite an anti-corruption law intended to bar politicians (and their spouses) from this exact type of business with state agencies. Although Thaksin pleads innocence, his exile and ousting from office during a celebrated coup speaks clearly of the public's perception.

Corruption is not only unique to Asia. For every rat that you see, there are probably hundreds hiding in the drains. This was true with financial scandals. The scandal at Enron was followed shortly by Arthur Anderson, Global Crossing, Adelphia, WorldCom, Tyco, HealthSouth, and ImClone.. Corporate fraud is a plague has swept across the entire global business landscape. It has spread to Europe, the Dutch grocer Ahold, Italian dairy-products company Parmalat and Hollinger International Inc, the newspaper company controlled by Conrad M. Black, a Canadian-born British Lord. Corruption also escalates into the form of insider trading, abuses of executive powers, trickery and executives in power to take advantage of the weaknesses in corporate governance and loopholes in financial systems. The solutions are transparency, accountability and tough laws against the law-breakers.

Few of us understand the Byzantine accounting methods Enron allegedly used to justify its earnings. Dennis Kozlowski and his gang received indecent salaries and perks. The lesson for all to learn is that power corrupts. Therefore those responsible for controlling large and small companies ought to be conscious of a fine line between corruption and ethical practices. Once you cross over this fine line and at the slightest hints of trouble, the whole system will come after you.

Corporate governance is extremely critical. Samuel A DiPiazza, Jr, the Global CEO of PriceWaterhouseCooper commented on the 29 February 2004 Channel News Asia programme "Agenda," that corporate governance emanates from the selection process of the CEO and board members. It should no longer select key personnel in the golf course. In the same programme, Michael Rake, the Chairman of KPMG International also said that the corporate culture needed to change as too much power was vested upon one person, therefore the suggestion on segregation between the Chairman and CEO positions.

On the other hand, one has to be careful that too much legislation, such as the Sabanes-Oxley Acts does not kill the golden goose. Bureaucracy should not rear its ugly head to impede businesses. A right balance is required.

The key to staying out of corruption is like avoiding contracting AIDS. You have to make a decision upfront not to fall into this trap. If you have decided to be ethical in your business practices, you will not succumb to the pressures and opportunities that may arise for you to earn a few million dollars if you can lie about certain information. You can also rest assured that you need not worry about how to extricate yourself from the quicksand of corrupt practices. Those who are corrupted should get out of it quickly. Those who are not in corrupted practices should not even think about getting involved with corruption. Corruption is a criminal offence and your future will be ruined if you commit this crime.

Principle No. 14

People – life and death matters. (Matthew 10:1 He called his twelve disciples to him and gave them authority to drive out evil spirits and to heal every disease and sickness)

Winning and high-performing companies share the belief that their core asset is the people who have the knowledge, skill and experience. Maximizing the value of those core assets is critical to business success. It takes the form of the strategy to acquire, retain, measure, manage and leveraging on the strengths of their people. It is no longer true that people are the key assets of the company. It is the good people that are the key assets and give life and vitality to the organisation. Bad people are the liabilities that spell death and trouble.

Jesus recognises the importance of people. He delegates to them to do God's work and fully entrust them with authority even to drive out evil spirits and heal every disease and sickness.
He even died for them so that they can be saved.

Competitors can catch up on core competencies. Benchmarking and reengineering may put them on the cutting edge. But only dedicated individuals can continuously produce new, creative and exciting ideas that allow a company to reinvent itself, manage its self-renewal process, and foster a true learning organisation. Yet, many companies still fail to use the right management and leadership strategies to motivate and retain their staff.

Creative talent, while arguably the most prized asset for any corporation, is probably also the most unrealized. Creative people are thought to be nonconformist, unpredictable, self-absorbed and therefore difficult to manage. Because many organisations are filled with conformists who tend to like other conformists, the frustrations and limitations of such stifling organisations drive creative people out.   Therein lies the organisation's loss. Attracting, developing and keeping maverick talents are a major challenge to any leader.   It is essential to create an environment that offers a high degree of freedom and encourages original ideas.

Company CEOs preached about people being their most important assets. However, their managerial actions do not match the rhetoric. Many quote examples of CEOs downsizing and firing of the people the first instance the company is in financial difficulty. Operating budgets are slashed on training and development. Employees can clearly see that the

Page 67

actions of the management action do not support the words. These CEOs got it all wrong. They should be hard on performance but soft on people.

When Richard Branson nominates his people as Virgin's greatest asset, he points adroitly to something that gives a corporation a long-term, inimitable competitive edge: the creative talent of its individual employees. He believed that loyal employees in any company create loyal customers who in turn create happy shareholders.

In 1993, Branson gave a speech to the British Institute of Directors. His audience no doubt expected to be amused. Instead, the speech began: "Let me share with you the philosophy behind our experiences at Virgin. The basic principles are 'People matter'."

When interviewed on Virgin's key success factors, Branson replied: "I'm absolutely certain that it is a question of the kind of people you have, the way you motivate them. I'm sure that is what can make any company successful. If you can motivate your people, you can get through bad times and you can enjoy the good times together. If you fail to motivate your people, your company is doomed not to perform well. I find that I spend a lot of time trying to concentrate on motivating. Part of Virgin's management philosophy is based on the fundamental belief that the individual is all-important in our company."

Sam Walton, the founder of Walmart took five hours at the shareholders' meeting to individually thank his four thousand excellent performing staff. Subsequently, he would invite them all to his home. Proctor & Gamble treated its staff as family members. All these top and successful companies truly recognise their people's contributions to the success of their companies.

Boulton, Richard E S et al said: "In 1978, on average, book value represented 95% of market value, while 10 years later it was 28%. Today, it is estimated that 80% of stock value is driven from assets that do not appear on the balance sheets, assets like people, brands, knowledge and relationships."

The issue relating to company is usually the "what and how" rather than the "who". This is the wrong emphasis. It is no use having all the correct strategies and resources when you do not have the right people to do the job. To compete successfully externally, you need to have people perform successfully internally.

Principle No. 15

People work hard for money, but they will die for a cause.(Acts 7:59 While they were stoning him, Stephen prayed, "Lord Jesus, receive my spirit")

Most people will work hard for money if properly motivated. Though it may help, more money is not the key to making your employees more passionate. It is a myth to think that you do not need passion if only you have good staff and pay them well. It helps to have good people and to pay them well. However, passion needs to be embedded in a cause that the people can invest themselves personally in. This will spur the employees on as they can grasp something out of this cause. It is not just about money. People simply would not follow someone for long if he is not chasing after a big and worthwhile dream.

Thus companies need to provide a deeper meaning or purpose to life for their employees to unleash their fullest potential. If the employees find a meaningful cause for what they are doing, many will be passionate and some will die for that cause. People through the ages have demonstrated this intrinsic desire to die for one's beliefs whether they are religious, political or social. In the same vein, good organisations are those that are great at rallying people around a lofty cause. And the magnitude of this cause can even turn into a crusade.

The Indian born founder of Hotmail Inc., Sabeer Bhatia could *only* offer a cause to the people who joined him in starting up Hotmail. He could not afford to offer them any salary. Many of his people decided to join him regardless of the lack of pay because of their faith in his project and the potential of the Internet. They had no goals for immediate monetary gratifications. Today, as a result of the huge success of Hotmail, the people who stuck with Sabeer have struck it rich. Sabeer Bhatia was able to turn the cause into a crusade with cult-like fanaticism. He was able to command the full dedication of his followers.

If what people do on the job is placed in the context of a good cause such as improving the quality of life, contributing to the betterment of mankind etc, the impact can be dramatic. Barnevik, the former chairman of ABB Brown Boveri, says that he is motivated by a desire to create a better world by generating employment thereby making the world more liveable with clean energy and transportation.

History has shown that there are many people who would die for a cause. They call them martyrs. Under King Nero of the Roman Empire in 64

AD, thousand of Christians were tortured and put to death because they believed in a faith – Jesus. Stephen as mentioned in the Bible was the first early Christian to be put to death (Acts 7: 59) for a cause that he believed in.

For Branson, too, social concerns are an important concept of his corporate philosophy. On many occasions, he has put his money where his mouth is. For example, Virgin produced low-priced Mates condoms in response to the AIDS crisis. He also bid for the national lottery franchise in the UK with the promise to donate all the profits to charity. The CEO of BP, David Simon has said that environmental protection is a significant corporate cultural value: "We have an action plan in which 50,000 BP employees participate. Our employees have hopes for the world and for their children." Some environmentalists concede that BP is at the forefront of multinational organisations taking global warming seriously. Anita Roddick, the founder of The Body Shop has also built a successful business that respects nature, animals, people and employees.

When your staff firmly believes in the company's cause, they will go beyond the call of duty.

Cholesterol is like the calibre of staff. LDLs are the dysfunctional staff and the HDL the good ones cleaning up the mess left by the LDLs. (Genesis 6:9-22 – God said to Noah, "I am going to put an end to all people, for the earth is filled with violence because of them. I am surely going to destroy both them and the earth.")

The human body requires some cholesterol to function properly. These cholesterol – "good" (high density lipoprotein or HDL) and "bad" (low density lipoprotein or LDL) ones – are found in all cells which help to carry fats in the body. Similarly, in every organisation, there are two categories of employees. There are the "bad cholesterol" employees as well as the "good cholesterol" employees. Those in the first category, the "bad cholesterol" are not natural self-starters and they require prodding by some external forces from the environment before they are compelled towards achieving certain goals. Too much of bad cholesterol can increase the risk of heart attack and stroke, as the bad cholesterol slowly builds up in the walls of the arteries that feed the heart and brain. Eventually, their vital supply of blood, oxygen and nutrients are cut off.

In the corporate context, the heart attack would be synonymous with a company suddenly waking up one day and finding that it has lost all its competitiveness. Usually the stroke or heart attack suddenly deals a lethal blow on their victims without any warning signs.

The "good cholesterol" employees are intrinsically motivated from within. They are intelligent, high achievers and will exercise initiative and assume responsibility towards achieving the goals. They are able to attain the goals even though the external circumstances may not be favourable or supportive of such actions. The "good" cholesterol carries the "bad" cholesterol away from the arteries and back to the liver, where it is metabolised from the body, thus minimising the clogging of the artery walls.

In the Bible, there are a lot of "good cholesterol" workers. Those who surrender to God, take responsibility and completely obey Him without compromising the quality of their deeds and their attitude towards it. In the sixth chapter of Genesis, we come across the character of Noah. Noah was instructed by God to build a huge ark, put two of every kind animal inside, gather his family and store food. God told Noah that there was going to be a flood that will wipe out the whole earth. "I am going to bring floodwaters on the earth to destroy all life under the heavens, every creature that has the breath of life in it. Everything on earth will perish (v.

17)." For the average person, this would be bizarre. We would be doubtful and probably mocking of what God had just declared. But Noah didn't ask any questions. He immediately obeyed God. "Noah did everything just as God commanded him (v. 22)."

The "good cholesterol" employees have a high level of internal energy or "qi" which propels them forward despite the external difficulties. The danger of not establishing the desired corporate culture is that it will not only fail to spur the "bad cholesterol" employees towards achieving the desired corporate goals but may even deter and demotivate the "good cholesterol" employees from doing so.

One way of perpetuating good cholesterol is to ensure that you have good genes and cloning at the recruitment stage. This is why Bill Gates of Microsoft hires the best, brightest and highly motivated of the new university graduates, mainly the "good cholesterol" personnel. He creates the environment where these individuals can thrive. As the critical mass of "good cholesterol" employees work in concert to share experience, stimulation and knowledge, the energy level "qi" shoots up. This also raises the contribution levels of the "bad cholesterol" employees and gets the whole company all motivated and charged up.

A good example of how the "bad cholesterol" players can be the "bad apple" to ruin the proverbial "barrel" is the culture of greed in Wall Street. Corporate America only views profit and growth in the short term. This is clearly evidenced through the quarterly reporting and results system which is prevalent in the American Stock Market. The head-honchos of many of the driving corporations on Wall Street such as Lethman Brothers, AIG, etc knew they were selling toxic assets…but they were simply following the greedy tenets of the culture which surrounded them. If they had avoided those toxic assets in the past few years while everyone around them were pursuing those bad-assets, the leaders of those organizations would have been seen as super conservative and they themselves would have been shunned. These corporations and their leaders were simply caught-up in the culture which they helped to create. And the downfall of their companies is the evidence that the culture must change by working out the bad cholesterol and building-up the good. ones,

A great way to develop good cholesterol is by training or exercising. Some people are not able to do their jobs well because they are not adequately trained for the purpose. Good training and development programmes like exercising increase the "good cholesterol" employees and reduce the dysfunctional personnel. To further foster the "good cholesterol" performance, your staff incentive scheme should be consistent in rewarding the good employees and penalise the bad ones.

Thus understanding the facts about "good and bad" cholesterol employees will help take better care of your corporate health. It will help you avoid a corporate heart attack or stroke.

Principle No. 17

To avoid having nightmares, do not go to bed with the devil. (Judges 16:1-21 – To Delilah: "See if you can lure him into showing you the secret of his great strength and how we can overpower him so we may tie him up and subdue him.")

Some businesses fail because the company teams up with the wrong partner. There are many principles in marriage that are equally applicable to seeking a business partner. As in a marriage, the wrong choice of parties can be very costly, messy and emotionally draining. It is easy to jump into bed with anybody, but one needs to pay a heavy price to split if it does not work out. Do not dance with the wolf, you may be eaten up alive. The marketplace is a jungle out there, if you are not careful, you can become the lunch or dinner for your competitors as well as your partners. The guiding principle in selecting a suitable partner is to allow your head instead of your heart to decide.

If you team up with the wrong party, you are bound to fail, no matter how favourable the circumstances are currently. Bad times and crises will always hit any relationships and partnerships. If the relationship is not built to last, it will not be able to withstand the test of time. Always do your homework well before teaming up with any partners. Check on their past experience and performance, particularly their track records of dealing with their business associates. A good reference and character check will save you tons of headaches at later stage. This is a better approach than to find out later to your despair that you have gone to bed with the wrong partner.

This is what exactly happened to Samson. We have heard about the popular story of Samson and Delilah in the book of Judges, how Delilah was bribed by the Philistines for 1100 shekels of silver to find out the weakness of Samson so that they could capture him and kill him. Samson was in love with Delilah, unaware of the harm that she could do to him. We can look at how Samson may have had doubts about and lied to Delilah three times when she asked about the secret behind his great strength, however was blinded by everything else which is what caused him to tell his secret anyway. Upon revealing his secret, Delilah immediately relayed this to the Philistines. "Then the Philistines seized him, gouged out his eyes and took him down to Gaza. Binding him with bronze shackles, they set him to grinding in the prison (16 v. 21)."

Similarly, strategic alliances can have profound impact on the businesses. To avoid problems relating to payment defaults, legal suits and quarrels, it is prudent not to deal with the "black sheep" of the industry in the first place. It is easy to identify these "black sheep" as their reputation stinks in the industry. It also pays to do careful checks on your business associates, customers and suppliers before entering into any partnership with them. If you go to bed with the devil, you will have nightmares.

Yet, many businesses fail primarily because of wrong partnership and strategic alliances. For example, many sub-contractors went bust because of business dealings with bad main contractors and errant owners in the construction industry in Singapore in the early 2000's. It is wiser to walk away from these businesses deals. It does not make good business sense to undertake a contract that may ultimately cost you major losses because you are unable to collect the money and face with back charges, liquidated and consequential damages. You may as well spare yourself of the headaches and agonies by not undertaking such contracts. However, this is often easier said than done as during the course of business, there are mounting pressures to take on projects because of shareholders' demands. Furthermore, the sales personnel are ingrained to clinch sales and it is a tremendous letdown for them if they are told not to canvass for businesses.

Similarly in the early 2000's, many joint ventures in China failed because of teaming up with the wrong equity partners. The local partners usually contributed land, factory and local manpower resources. The foreign parties contributed the financial resources and technical expertise. The problem in this situation was that for a partnership to work, it goes beyond mere tangible contributions. It requires good rapport, cultural understanding as well as the mettle to undergo the ups and downs in business challenges.

In family businesses, employing your own family members can pose lots of complications and challenges. You will be asking for a lot more trouble if you employ your sons-in-laws or daughters-in-laws. In some businesses, the bosses even employ their mistresses as employees. It is a sure-fire way of breeding discord, quarrels and trouble in the company which could then also extend into the home if you are not honest in your dealings.

The Japanese spend a lot of time to establish rapport and understanding with their partners before entering into business relationship. The purpose is to establish that the "magic and chemistry" are in alignment. When businesses have such alignments, they can go through difficulties which are bound to hit them one day. Just like in a marriage, if there are already cracks in the couples' relationship, when the pressures come on, the couple will break up as they are unable to handle them rationally.

The bottom line for business partnership to work is to select your partners carefully and judiciously. Working well with your partner can be very taxing emotionally and physically. Do not play with fire; similarly do not enter into relationship with the devil unless you wish to have endless bouts of nightmares.

Principle No. 18

Talent management functions like the kidney that hires the good personnel and fires the bad ones. (Mark 3:14-15, 14:10, 14:18– "Then Judas Iscariot, one of the Twelve, went to the chief priests to betray Jesus to them")

The two kidneys are the vital organs in the body that, amongst other functions, cleanse the blood of toxins and keep it chemically balanced. The kidneys are sophisticated reprocessing machines that process the blood to filter out the wastes and extra water. Similarly a good talent management system will hire the good personnel, retain them and remove the bad ones.

Good management is not just about recruiting the right people to do the right jobs. This is particularly important during challenging times when staff budgets are cut to the bone. A strong management team must also have the discipline and insight to identify the dead wood in the company, and to be able to take firm action to remove them. These executives are those who have being entrenched in the system because of their job security and seniority are just cruising along and marking time. They do not have active and productive contributions as well as add value to the company. Most managers acknowledge that the most difficult task is firing of employees, particularly somebody that they have worked with closely for several years. Usually, the people that you did not fire are the ones that make your life miserable.

In the Bible, we know very much about the twelve apostles appointed by Jesus. These twelve have been observed and trained by Jesus; He tested their faith, their capability to lead others, their loyalty to him, all the way down to the very last quality. He had selected twelve apostles who will carry out the mission he had called them to do. "He appointed twelve — designating them apostles — that they might be with him and that he might send them out to preach and to have authority to drive out demons (Mark 3:14-15)." And true enough, just like in the corporate world, the one Jesus didn't fire, Judas, was the one that betrayed him. We must not forget, however, that this was part of his plan. He was able to foresee everything before it actually happened. He knew that Judas was going to betray him (Mark 14:18).

We in this world, however, should not wait before somebody actually "betrays" us. Unlike Jesus, we don't have the power to foresee these things and this may lead to serious damage to the company. It would be best for us if we could weed out in the beginning those who we think would not be competent enough, else it might just be too late.

In many organisations, the decision-making power resides at the top. Empire-building by yes-men becomes the main preoccupation of the day. In the corporate intrigue of power struggle for status and position, the good personnel who may have differing views are stifled.

In talent management, the CEO has to look beyond himself and his abilities. He is smart if he hires the right people who may be better than he in those competencies to execute tasks that he himself is unable to do. He is then able to extend "his arms and legs" within the organisation to get things done in more efficient manner.

This philosophy is shared by Jack Welch as he felt that smart people hire smart people. He said: "Every time you hire someone that is not better than you, you have missed an opportunity, because if you got all the answers, who the hell needs anybody else." GE's core competence is the development of people and Welch's greatest legacy was to transform GE as the training ground of the world's top business honchos. For example, the other two candidates, namely Robert Nardelli and James McNerney who did not get Welch's job left GE to become CEO of The Home Depot and 3M respectively.

Hiring the right person takes good skill in recruitment. Sometimes, even with good evaluation and hiring efforts, the employers do make the wrong hire. In such situation, you need to try to redeem the situation or live with it or fire the employee and start the recruitment process all over again.

However, in the situation of lean staff budget, you do not have the luxury of carrying "dead wood". It maybe necessary to fire the wrong recruit. Jack Welch saw nothing wrong in delayering and downsizing incompetent people. To him, downsizing and delayering were absolutely necessary, and not firing workers who were a part of a losing business would have been more heartless than letting them go past the age of 50. Welch the self-actualizer is also Welch the pragmatist and he sees these decisions as necessary threads in the fabric of business. "That is business," stated the GE Chairman. He also explained it this way: "I think the cruellest thing you can do to somebody is give them the head fake….nice appraisals….that's called false kindness. A removal should never be a surprise."

On the other hand too, retaining the people that you want to keep has become a critical issue for organisations. When the key and talented people leave, there is a loss of experience and knowledge as well as continuity. Yet, companies would rather spend the valuable resources to recruit new talent from competitors than retaining the talent that they already have.

Principle No. 19

If you find a rat on the top of the pole, somebody must have placed it there. (Judges 20:15-16 – "Among all these soldiers there were seven hundred chosen men who were left-handed, each of whom could sling a stone at a hair and not miss.")

Troubled companies are often the result of incompetent management. The rot at the top will fester downwards as they also hire incompetent sub-ordinates. A good leader must ensure that the right people are in place or there is good talent management. Then the rest of the business will take care of itself.

When the Benjamites were preparing to fight with the Israelites, they didn't just send out any army they had. They made sure that the soldiers they send out can really battle it out there. From the 26,000-strong army they had, they've chosen 700 who were surely enough the best of the best. "At once the Benjamites mobilized twenty-six thousand swordsmen from their towns, in addition to seven hundred chosen men from those living in Gibeah. Among all these soldiers there were seven hundred chosen men who were left-handed, each of whom could sling a stone at a hair and not miss." Now that's good talent management.

Management failure, loss of market share, bad debts and poor financial management are the common manifestations of incompetent CEOs. Incompetent CEOs usually hire incompetent managers who may lack the necessary expertise, business acumen and skills to run the company's operations. These may result in untimely decisions and diminish the company's opportunities for growth and expansion in the ever-changing world of business.

It is good for companies to rotate the positions and management posts regularly. This will allow for the people to be rotated in order to handle new challenges and portfolio. It brings fresh perspective to issues not seen by the predecessors. It is also one good way to identify leaders. Exxon-Mobil has an executive development programme for the staff rotation every two to three years. Engineers are asked to be financial analysts and economists asked to become logistics executives, computer analysts, etc. Through such rotational programmes, the corporation's staff is better groomed for higher positions and responsibilities.

Turnaround expert Peter Tourtellot suggested over the years, companies tend to promote cadres of yes men to ever-higher positions. This happens because upper management likes being told it is on track. Being a part of the organisation for years, the acquiescent hires are finally promoted to their level of incompetence. At that point they become fearful of losing their jobs and make them even less likely to criticize the company's leadership constructively. Company heads should hire people with dissenting views if they want to have more balanced outlooks.

Most firms suffer from the weakness of having a team of homogeneous executives at the helm. Many of Compaq's top executives came from Texas Instruments and Firestone managers were "gum-dipped." This uniformity was no coincidence as these executives were the products of management selection and promotion processes that produced a standard product. It deprives the company of the much desired diversity of views and catalysts for effective response to market changes.

Consensual decision making works extremely well when there is the luxury of time to obtain to the "right" decision. The bad news is that the right decision often comes too late and becomes the wrong decision. Consensual decision often proceeds at a glacial pace.

In a company, the 'yes' men tend to find favour with the top management. However, they are usually promoted to their level of incompetence. To protect their "rice bowl", they are unlikely to offer critical or dissenting views. This is why top management should encourage people with different views, especially if these are supported by sound facts.

Take the sub-prime problem. Everyone involved in taking sub-prime lending deals knew the bubble was going to blow. And the dysfunctionality of the leadership only promulgated the use of these lending methods. All parties wanted to portray themselves as 'yes' men and refused to acknowledge that they were going down a path to disaster. Even the American government refused to regulate, espousing terms like "free-market economy" and allowing the world economy to creep closer to downfall with every new day. Even Alan Greenspan admitted that there was an oversight and mistake. Management within the organization of the banks continued to deceive themselves and others that the party was not going to ever end, so they continued to sell toxic assets and lead others to do the same.

To prevent a rat from getting up the pole, top management should have the discipline to remove "dead wood" in the company. Good management means not just hiring the right person but also firing the wrong one. This is good talent management.

Stage 2: Diagnosis

Principle No. 20

The first step to health is to recognise that you are sick and need treatment (Exodus 5-12 – Pharaoh: "Who is the Lord that I should obey him and let Israel go? I do not know the Lord and I will not let Israel go.")

The first step to good health is to acknowledge the presence of pain and that all is not well with the body. In many ways, the job of the turnaround manager is akin to that of the physician. The first step is to diagnose the corporate patient's condition before even attempting to prescribe the right medication. For prescription without proper diagnosis is malpractice.

The starting point is crucial to ensure that you have the right footing. To learn any skill, one has to take that first step. If you want to learn to swim, you have to take the first step of plunging into the water. To learn to parachute, you have to take the first step of jumping out of the airplane. One can read about and rehearse all the knowledge about swimming and parachuting or any other skills. However, one will never learn the skills if the first step is not taken to do the "real" thing. Ironically, it is found that the first step is always one of the most difficult steps to take in any venture, for it entails stepping into unknown territories and unchartered waters. Whether it is taking the first step to recognise that one is unwell or taking the first step to learn a new skill, the first step is also one of the most rewarding.

However, diagnosing the company's health is not as straightforward since many qualitative factors are involved. Oftentimes, the management also plays the game of denial and deception. Usually there are ample warning signs or symptoms of impending trouble such as high attrition of good staff, declining brand value etc. However, the management may be in the state of self-denial or does not wish to let out the knowledge of the company's predicament. Admission of the failure may expose them to criticism by the company's board of directors, shareholders and their peers. Unfortunately, this may result in delays in implementing the vital remedial actions during the early stage of under-performance. Adoption of prompt actions may have significantly improved the company's quandary and chances of survival.

Denial and deception remind us of the former Iraqi Information Minister, Muhammed Saeed al-Sahaf who made comical and untruthful remarks about the realities of the outcome of the US-Iraq war: "There are no American infidels in Baghdad. Never....They are coming to surrender or be burned in their tanks....Who are in control, they are not in control of anything – they don't even control themselves....Be assured. Baghdad is safe, protected." These statements were made despite the fact that the American forces have already landed at the Baghdad airport and within days Baghdad was captured by the allied forces.

Some sick companies play another game of "don't know and don't care". This is ignorance and apathy. Similar to taking care of physical health, these companies fell sick because of not knowing what to do as well as neglect. Their "cannot be bothered" attitude was perhaps the result of having been distracted by politics, mesmerised by new acquisitions or focused on the wrong strategies. These have misled the management from doing what is right for the company. As a result the company falls into ruins and tatters.

In Exodus, we see how the pharaoh played his own game of "don't know, don't care." When Moses and Aaron came to Egypt to tell Pharaoh what God had instructed them to, which is, to let the Israelites go, Pharaoh didn't listen to them, and instead, gave the Israelites even harder work. "Pharaoh said, "Who is the Lord that I should obey him and let Israel go? I do not know the Lord and I will not let Israel go." "Make the work harder for the men so that they keep working and pay no attention to lies."

Even after Moses performed various miracles, like turning his staff into a snake, turned the Nile River to blood, Pharaoh still didn't listen. Because of Pharaoh's neglect, the Lord sent out different plagues. Egypt suffered 10 plagues because of Pharaoh's stubbornness. God had to resort to great measures, like the killing of all the firstborn children, including Pharaoh's, just so he would let the Israelites go. Just like a sick company, Egypt needed badly a treatment as they have come to ruin because of their ruler's neglect and inability to recognise the need for his own treatment.

National economies also need to acknowledge that they are sick and need help. In the most recent economic crisis of the late 2000's, Japan was one of the first Asian nations to admit that there has been a substantial change in their economic fortunes. Simply said, the Japan economy is in recession. By admitting that there is a problem, they can now begin to heal – and heal aggressively.

And that is also how a company should respond. However, after recognising that the sick company needs treatment, sometimes the beleaguered management's vision may be limited by the symptoms and not addressing the cause. To maximize the benefit of finding a cure, at this juncture, it will be useful to probe further with broad questions such as:

Is the company in trouble with the law, bank, creditors, etc?

What is the cash flow position?

Is the company up for sale?

Can the company be turned around?

Should the company be closed?

Once these broad issues are determined, the turnaround manager then ventures into deeper issues relating to finance, marketing, operation, etc before deciding the appropriate treatment.

Proper medicine can only be administered after the acknowledgement that there is pain.

Do not blame your parents if you have no food, do not blame the government if your business is bad. (Jonah 1 – "Pick me up and throw me into the sea," he replied, "and it will become calm. I know that it is my fault that this great storm has come upon you.")

In Singapore, some business people could be heard saying at the coffee shops: "Blame your parents when you have no food and blame the government when your business is bad." Such wrong attitude provides a bad start to solving your problems. Shame and blame are not justifiable. Take responsibility.

Much of the world's trouble arose as people blame others for their misfortunes. When criminals are jailed for murder, they blame it on their childhood abuses that have caused them to be angry against society. Teenagers got addicted to drugs and they blame it on their divorced parents that caused them to be delinquent. People get obese and sue McDonalds for serving fat-laden hamburgers. No wonder, we are increasingly becoming such a litigious society. During the Asia financial crisis in 1998, some Malaysians were blaming the IMF, or "It's all Mahathir's Fault" for the crisis.

The buck should stop with you. Troubled companies should take responsibility for their pathetic state of affairs because of their past actions. Otherwise, there is no accountability and recognition of one's mistakes. Every action results in positive or negative consequence. Learning will not take place if one does not take cognizance of one's erroneous ways.

One of the most popular characters in the Bible known for this is Jonah. When God called out to him to take on a mission to preach against the city of Nineveh, Jonah ran away from the Lord. He went to another city and sailed away instead. The Lord however, sent out a great storm that threatened to wreck the boat he was riding. The crew who was sailing with him got scared and was desperate to find out what is behind the calamity they are experiencing. Jonah took responsibility for it, saying that it is because he ran away which is why the Lord sent out the storm. To save everybody else, Jonah told them to throw him in the ocean so that the storm will calm down. "Pick me up and throw me into the sea," he replied, "and it will become calm. I know that it is my fault that this great storm has come upon you." True enough, when they threw him overboard, the storm died down.

To keep Jonah safe, the Lord provided a fish to swallow him. It was while inside that fish that Jonah had learned his lesson; he had realized his mistakes and now recognized God's power, having more faith in him and his plans.

Many executives think that "corporate wellness" is a question of the economic situation, competition and customers' behaviour. Companies often fail to discover the real issues by refusing to self-critique corporate culture and management. Similar to physical wellness, most people think that genes determine health. However, they could not be more wrong. These same people will not change to more healthy eating habits, exercise regularly or maintain good mental health, thereby reducing themselves and losing-sight of their own ability to change their health for the better proactively. To these people, the individual and likewise the corporate efforts, the internal efforts, are not as important, as the external ones. However, this belief is an illusion – we are each responsible for our own physical or corporate wellness.

It is clear that our behaviours as well as emotional and spiritual make-up can affect our physical health. Corporations too should take responsibility for their own wellness by taking personal accountability for the outcome. As an author Robert H. Schuller once said: "If it is going to be, it is up to me."

Once you acknowledge the problem and take responsibility for your action, energy can be focused and channelled toward active and constructive remedies. Energy is sapped away when one plays the game of shame and blame or in medical terms, licking your own wounds. Blaming is like the bad cholesterol of the mind as it is directs the corporation toward vengeance and negativism. On the other hand, nothing is more beneficial to a good organisation than having a solid system of accountability.

Accountability is making good on one's commitments and promises and dealing with the consequences if these are not duly delivered. When this message is communicated clearly throughout the organization, the message will then be respected by all.

Business leaders must develop a strong sense of accountability. First, they must take responsibilities for their own decisions and know that the buck stops with them – at the end of the day, there is no one that more responsible for a bad decision than the leader. The leaders must not only know what tasks to assign, they must ensure that their senior colleagues take due responsibility for getting these tasks implemented effectively and efficiently. They must deliver results. When things go wrong, business leaders must not exonerate their guilt by finding scapegoats or through witch hunts.

Moving down the line, all the staff must be held accountable for their plans, commitments and actions. They have to deliver based on the financial budget committed for the year. They have to deliver to customers what they promise them. They have to take the rap for their actions.

Customers are generally quite forgiving if you admit to a mistake and try to make amends. No supplier is perfect and customers know that. However, customers can be vengeful if mistakes are "swept under the rug." Take the several late 2008 retreat trips made by AIG executives – each costing in excess of 500USD. Although this may be normal operating procedure for AIG, the American public has been stunned and vengeful in attitude toward this failing firm. The American public feels as if AIG, which has received a significant bail-out from the US government, should be tightening their belts, admitting mistakes and repairing the failing business. However, what the American public sees are AIG executives flaunting the money that has been provided by the taxpayer – and none of it going to repair the failing economy. The AIG management is merely good at getting handouts from the government and not taking responsibility by this action.

The important thing here is that you take responsibilities for any mistakes, rectify the mistakes, make restitution if necessary and ensure that the problems do not recur.

Taking responsibility is the first step to recovering from a mistake. Then, it is necessary to create a plan to rescue. For economies which falter, the same must be said. The financial tsunami of the late 2000's is a good example. The Singapore government recognized the need to introduce an expansionary budget in 2009. This expansionary budget should be implemented soon to avoid the continued wanton increase in both individual and private company bankruptcy. By admitting that there is a problem, taking responsibility and establishing a strong response, the Singapore economy's recovery can be strong in the face of the harsh economic times ahead because the leaders have taken action and responsibility to fix the problem..

Principle No. 22

A company in crisis is in a nightmare, but this nightmare does not disappear when the company wakes up (1 Peter 4:7, Habakkuk 2:3, Matthew 4:17 – "For the revelation awaits an appointed time; it speaks of the end and will not prove false. Though it linger, wait for it; it will certainly come and will not delay")

Crisis is visibly recognised when the company faces credit squeeze, negative profitability, cash flow problems and collection concerns. However, before the full crisis manifests itself the management of failing companies goes through four stages of crisis development: Hidden or ignorant crisis occurs when senior management overlooks the signals of impending failure; denial and excuse crisis, when the crisis is explained away in the belief that it will disappear and therefore, no action is necessary; financial and blaming crisis happens when some token actions are taken as "stop-gap" measures without implementation of large-scale or radical change; and bankruptcy or surrender crisis, characterised by the inability to take action as the situation may be beyond redemption.

Necessity is the mother of invention. A crisis is often necessary to stimulate new initiatives and to persuade management to radical measures, accepting new approaches that they would not normally be prepared to consider. When a man knows that he is going to die in a month, usually his mind becomes much more focused as he has limited time to resolve outstanding issues in his life.

Once there is awareness of the onset of a crisis, the company needs to adopt changes similar to those of a sick and dying patient. As outlined by Elisabeth Kubler Ross, MD, in her classic book *On Death and Dying,* those stages begin with denial and progress through anger, bargaining, depression and acceptance.

Hidden and denial crises might first surface when shareholder or subordinates question the company's latest results or when a creditor such as a banker points out a disturbing decline in sales. The management's normal reply may be "We have seen this before; there is a little hiccup in the economy and our business is seasonal; or nothing has gone wrong." There is a prevailing ignorant and apathetic response towards the impending crisis.

Anger, on the management's part, during the financial crisis, is sometimes manifested in defensive posture, particularly when the level of criticism becomes amplified. Bargaining is a last-ditch effort on management's part to regain control. This stage shows itself as a variation of blaming, because the remedies that management contemplates are beyond its means and the management blames it on the poor economy. The CEO may be asking for some more credit from the bank or waiting for a white knight to save the company from certain death.

When bargaining has failed, depression sets in. Creditors and bankers start to demand payments; next customers, suppliers and good employees defect. As the bankruptcy stage sets in, managers begin to accept its fate. They simply give up. The acceptance stage is marked by a sense of forthright preparedness for the inevitable. This is the time when management has to accept that it is unable to do the job and surrender to the unpleasant circumstances. They are either to be ousted unceremoniously or let the company enter into bankruptcy proceedings. Thus this final stage is usually followed either by failure or successful recovery usually led by a new management team.

There are numerous instances in the Bible where Jesus and his disciples warn us about the coming revelation. In his first book, Peter tells us: "The end of all things is near. Therefore be clear-minded and self-controlled so that you can pray (1 Peter 4:7)." Habakkuk tells us a similar message: "For the revelation awaits an appointed time; it speaks of the end and will not prove false. Though it linger, wait for it; it will certainly come and will not delay (Habakkuk 2:3)." And ultimately, Jesus tells us himself: "Repent, for the kingdom of heaven is near (Matthew 4:17)." Just like crises in the corporate world can be devastating, so will Jesus' revelation be apocalyptic; therefore we must prepare for it.

No matter the current market, crises are very rampant, laying hidden beneath the surface and can destabilize a company at any time. No one in Asia in 2003 predicted or pre-empted the devastating economic impact of the SARS epidemic. Several Asian economies were literally crippled as people feared for their lives and shunned public places and curtained all overseas travels. The crux of a good crisis management is to be prepared at all times. The Asian governments got wiser in 2004 and although there were some isolated reports of SARS infections, another major disaster or crisis was averted due to better control and preparation.

Likewise with the current financial crisis we are seeing in the late 2000's. Only the wise financial advisors foresaw that there would be issues with the American lending industry, but even those wise advisors could not have foreseen the following global economic crash which occurred due to the American government's fumbled response. Even now, after the crisis is in full-bloom, bankrupt and collapsing firms are ignoring their pain and the economy's struggles and continuing with business as usual – never realizing that their own crisis is leading to the world economy's doom.

The message to be gleaned from this: Wake up and be prepared for crisis because it can strike any company at anytime.

Principle No. 23

The key to successful turnaround is early intervention. (Matthew 6:33, Psalm 139:13 – "But seek first his kingdom and his righteousness, and all these things will be given to you as well.")

Most diseases including cancer and heart problems are easier to cure if detected early. Similarly, most sick companies can be turned around if the problems are discovered early. Sick companies need to be placed urgently into the intensive care units as the normal treatment regime is ineffective.

The Bible tells us about the "early detection program" of coming to Jesus. In Matthew chapter 6, verse 33 tells us: "But seek first his kingdom and his righteousness, and all these things will be given to you as well." After all, who can specialize in us more than our maker Himself? In the book of Psalms, David reminds us through his words: "For you [God] created my inmost being; you knit me together in my mother's womb. "This means that in all things, we must go to God first. Be it a problem, a sickness, or a crisis, our immediate shoulder should be God.

Unfortunately, owing to denial, ego or pure ignorance, many sick companies do not seek help till it is very late. Troubled businesses usually try to conceal their problems from others for obvious reasons – the creditors may stop their loans, suppliers may stop supplies, employees may jump ship etc. However, like sick people, sick company need to seek urgent help. They need to engage specialists to facilitate the restructuring programmes and to face the new harsh realities before it is too late.

Much like human health, more businesses are also destroyed by neglect than any other causes. This is why regular health check is vital to prevent any unexpected health problems, detect them early so that appropriate remedies can be administered.

The traditional accounting methods such as balance sheets and profit and loss statements only capture the measurable financial aspects of the company at a certain point in time. Furthermore, the real financial health of the company can be masked by deliberate accounting irregularities as in cases at Enron and WorldCom. By the time the sickness is visibly evident in the company's accounts, it may already be too late to take corrective action to reverse the situation. Oftentimes, when the accounts show red, the company is extremely sick or suffering from haemorrhage. There are many other non-quantifiable financial factors that may impinge upon the health of the company. These may include high staff attrition, low morale or an incompetent CEO. Usually, there are ample warning signs or symptoms of impending trouble. However, these warning signals are often ignored or suppressed; hence the onset of a crisis comes as a surprise.

In 2000, with the dotcom crash, the American Federal Government lowered the interest rate and the economy recovered swiftly, the overall world economy not suffering overly much. Unfortunately, the rate was kept low and banks began to lend irresponsibly, starting a trend of lending to people which could not afford to service their loans. As the housing bubble started to show signs of faltering throughout the mid-to-late 2000's, the problem was not arrested. The Fed waited to increase the rate until 2005, and by then, it was too late to save the economy as the housing bubble was already well on its way to bursting. The downfall of the world economy should have been recognized and halted in the mid-2000. Early detection and solid action to avert disaster was possible, but just not taken into consideration.

Early detection of business problems is vital to sustaining a company's growth, manage the crisis effectively and to contain the economic distress. Business problems rarely occur suddenly. Most problems develop over a long period of time due to a series of financial, legal, operational and strategic errors or miscalculations that went largely ignored or undetected by management. Some obvious examples that a company is heading down the wrong course include persistent operating losses, high key staff attrition, and loss of morale and market share.

It is important to pre-empt any problems from arising by looking out for warning signals. Therefore, a proverb that says: "The superior doctor prevents sickness. The mediocre doctor attends to impending sickness. The inferior doctor treats the actual sickness."

Principle No. 24

Companies should go for regular health checks. (James 3:1, 1 Corinthians 3:12-15 – "If what he has built survives, he will receive his reward. If it is burned up, he will suffer loss; he himself will be saved, but only as one escaping through the flames.")

Many companies have annual medical examinations and health screening for their employees but are negligent when it comes to their own corporate check-ups. Poor management and financial information systems typically get blamed for management's inability to "see it coming." This is because the checks were done too late.

Companies should know their current fitness level as part of the regular health check. The fitness level assesses the state of health of the global, local economic and political arena, the industry specific issues and dynamics as well as the issues relating to the company. The trouble is that companies do not know their state of fitness and often adopt a "fire-fighting" approach whenever the companies are in trouble. Early diagnosis is always better than a post-mortem.

Jesus' teaching to his disciples emphasized that accountability was a big part of their fellowship with one another and their pact of faith with Him. Keeping others in check before they go off-track is important, especially for the teachers and leaders of both our spiritual and secular institutions. Which is why the Bible tells us that teachers will be judged more strictly, because they are the ones leading the people, therefore they should be more careful. "Not many of you should presume to be teachers, my brothers, because you know that we who teach will be judged more strictly (James 3:1)."

Paul teaches us in 1 Corinthians 3:12-15 this analogy: "If any man builds on this foundation using gold, silver, costly stones, wood, hay or straw, his work will be shown for what it is, because the Day will bring it to light. It will be revealed with fire, and the fire will test the quality of each man's work. If what he has built survives, he will receive his reward. If it is burned up, he will suffer loss; he himself will be saved, but only as one escaping through the flames." That is why, to prevent this, teachers, or disciples, must keep each other in check, before anything even happens, to them or to their disciples.

On the economic front, the check should evaluate some of the leading economic indicators such as GDP growth, consumer confidence and stock market growth. Political stability is also critical as political chaos can severely upset economic and business confidence. On the industry front, the check should include reviewing the business trends, consumer spending, the competition as well as the product life cycle. At the company level, the check should reveal a full picture of the company's profit and loss, balance sheet as well as cash flow positions. The use of financial ratios as key performance indicators will help to identify current and potential troubles. Control procedures should be reviewed to ensure that the company does not undertake too much risks and financial burdens.

Additionally, business models become obsolete very quickly due to changes in the market landscape. As discussed previously, early detection of a problem is a must. However, in some organizations, the staff dare not tell the CEO or Founder that he is naked – but when the tide recedes, the companies which are swimming naked are exposed. Only through calling-in an outsider to do a health check can you is sure you are getting an unbiased opinion. Those who rely only on their internal checks and balances may be preparing to stand in the market without their clothes.

Through these fitness checks, the company can then determine whether the impending problem is financial in nature, which may be a case of over-gearing and cash flow problem. Operational and control issues may be involved too, such as frauds, financial scandals, etc. These checks can prepare the top management for some exigencies such as a change of political regime, government or terrorist attacks, etc.

When the checks revealed any areas of weaknesses, the company needs to prescribe the appropriate treatment. The company may need to employ some form of financial re-engineering to resuscitate the company. If necessary, enlist the assistance of turnaround specialists. Therefore knowing the state of one's health is inadequate, one needs to take appropriate actions to remedy the situation.

Have you done your health check lately and got your temperature checked?

Principle No. 25

Knowing the type of viruses that are plaguing the company is half the cure. (Deuteronomy 29:1-18 – "Make sure there is no man or woman, clan or tribe among you today whose heart turns away from the Lord our God to go and worship the gods of those nations; make sure there is no root among you that produces such bitter poison")

Just as a competent medical practitioner needs to understand the causes of a disease, a competent turnaround manager must understand the causes of the company's decline. Much like human beings, companies are perpetually faced with all kinds of viruses or threats to their health; some are internally created whilst others are externally generated.

The human body is always battling all these threats so as to maintain the equilibrium of health or homeostasis. Likewise, an organisation that is able to successfully address both internal and external problems (from operational hiccups to market threats) is bound to enjoy corporate health and longevity.

The troubled company usually gets attacked by two types of problems – internal and external viruses.

Many of the internal viruses are generated by the company and are actually within the company's control. They are usually associated with weak management and poor financial system. The onslaught of such viral attacks can lead to bad or untimely business decisions, poor financial control and other related problems. The medical analogy for eliminating internal viruses may merit the use of surgery such as downsizing, restructuring or change.

For example a poll of the members of the Turnaround Management Association, people whose job is to rescue troubled businesses revealed that while 22 percent of turnaround professionals cited increased competition as a reason for business failures, a full 58 percent squarely put the blame on faulty management decision-making. Similarly, other studies have found that internal, rather than external causes are behind up to 90 percent of company failures. Peter Tourtellot, a turnaround manager, noted that one of the most common mistakes was that troubled companies did not listen to their customers. He also found that communication was sadly lacking in most of the troubled businesses.

Business journalist, Bruce G. Posner cited some of management's most embarrassing mistake. "What kills companies," he said, "has less to do with insufficient money, talent, or information than with something more basic: a shortage of good judgment and understanding at the very top."

External viruses being macro in nature are often beyond the company's control. The entire industry or marketplace or even the whole country may be stricken by the same type of external viruses. The attacks can be silent, swift and often appear non-threatening at the beginning. Examples of external viruses include economic recession, change in technology and consumer behaviour, political turmoil, natural disasters and terrorist attacks.

Such external viruses are harder to eliminate and predict. Sometimes, even having a strong management team is inadequate to cope with external viruses as the corporate culture is unable to manage change expediently. The remedy is to foster a strong and healthy corporate culture that is the immune system of the company.

God considered Israel as his people. He freed them from the clutches of Egypt and saved them from hundred other tragedies that befell them. In the book of Deuteronomy, as God instructed Moses to make a covenant with the Israelites, Moses warned them that there should be no one among them who is against the Lord. "Make sure there is no man or woman, clan or tribe among you today whose heart turns away from the Lord our God to go and worship the gods of those nations; make sure there is no root among you that produces such bitter poison (v.18)."

He had declared this as he knows that this will be destructive among the Israelites; corruptive, that each one and ultimately all of them can turn away from God and worship idols, just like what they have witnessed in Egypt and in the countries they've passed. This is much like a virus, and God was aware of it. He knows that Israel have fallen on this sin, and he knows that it can happen again. He understood what downfall the Israelites could end up into and thereby made a pre-emptive strike to prevent it.

Thus the best prognosis is to identify the viruses, predict their potential damage and eradicate them before they are able to penetrate, attack and wreak havoc to your system.

Principle No. 26

Tradition and past business assumptions may be the root causes of the disease in the ailing company. (Micah 6 – "You have observed the statutes of Omri and all the practices of Ahab's house, and you have followed their traditions. Therefore I will give you over to ruin and your people to derision; you will bear the scorn of the nations.")

For a troubled company, it is prudent to challenge all "sacred cows" – those old and sacrosanct business assumptions. It is probable that some of these old "sacred cows" which were based on prior erroneous perceptions and assumptions that got the company into trouble.

In times of rapid change, a strategic failure is often caused by an incorrect or false assumption. We console ourselves by telling ourselves that we have gone through the present problem before and hence are able to tide through it again. Often, we also falsely assume that this change is temporary, or that the impact would be limited and hence can be ignored. Success has got into the management's heads and become their greatest root cause of the disease. The prevailing mindset is that "we have been successful and everything worked in the past and failures will not happen here." Then the company's profit erodes and their stock plummets.

In a similar vein, we may dismiss the pain in our body such as a headache or stomach ache and just treat it with simple over-the-counter medication without noting its severity. Sometimes, this could well turn out to be more serious or life-threatening such as stomach cancer or prelude to a heart attack and stroke. The high death toll during the SARS outbreak of 2003 was also partly attributed to the initial dismissal of the symptoms and nonchalant attitudes adopted by some of the infected victims causing it to spread rapidly.

There are lots of traditions in the Bible that the people then followed, but not all of them were approved by God. Israel, on the one hand, made a mistake by following a tradition which defied what God had specifically told them not to do – the worship of other gods, that is. "You have observed the statutes of Omri and all the practices of Ahab's house, and you have followed their traditions. Therefore I will give you over to ruin and your people to derision; you will bear the scorn of the nations."

Many of these old and obsolete assumptions happen in large and well-known companies whose traditional cash cow businesses have become sacred cows and end up as sacrificial cows or mad cows when market forces turn against and overwhelm them.

Time and again, some wrong business assumptions and perceptions by experts have led many companies astray. For example, Ken Olson, president of Digital Equipment said in 1977: "There is no reason anyone would want a computer in his or her home." Chairman of IBM, John Akers added in 1983: "The world market for computers is about 275,000." Because of these erroneous assumptions and perceptions, it is no wonder both Digital Equipment and IBM were late in entering the personal computer market.

Gary Hamel said: "One of the things that I believe is that whatever you need to know to create the future you can know. By definition, whatever Microsoft needed to know, it knew. Whatever CNN needed to know, it knew. Take an example. Why was it CNN rather than BBC that created the global news network? I do not think it was a prediction issue for CNN. It was not somehow they had some wonderful planners who saw what the BBC could not see. All the things that you needed to create CNN were totally visible. You had cable television eroding the monopoly of the traditional broadcasters. You had satellite technology that made it possible to put a team anywhere in the world and get signal out. Anybody who was willing to challenge their own assumptions could see those things."

Michael Dell believes that the status quo is never good enough, even if it means painful changes with loss of his reputation. Success is greeted with five seconds of praise followed by five hours of post-mortem on what could have been done better. To Dell, celebration breeds complacency. He once rejected an idea to display Dell artefacts in the company's lobby because "museums are looking at the past." Says Michael Dell: "Celebrate for a nanosecond. Then move on."

Continued use of the "business as usual" principle has sapped the American Big 3 automaker's business for the past twenty years. Each year they would acknowledge that more and more of the automotive market in America was being lost to the Japanese automakers, but do nothing to stop the trend. They would continue to do business as usual and never acknowledge that the American people were changing – until it was too late. And now, the automotive chiefs are in trouble. Between this arrogance in the face of a changing market and the heavy toll that the economic downturn has taken in the automotive industry, they decided that they needed a bail-out from the US government in order to keep their employees in jobs. However, still, they have not realized that business as usual is not a viable business model. All three executives appeared before the American congress in late 2008 to ask for financial help – and all three rode to this meeting in private jets. The American populace was outraged and appalled – and so, too was the American congress. Not only did congress tell the automakers "no," but they also indicated that they should come up with a new business model if they were to approach congress again with a request for help.

Hence, companies sow the seeds of failures and arrogance during good and successful times. Managers get addicted to the old formula of success and refuse to change when the competitive situation changes. To ensure its effective and successful implementation, the troubled company must critically re-examine and re-visit every business assumption.

Principle No. 27

To treat the symptoms, know your competitors and customers. To eliminate the root cause, know the market. (Proverbs 24:17-18 – "Do not gloat when your enemy falls; when he stumbles, do not let your heart rejoice, or the Lord will see and disapprove and turn his wrath away from him.")

Sun Tzu, the strategist in the Art of War said: "If you know yourself and the enemy, you need not fear the result of a hundred battles." Though it is important to know your competition, one should not do so at the expense of neglecting the customers. By merely knowing the competitor, it is like a person driving a car and constantly looking out for the competitor's car at his side. He is so pre-occupied with the competitor that he fails to look at the road ahead and may run into hazards.

It is easy for us to direct our attention on our enemies and lose sight of the things that we should be focusing on, particularly our own selves. This has proven to be destructive as well in the Bible. In the book of Proverbs, it is written that if our enemy fails, we shouldn't be happy about it because God doesn't want us to be that way. "Do not gloat when your enemy falls; when he stumbles, do not let your heart rejoice, or the Lord will see and disapprove and turn his wrath away from him." God fights off our enemies, but as it is written, he will turn his wrath away from our enemies if we ever rejoice at their downfall.

Red-blooded managers harbour a healthy competitive streak. However, when rivalry hardens into hatred and competitors become enemies, companies can be lured into a trap. Apple Computers viewed IBM as the evil empire that stood for everything that Apple employees hated – conformity, bureaucracy and dull gray boxes. Recall Apple's Orwellian advertisement during the 1984 Olympics. Even Apple's motto 'think different' contradicted IBM's slogan 'think'. Apple's anti-IBM ethic may have slowed employees' ability to recognise the threat posed by Microsoft. And based on the new ads which both companies are showing in the more recent times of the late 2000's, we can see that this hatred is still simmering under the surface and holding both companies back.

Similarly, in the US automotive industry in the 1960s, the General Motors, Chrysler, Ford Motors were after each other's throat. However, they totally neglected to protect their turf in the small car market and allowed the Japanese cars to penetrate and takeover this market segment.

Knowing the customer's present needs is also merely treating the symptom and not the ailment. Today's customers are more demanding; they want more of those things they value. If they value cheaper prices, they want even lower ones. If they value convenience or speed at the time of purchase, they want it even easier or faster. To meet customers' one hundred percent demands, most companies will lose their shirts and pants. Also, every product becomes a commodity or marginalized because of competition. Hence, companies' efforts may yield temporary results if they only deliver what the customers want currently. These attempts may not sustain the company's long-term growth, as they are unable to optimise on profitability, resource allocation and opportunities.

To ensure vibrant business and continued long-term growth, companies must strive to drive the market and generate the demand. They need to pre-empt both the customers' and competitors' present and future development. 3M's Post It notes are now one of the most commonly used office products, which nobody had asked for previously. Microsoft's operating software Window came not from responding to customers' demands or competitors' threat, but from anticipating them.

The 1980 launch of CNN by Ted Turner was ridiculed by American TV veterans CBS, NBC and ABC. The latter failed to tap a niche that no one had yet asked for: a 24-hour news service. Other great innovations of our time including the personal computer, jetliner and Internet; all created without any customers or competitors in sight.

Knowing the market and staying ahead of the curve is what has kept Google from falling with all the other American companies in the economic depression of the late 2000's. Because they have continued to foster innovation and have taken conservative risks in their business model, they have done well in 3Q 2008, a rare thing in the American economy. This also clearly shows power of the internet. This evolving medium is by no means insulated from the normal economy, however, that Google has managed to continue to grow in the face of an economic crisis speaks not only good for the company, but also for the medium and the focus on the market in which it thrives.

By simply knowing the customers and competition, you are merely treating symptoms, an ineffective and temporary solution. To assure long-term prosperity, it is important to treat the cause of the disease that is the negative results brought about by the market. Therefore, it is better to understand the market and envisage any potential problems, otherwise it may destroy you.

Principle No. 28

To understand the disease, learn to be the patient. (Hebrews 2:17-18 "Because he himself suffered when he was tempted, he is able to help those who are being tempted")

There is an old saying in Spain: "To be a bullfighter, you must first learn to be like a bull." You want to be a good fisherman, think like the fish. Then you will understand where the fishes normally like to hide so that you can cast your line or net at the right spot. In the medical context, the best way to learn about the disease is to learn to be the patient. Usually, the patient knows very well about the disease that is afflicting him. Besides researching about the disease, he will also strive to find a cure for the ailment as he is suffering from the pain of the disease.

For most people, it is hard to understand how we say that our God can relate to us. As a matter of fact, if we think about it, how can such a great, all-powerful, all-knowing and all-present God be able to know what's best for his people? It is because he suffered like how we do now, tempted like how we are too; which is why he is able to help us and understand where we are coming from, because he himself experienced the same things. "For this reason he had to be made like his brothers in every way, in order that he might become a merciful and faithful high priest in service to God, and that he might make atonement for the sins of the people. Because he himself suffered when he was tempted, he is able to help those who are being tempted."

In business, a manager needs to be on the ground – talk and interact with the various people: staff, suppliers, customers, business partners and even competitors. Through these various channels, the manager is able to acquire more knowledge of the industry and have better feel of the market. The manager does not operate in a vacuum and is better equipped to make sound decisions and take timely action. All these will curtail declining trends and may even result in future improvements. This is why the worst place for a manager is his air-conditioned room, where he is cut off from the realities and dynamics of the marketplace.

During his tenure, Lou Gertsner, the turnaround CEO of IBM became IBM's most hardworking salesperson – logging thousands of miles to visit key customers and prospects. His approach sent an unmistakable signal to every employee to be hands-on and created a new image for IBM. By staying in contact with the market, Gertsner was able to make the right decision to turn troubled IBM around.

Sun Tzu, in the art of war also advocated a "staying on the ground" policy. "Generally, in the case of armies you wish to strike, cities you wish to attack, and people you wish to assassinate, you must know the names of the garrison commander, the staff officers, the ushers, gatekeepers and the bodyguards. You must instruct your agents to inquire into these matters in minute detail."

A design engineer who never goes out to see the machines and work with the technicians, the banker who never uses the online services or queue up at the banks, the taxi owner who has not driven the taxi but takes his own car, the restaurant owner who has not been to the kitchen – these people will not understand and make good decisions about the customers' needs and the issues encountered by the staff.

Many managers do not know the actual situation on the ground and only blame and fire their staff whenever the company encounters financial difficulty. This does not solve the problem as they do not know the actual cause and make the situation worse by making hasty decisions. Taking impulsive actions taken without full understanding of the events on the ground is like dispensing the wrong medication to the patient. It may cause more harm as the disease spreads unabatedly.

Good decision can only be made when you possess first-hand knowledge on the ground. Many senior managers particularly those in the staff functions such as the financial, accounting, human resource and legal departments do not meet with the customers. By exposing these support staff to the problems on the ground, it will help them immensely in understanding the problem faced by the line personnel such as the sales and operations staff. This will in turn foster better rapport and co-operation among the line and support staff.

Therefore, get your feet wet by going to the grounds.

Principle No. 29

People tend to do what you inspect rather than what you expect (Matthew 26:36-45 -"Then he returned to his disciples and found them sleeping. "Could you men not keep watch with me for one hour?" Jesus asked Peter.")

Expectation sets the height of the bar, but it is regular inspection that resets the height of the bar so as to ensure it is achievable. The common notion is that what gets measured gets performed. This is why it is useful to have key performance indicators. They serve to inform management which aspects of the business are performing according to its intended objectives or otherwise. They act as a preliminary diagnostic tool that enables management to identify areas for improvement. The roles of the key performance indicators also add meaning to the financial and accounting information as well as to provide a quick overview of the company's performance.

In theory, if you need to inspect, supervise and manage the staff frequently, the chances are you have hired the wrong candidates. In reality, it is difficult to obtain a good fit of the right people and therefore inspection is necessary.

This was also true in the Bible. When he and three other disciples went to the garden of Gethsemane, he asked his disciples to keep watch while he went away to pray. When he came to inspect and check up on them, he found them sleeping and not keeping watch like how he instructed them to. He checked up on them two more times and still found the same thing. For Jesus, he knew that he needed to check up on them and see over what they were doing because he knew that they aren't able to follow what he had commanded them.

The key performance indicators used by the company may include financial as well as operational parameters. Financial ratios are common yardsticks derived from financial and accounting statements. The operational parameters may include more generalised criteria such as quality goals; reject rates, production targets as well as balanced scorecards, etc.

Most companies use the budgeting process to formulate the key performance indicators. However, the problem is that the key performance indicators in the budget are artificially stretched so that they become 'management' goals. The people who are supposed to deliver those goals on the ground may not be committed to them. This renders the whole budgeting exercise futile and a waste of time. Yet the irony is that companies expended immense resources and months of preparing for the annual budget.

Good companies focus on measurements in many ways. They share the information on the key performance indicators to their staff so that they are aware and can be committed to achieving those targets. These good companies hold their staff accountable to achieve those indicators. Although stretched, they must be achievable. The key performance indicators are regularly tracked and monitored. Strategies are reviewed and changed periodically to ensure alignment with the market dynamics.

Inspection should be followed with carrot and stick programmes to ensure that staff are rewarded or penalised for not achieving certain measurements. If the staff are unable to achieve their goals, one needs to also enquire whether it was a question of lack of proper training or motivation or unrealistic goal. This is why goals need to be inspected as well as measured if possible.

Principle No. 30

Life is Simple. And in business, the simpler the better (Psalm 19: 7 The decrees of the Lord are trustworthy, making wise the simple)

If there is one guiding motto in life, it is simplicity. This principle should reign supreme in all areas of life, from language, ideas to business and strategies. Yet, the irony remains that most people are attracted to complexity, thinking that simple efforts run the risk of being ridiculed as being obvious, simplistic or unoriginal. Contrary to what some may think, simplicity is hard to achieve. In fact, Karl von Clausewitz, the famous military historian, once said, "Everything is very simple in war, but the simplest thing is difficult."

The Bible always encourages simple living as epitomized by the life of Jesus. The Bible also makes simple things very wise as in Psalm 19:7 The instructions of the Lord are perfect, reviving the soul. The decrees of the Lord are trustworthy, making wise the simple. This was clearly evident in the conversation between Thomas and Jesus wherein Thomas asked Jesus about not knowing the way. Jesus replied to Thomas simply: "I am the way and the truth and the life. No one comes to the Father except through me."

In business, the most successful ideas are usually stunningly simple. In fact, simplicity is at the heart of many success stories in business. Management consultants are often guilty of clouding things with technical jargon and complex concepts. There is a tendency among business people to indulge in complicated and high-sounding buzzwords that give the impression of being smart and polished. Jack Welch, the chairman of General Electric, hit the nail on the head when he said, "Insecure managers create complexity. ... Real leaders don't need clutter. People must have the self-confidence to be clear, precise, to be sure that every person in their organization understands what the business is trying to achieve. You can't believe how hard it is for people to be simple, how much they fear being simple. They worry that if they're simple, people will think they're simple-minded."

The tenet that "business is simple" is one of Welch's fundamental beliefs. After all, "this is not rocket science," insisted Welch. To further his point, Welch has said that if you gave the same information to a group of business people, they would likely come up with the same answer to any problem put before them. Simplicity and informality have been constants throughout Welch's years.

Very often, the answer to improving company performance boils down to introducing simple ideas and making sure they get done. Success in business usually comes down to the ability to find a simple idea that distinguishes one from the competition. And while the idea differentiates your business from your competitor's, strategy gives wing to the idea that can make your business soar. While it is true that new ideas drive businesses, is the process of finding a new idea as complex as some have made it out to be? The simplest way to invent a new product is to borrow and adapt an existing idea.

Take for example, Papa John's Pizza, which was voted as the "Best Pizza Chain in America" for two years running in the early 2000's and whose simple approach to business generated almost US$900 million in annual sales. Its founder, John Schnatter, has this to say about his success, "There are no secrets to our success. It is all about better ingredients and quality and good old-fashioned hard work. The biggest thing we do differently is that we keep things simple."

Indeed Ralph Waldo Emerson captured the essence of simplicity superbly when he remarked: "Nothing is simpler than greatness; indeed, to be simple is to be great". Successful companies rely on simple concepts of clear focus on it core competence, do it much more efficiently than its competitors and have the right people to run the business.

Remember the acronym, KISS, 'keep it simple and short'. We need to keep businesses simple and more importantly, to make it simple for the customers to do business with us.

Principle No. 31

The greatest lesson is to learn faster than your competitors. (Proverbs 24:30-37 – Solomon: "I applied my heart to what I observed and learned a lesson from what I saw: A little sleep, a little slumber, a little folding of the hands to rest- and poverty will come on you like a bandit and scarcity like an armed man.")

Peter Drucker said: "Every few hundred years throughout Western history, a sharp transformation has occurred. In a matter of a few decades, society altogether rearranges itself, its world's views, its social and political structure, its arts, its key institutions. Fifty years later a New World exists. And the people born into that world cannot even imagine the world in which their grandparents lived and into which their own parents were born."

Unfortunately, for most people who live in a hierarchy, the speed of learning tends to be limited by those at the top. If they were a smart Henry Ford or Thomas Watson Jr., the organisation could learn faster than their world changed. If they were not that smart they might get an initial foothold but eventually competition and change would weed them out.

We cannot learn faster than the world changes. Many outcomes/outputs especially for business organisations depended on a much wider range of knowledge, skills, values, technologies and competencies. This forces us to learn and grasp a broader range at a faster speed. Why was Bill Clinton so concerned over a cloned sheep? Why was a commission set up to investigate cloning? Only because they were surprised by news, for what was assumed to be possible only in science fiction, and by the fact that no one in the government has the faintest clue on the likely consequences. Today change is non-linear and not first order.

Otto von Bismarck, the German statesman (1815-1898) said: "Fools say they learn from experience. I prefer to learn from others' experience." Therefore, you too can profit from your competitors' success and failure. The incandescent light bulb first emerged some thirty years before Thomas Edison found the right filament. Henry Ford's revolutionary assembly line emulated Singer's sewing machine and Campbell Soup meatpacking.

King Solomon was the wisest king in the Bible. Like Otto von Bismarck, he used another's experience, in this case, failure, to teach himself, learn from what he had seen and make his own principles. He narrates to us in the book of Proverbs, "I went past the field of the sluggard, past the vineyard of the man who lacks judgment; thorns had come up everywhere, the ground was covered with weeds, and the stone wall was in ruins. I applied my heart to what I observed and learned a lesson from what I saw: A little sleep, a little slumber, a little folding of the hands to rest- and poverty will come on you like a bandit and scarcity like an armed man."

David Kearns former Chairman of Xerox in 1989 said: "We realize that we are in a race without a finish line. As we improve, so does our competition." But having done that, one has to quickly outpace your competitors in learning. Successful organisations are not only more profitable than their competitors but also grow faster than they are. Many companies who are unable to learn faster than the competition degenerated from fast track to derailment as their competitors overtook them.

It is insufficient for a company to be merely a learning organisation, particularly, if it is learning the wrong things. During the pioneering days in China, some foreign investors resorted to cheating the tax authorities on import duties and declarations because everybody was doing it. It was easier for the local small operators to close down their operations and disappear into oblivion to evade the authorities. It is equally easier for them to sprout somewhere else in China. However in the case of the foreign investors, they could not just disappear overnight as they had bigger investments and landed up paying the hefty fines for their misdeeds. These foreign investors learned the wrong things from their small local counterparts.

At times too, the company needs to unlearn some of its earlier erroneous philosophy and lessons. In this fast changing world, the key question to survival is how fast this company can unlearn and relearn the new models and policies that can ensure its survival. Therefore it is also important to unlearn faster than your competitors.

Unfortunately, companies fall into the trap of learning the fads of management of downsizing and re-engineering. The vicious cycle continues with staff downsizing resulted in a skeleton force too weak to do anything then to further re-engineering of the processes which results in the remaining staff being frustrated and leaving eventually. These fads are much like your photos during your own teenage days and when you reminisce, you wonder how in the world you ever got involved with that

Page 109

Company CEOs need to understand the basics in running businesses remain unchanged – handed down from our father, grandfathers and forefathers. CEOs should by all means learn from the various new management theories but not to be mesmerised by them or to blindly apply them.

Therefore, you need to learn faster than your competitors. Also ensure you stop unlearn the wrong things and doing them.

Principle No. 32

Do not suffer from competitive myopia. Have 20/20 vision. (Ephesians 6:11, 1 Peter 5:8 – "Be self-controlled and alert. Your enemy the devil prowls around like a roaring lion looking for someone to devour.")

Competitive myopia occurs when companies do not monitor their competitors systematically. Information on the competition needs constant updating. One should always try to ascertain the competition's next move.

We should keep the same attitude and always be aware of the devil and what his next move is. If we are not ready for his strikes, we just might be tempted to sin, or worse. The Bible talks a lot about being prepared for what the devil might do. In Ephesians, it is written "Put on the full armor of God so that you can take your stand against the devil's schemes." Jesus doesn't want us to fall for the devil's traps, which is why he tells us to always be prepared. Knowing the devil, he would really persist, especially if he knows that he can get what he wants. Like a business close competition, the same principle applies to us. We should keep in mind this verse we find in 1 Peter 5:8: "Be self-controlled and alert. Your enemy the devil prowls around like a roaring lion looking for someone to devour."

Most troubled companies lose sight of the fact that they do not operate in a competitor vacuum. Their very existence depends on whether they can add more value at cheaper price to the customers' vis-à-vis their competitors. Therefore do not suffer from competitive myopia.

In the early 2000's, Reuters lost its market share to newcomers such as Bloomberg. Reuters should have seen the threat of Bloomberg years prior as the latter's concentration and focus enabled it to deliver a high quality, consistent product in a hard-hitting manner. In short, competitive myopia played a large part in Reuter's loss of market dominance.

Many companies have no programmes at all for the systematic monitoring of their competitors. They might have massive volume of information on market movements and feedback from the sales force. However, they deluded themselves and became complacent that they had all the market information. Then, they had rude shocks and got stunned by pressures from unexpected sources and direction.

Polaroid got into trouble as the photography market changed throughout the new millennium because it failed to diversify sufficiently beyond its instant firm process, which had propelled the company to greatness. Kodak may face the same fate. In a world where people want to e-mail photos to friends, digital cameras make far more sense than plain old film. And both of these previous photography giants were so slow to respond to their start-up competitions that they have been supplanted and now the majority of the market is held firmly by digital camera companies that didn't even exist in the late 1990's.

However, not all companies fall into the trap of competitive myopia. Intel founders Andy Grove and Gordon Moore realized that their company's core business in memory chips was being attacked by cheaper Asian imports. They transformed the company into a maker of microprocessors.

In 2005, Citigroup broadened it's appetite for risk, moving aggressively into Collateralized Debt Obligation, a risky venture. Increases in staff to handle these transactions and changes to the bonus system (sometimes doubling and tripling bonuses) were among the first moves that Citigroup took to maximize its profit in this sector. But not far behind these first steps, risk controls started to dissemble, and the risks were being ignored. And with high bonuses and increasing salaries, no one wanted to point out possible flaws. Even potentially massive flaws such as the fact that none of Citigroup's risk modelling included the possibility that the national housing market might take a downturn. But in late 2007, thousands of homeowners did default and the national housing market did take a downturn. And Citigroup, with $20 billion USD of securities in mortgage-linked accounts, is left holding the bag while the bulk of these mortgage holdings are being marked-down to anywhere between 21 to 41 cents on the dollar. On top of that, Citigroup is also facing the possibility that auto and credit card loans may also start to falter as the global economy is in a tail-spin. Because they wanted to be competitive, they became overly competitive and lost sight of the risk-management side of their business.

CEOs always claim that they are doing better than their competitors. Often times, information on the performance of industry players is quite difficult to obtain and verify. The issue here is that doing better than some competitors is just not good enough. Do not suffer from competitive myopia by not fully understanding the performance of your competitors or yourself.

The feedback from the ground sales force is sometimes like fresh milk. It has a short shelf-life if no action is taken to counter act against the competition. We may have all the competitors' action all mapped out such as their products and services, production/sourcing, business strategy, positioning, customer service, etc.

But what are our next specific moves? Instead of having competitive myopia, have 20/20 vision.

Principle No. 33

Just as a heart ailment is a major killer, competition is the silent killer leading to corporate failures. (Ephesians 6:13 Therefore put on the full armor of God, so that when the day of evil comes, you may be able to stand your ground...)

The management mantra of the 1980s was product quality, and activities involving Quality Control (QC) circles, Total Quality Management (TQM) and ISO 9000 were the order of the day. Back then, consumers were willing to spend enormous sums for quality products. However, product quality has significantly improved and today, having a good, quality product is mandatory for the company's effective participation and survival in the marketplace.

Subsequently, the management slogan in the 1990s embraced technology as the cure-all. Companies then tried to distinguish themselves from their competitors through the use of technology, by offering better and more sophisticated features, use of the Internet and other communication systems. Huge sums were channelled into technology to build a better mousetrap with more superior state-of-the-art features. Today, the world does not beat down the door of the better mousetrap developer. The collapse of the high tech stocks on Nasdaq in the early part of 2001 illustrates the vulnerability of technology.

The thrust in the new millennium is competition. Competition intensifies with the emergence of a better range of products that are often of superior quality coupled with attractive and affordable pricing. In such a scenario, many products become marginalized, and like commodities, pricing becomes a key determinant in a shrinking market.

In today's competitive environment, your margins for errors are also thinner. In the past, three strikes or major mistakes and you are out, but today, one strike or major mistake and you are history. Customers have many choices and they will switch their suppliers at the turn of the dime if you make a major error in quality, delivery, etc.

The Bible also warned us to be on the alert in Ephesians 6:13 against the enemy. Therefore put on the full armor of God, so that when the day of evil comes, you may be able to stand your ground and after you have done everything, to stand. The competitor can sneak in on us if we are not alert.

Oftentimes, the elusive competition quietly sneaks in by the back door. You may have been losing trickles of disgruntled customers and one day, you come to the sudden realisation that even your major customers are gone.

PSA Corporation learnt too late to retain its number one customer, Maersk from switching to Port of Tanjong Pelepas in Johore in the early 2000's. After PSA Corporation rejected the requests for better terms of AP Moller Group, parent of Maersk Sealand, the world's largest operator of container ships, the Copenhagen based company moved the operations to Tanjong Pelepas and also took a stake in the port. This was a double whammy for PSA Corporation as it not only lost its biggest customer; it had to compete against its former ally. With the help of Maersk, Tanjong Pelepas was also able to capture Evergreen, PSA Corporation's second largest customer. PSA had tried to compete on efficiency and fast turnaround of clients' ships. But this could only justify for some price premium for up to a point. Consequently, PSA Corporation had to downsize in order to stay competitive, a tad too late as it lost its top two customers within a short period.

Competition may lead to opening up new markets. For instance, with the advent of low budget airlines in the late 1990's, more poor Indonesians were able to travel overseas. This is the market segment, which most major airlines such as Singapore Airlines wished that they had targeted. But one should never under estimate or take the competition for granted.

Competition is a silent and sudden killer like heart attack; it can creep up on you without warning. However, just as an individual can prevent this disease by adopting a healthy lifestyle, a company can stave off competition by remaining alert and adopting appropriate strategies to combat it. When you are faced with increasing competition, you may still survive, prosper and succeed, but it is no longer business as usual.

Principle No. 34

You can have wealth and wisdom, but you better have health. Similarly, you can have performance and quality but you better have pricing.. (Matthew 26:6-13 – "The poor you will always have with you, but you will not always have me. When she poured this perfume on my body, she did it to prepare me for burial.")

It is rather common for companies selling in Asian markets to encounter the following problem: Why are their high-margin, high-quality products, which are the rage in the United States and Europe, not fetching high prices here?

Having the right products does not always guarantee successes in Asia as the markets are heavily biased towards pricing. Perhaps, this is ingrained in the "cheap and good" mentality advanced by mothers. Mother always knows best. Therefore, in order to penetrate the Asian market, companies must not neglect the right pricing for their products.

Henry Ford knew about pricing. He said: "There is only one rule of business and that is: "Make the best quality at the lowest cost possible." The early Ford Motor Company was a paragon of the lowest possible prices. This is because the founder's business model was tuned to a single purpose: delivering an acceptable product at the lowest possible price. As Ford's costs fell, the retail price of its model T car fell too.

In the book of Matthew, chapter 26 verse 6 talks about a woman who "priced right." When Jesus was in Bethany, in the home of Simon the leper, a woman came over to him and poured expensive perfume on his head. The disciples were appalled when they saw this, because they know that the perfume can be sold at a high price and that she just wasted it. However, for the woman, it was that she knew that she was spending this expensive perfume on a "highly-priced man" – Jesus, that is. And because she did this, Jesus found favor in her, and rewarded her accordingly. "I tell you the truth, wherever this gospel is preached throughout the world, what she has done will also be told, in memory of her."

There are many ways of lowering cost without compromising quality. For example, costs can be reduced by manufacturing or sourcing for parts and components in some low-cost countries. The company can still maintain its brand names and produce the desired products at the right price as nowadays as many customers do not really bother where the components and parts are coming from. Other ways may include franchising, teaming up with other local partners, etc.

The Internet has also rendered pricing information transparent. Customers can compare prices of products that they wish to purchase by logging on to the Internet. Auctions are also offered online. For instance, in the United Kingdom, private cars are sold more expensively to individuals than corporations. Corporations are able to negotiate for a lower price as they order in large quantity for their executives, whereas individuals do not have the bargaining power. With the onset of Internet in the late 1990's, consumers can shop for the lowest prices of cars on the Internet. They were able to order cars from Scandinavia countries for shipment to the United Kingdom. Consequently, the car prices plummeted by 20% to 30%.

In the early 2000's., there was a large pool of skilled Indians in the Bangalore software park whose salary was one tenth of that of the developed world and they can perform tasks as well if not better. Customers made this switch to Bangalore unless there were compelling reasons for them to continue doing business with their previous sources. Similarly, with the Chinese in the Suzhou Industrial Park during the same time frame, who could design and develop sophisticated electronic components and parts at one tenth the cost of the developed world. Many consumers demanded the lower prices allowed by switching to these lower-cost sources and your customers will demand that kind of costing from you too.

Pricing is not everything but it is an important thing.

Principle No. 35

Your low cost competitors are not after your crumbs, they want to eat your lunch. (Numbers 25:1-5 – "While Israel was staying in Shittim, the men began to indulge in sexual immorality with Moabite women, who invited them to the sacrifices to their gods.")

Many industry leaders are faced with a sea of changes in the marketplace, particularly the onslaught of many low cost competitors. They are minnows and will grow to become sharks if they are not nipped in the bud. Examples abound on the proliferation of the Chinese products in the world market.

The way to handle these manufacturers is to try to nip them in the bud. It is like war. You must not allow your competitions to establish a beachhead. For once they succeed in doing so, it will be so much harder to dislodge them. You want to knock them out in the waters where they are most vulnerable. When customers try the low cost products and they like them, it will be very difficult and expensive to entice them to switch back to your products. If you cannot beat the low cost competitors in the price game everything else being equal, then better to identify another premium niche.

Johnson and Johnson, the health-care multi-national company also faces stiff competition and a long wait for the next drug blockbuster. As part of its strategies to hold off competition in the late 1990's and early 2000's, it gobbled up 34 companies in a period of 5 years and kept acquiring. Johnson and Johnson also put existing drugs to new uses – epilepsy drug Topomax was used to treat migraines. Workers were made to cross divisional lines to develop products and drug-delivery systems including treatments for stroke, diabetes and schizophrenia. Teamwork between pharma and device divisions led to the billion-dollar coronary stent. Cost-cutting on the 200-plus units, merger of the back-office operations and centralized purchasing helped to save $1 billion in two years – funds that it will use in the development of badly needed new pharmaceuticals.

On the other hand, Hoover, which makes vacuum cleaners since 1907, shrunk its unionised staff strength from 1,800 to just over 1,500 in 1994. The Chinese competitors were undercutting Hoover's market and selling cheap vacuum cleaners at $79. Hoovers with price tags of $200 and higher could not compete and was caught unaware. These Chinese low-end models had 40% of the market before Hoover could adequately respond. Hoover tried layoffs, new vacuum-cleaner features etc, but to no avail. On the other hand, the market leader Whirlpool during that same time period was up 38% in sales revenues and boosted its 2004 profit outlook unexpectedly. Whirlpool no longer sells vacuum cleaners and diversified into other household appliances, keeping out of the cut-throat competition.

We can make a comparison of Hoover with the popular nation of Israel. Israel was doing fine – they worshipped God, followed his commandments, and God found favor in them; just like how we can say the general public found "favor" in Hoover – buying and patronizing their products. However, just like how Chinese manufacturers offered what seemed like a "better" deal, people shifted.

The Israelites, later, seemed to have found a "better deal" in the country of Moab – where religion, is probably more "relaxed." When they arrived in the city of Shittim, the men indulged in sexual immorality with the women of Moab. In addition to this, these women invited them to offer sacrifices to their god, Baal of Peor. And these Israelites did. Because of this, the Lord became furious with them. "The Lord said to Moses, 'Take all the leaders of these people, kill them and expose them in broad daylight before the Lord...'"

We can draw from here the same principle discussed earlier. The Moabites didn't want Israel to just party and have fun with them; they wanted them to sacrifice to their gods as well. Like in the corporate world, they don't want just a bite, they are want to eat the whole sandwich!

As mentioned earlier, the Port Authority of Singapore (PSA) also lost its competitiveness when Tanjong Pelepas in Malaysia stole away PSA's number one and two customers with cheaper pricing in the early 2000's. The Singapore government learnt this lesson and responded quickly to the threats of low cost budget airlines and regional air hubs. Airlines also had the option to bypass Singapore Changi Airport and fly directly from Australia to Europe or Middle East to US avoiding stopover in Singapore. Singapore Airlines introduced the budget airline Tiger to compete in this sector as well as to boost its premier airline image through the offers of new planes and non-stop direct flights to the US. Singapore Changi Airport even built a terminal for budget airlines. The Singapore government came down hard on the Singapore airline pilots to ensure that the national airline is not dragged down by labour disputes. The airport terminals also underwent renovation and upgrading. All these proactive measures have not effectively maintained the competitiveness of the air transportation and aviation industry in Singapore. Still today, in the late 2000's, Changi Aiport is still struggling to maintain its competitive edge and has recently announced that it will undergo a corporitization in an effort to compete in this uphill battle. It may seem like Singapore's premier airport is always struggling to maintain its leverage in the market, however, this is better than waiting for the low cost competitors to gobble your lunch right under your noses.

Another case in point is the ball-point and fountain pen competition. Ball-point pens were much cheaper, easier and less messy to use. The fountain pens were beaten face down and lost almost all the market share to ball-point pens. Then somebody thought of making the fountain pen a luxury item. The fountain pen was sold for US$ 400 and positioned as a prestigious and luxurious item, similar to the jewel wear. The manufacturers of fountain pens such as Parker, Sheaffer and Mont Blanc have then comfortably locked into the high-end segment which the ball-point pens cannot penetrate. Today, both the fountain and ball-point pens co-exist each has its own market niches.

You need to be wary and be prepared to thwart off the moves of these low cost competitors. This is why Howard H. Stevenson in his book said: "Do lunch or Be Lunch."

Principle No. 36

The tongue is the window of your health. (James 3:5-6, Psalm 52:2, Proverbs 18:21 – "The tongue has the power of life and death, and those who love it will eat its fruit.")

The doctor often examines the tongue to determine the general state of health of the patient. The tongue is the organ used by the body for communication. Similarly, we determine the morale level and state of mental health of the company by examining the manner of its communication. What the heart and mind think, the tongue speaks.

In sick companies, negative comments and rumours abound. Such negative energies can sap away the morale and fruitful concentration of the company. It is quite easy to ascertain the state of health of the company. If you spend some time talking to the staff individually and you will soon be able to learn about the negative state of health of the organisation. Staff will usually understand the cause of the problems and the solutions to them.

In addition to talking, the tongue can be used to chew, mix, taste and swallow food. Even when you are sleeping, your tongue is busy pushing saliva down the throat to be swallowed; otherwise you will be drooling all over the pillow. Similarly corporate communication is the tongue of the organisation and is the way all business entities interact with each other during the course of business. Corporate communication also serves multiple functions of improving corporate image, strengthening teamwork and corporate culture as well as handling difficult situations and customers. How an organisation communicates with its employees, its extended audiences, the press and the public at large will reveal its corporate character and values.

In the Bible, the tongue is regarded to be powerful as well. It goes as far as an untameable part of our body; that no man can ever tame the tongue. Even with its size, its immense capability to the extremity of turning the whole person's fate around is not far-fetched. In James, it is written: "Likewise the tongue is a small part of the body, but it makes great boasts. Consider what a great forest is set on fire by a small spark. The tongue also is a fire, a world of evil among the parts of the body. It corrupts the whole person, sets the whole course of his life on fire, and is itself set on fire by hell."

Psalm 52:2 reads "Your tongue plots destruction; it is like a sharpened razor, you who practice deceit." Similarly, the book of Proverbs tells us

"The tongue has the power of life and death, and those who love it will eat its fruit."

There are many other passages in the Bible that speak about the wrong and right uses of the tongue; as it is through the tongue that you are bound by your words and by your declarations. It is by this means that we see the importance of communication, especially the spoken word, which cannot be over-emphasised.

Oftentimes, relationships break down because of poor communication. Marriage counsellors can testify that the poor communication is frequently the cause of marital conflicts and failures. When communication breaks down, it results in misunderstanding, rumour mongering, negative comments or verbal diarrhoea, which all eventually leads to ill health. Also, when communication breaks down in the company, the rapport, metabolism and chemistry of the people suffer.

The turnaround manager needs to create a culture marked with candour and straight talk. In the modern world, market information and ideas are precious and highly perishable commodities that need to be speedily exploited and acted upon in order to fully harness their value. Therefore, the organisational communication lines must be short, direct and healthy.

When you are thirsty and water is available, you are not going to argue over the temperature of the water. (Proverbs 17:14 – "Starting a quarrel is like breaching a dam; so drop the matter before a dispute breaks out.")

This seems to be an obvious principle. Yet, many troubled businesses are the result of petty quarrels and disagreements amongst partners and major shareholders. There are also many family-run companies where the family members soured their relationships ruining the business.

Oftentimes, the trouble does not start with the competition or the staff, but arise out of major disagreements amongst the key shareholders. Disagreements can be healthy if they are properly controlled and managed. However, the disagreements can become dysfunctional when they are not properly resolved and allowed to fester. These can result in the break-up of the entire company. For instance, the famous Swedish pop group ABBA was once the largest export revenues for Sweden in the 1980's, however the group broke up and its fame went with it. Also Simon and Garfunkel were very popular pop singers as a team in the late 1970's and early 1980's. But when the partners broke up, they also lost their popularity.

When the major shareholders disagree, a feasible solution is to bring in professional managers from outside to run the business. However, they have to be given the full autonomy to run the company.

Other suggestion to get out of the quandary may include buying out the other dissenting shareholder. Businesses are already fraught with all kinds of challenges. As a house divided cannot stand, a company that has divided teams will not be able to handle the vagaries of the market dynamics. All the energies and valuable resources will be expended on office politics and putting out fires, when these should rightly have been directed externally to manage competition, etc.

In tough times, at one point, everybody has to compromise and set aside their differences. Political fights should not be allowed to get out of hand. People should concentrate their energies to quickly getting the organisation back on an even keel. A right dose of internal conflict and competition can be healthy, engendering new ideas as well as generating checks and balances. However, they have to be controlled and managed within boundaries. Otherwise, too much backstabbing and sabotage will rouse suspicion and faultfinding. Then the atmosphere becomes unhealthy with self-interest and politicking overrides the interests of the company.

Even in good times, the finest plans can be derailed through petty disagreement such as the assignment of responsibility. During bad times, harmony and co-operation amongst all the key members are imperative.

It is not only in the corporate world that disputes can be destructive. In the book of Proverbs it is written: "Starting a quarrel is like breaching a dam; so drop the matter before a dispute breaks out." It is evident in the Bible that when there are disputes, whoever is involved is encouraged to get a judge to settle disputes before them, as these can turn out into something even bigger – which is what they aim to prevent in the first place.

Dynamic organisations are the ones that actively challenge the status quo as a means of staying competitive. This requires leaders who can positively use conflict and tension. They must be able to stimulate a climate that challenges and spurs staff on without stifling them and causing them to be dysfunctional.

Therefore, when you are thirsty and water is available, you do not argue over the temperature of the water or the type of water container. You quench your thirst by drinking the water that is available to you.

Principle No. 38

Rumour is like the SARS virus, it can spread by mouth, by phone and sometimes pop up in the most unusual places. (Proverbs 16:28, John 21:22-24 – "A perverse man stirs up dissension, and a gossip separates close friends.")

Troubled companies are often plagued with negative unverified information, otherwise called rumour mongering. This is extremely unhealthy and can be deadly and infectious like the dreaded Severe Acute Respiratory Syndrome (SARS) virus. Misinformation and rumour are very dangerous for companies. In this information era, rumours can spread at an amazing speed through modern communication facilities such as the mobile phone, telephone, fax, computers and satellites.

The rumours of the outbreak of SARS in China started in Heyuan, a small city in Guangdong Province in December 2002. The health authorities diagnosed the disease as "Atypical Pneumonia" but the medical diagnosis was not released to the public immediately and rumours on the outbreak of a terrible, unknown disease began to spread resulting in panic buying of drugs. The crisis and panic peaked after the Spring Festival holidays and the central government had to make a public announcement of a public health crisis. This was a tad too late as the Chinese government was then criticised by its own people and the international community for not officially warning the public of the SARS hazard earlier.

Rumours, or more commonly referred to as gossips in the Bible, are condemned. About 6 verses in proverbs in the Bible are dedicated to gossip and the threats it poses. In chapter 16 it is written "A perverse man stirs up dissension, and a gossip separates close friends." It is in gossip that we find all the twists and turns that can be said of a story. Most of the time, it is a perverted account of the truth. In the book of John, Jesus became a victim of gossip as well, as his words were distorted regarding the death of a disciple. It was John who had to testify against all these rumours and claim its invalidity.

The only way to stop rumours is to let the staff or public know the truth. It is always useless to hide the facts or deny the truth as this creates the environment for rumours to flourish.

Uncertainty of the future fate of the company also results in rumours. Rumours are dysfunctional, sapping away the energy of the staff. As a result, rumours rob you of constructive thinking and action. They are very detrimental to staff morale.

The most effective way to stem rumours is communicate directly with the staff. Let them hear from the horses' mouth. In some cases, as a turnaround manager, you may not be aware of the rumours that are circulating in the company. Furthermore, in the Asian culture, normally, staff does not openly let the management know the rumours in an open dialogue. In such cases, the use of a questionnaire survey may be useful in ferreting out the undercurrents and root causes of the rumours. Staff can feedback their suggestions for improvements, concerns, etc anonymously without fear of reprisal from their supervisors or managers. Corporations are increasingly supporting the whistle-blowing programs for staff to alert the board and management of any malpractices.

In many ailing businesses, where dissatisfaction and complaints abound, poison letters are also common. These are also a form of rumour. However, if the poison letter intending to assassinate somebody's character has no signatory, it is difficult to investigate or pursue the matter.

The greatest harm from rumour whether they are truthful or otherwise is the creation of negativism in the corporate environment. In troubled businesses, the dilapidating disease afflicting executives is not alcoholism but negativism.

Positive thoughts bring health, happiness and vitality, laughter and success and real life. On the contrary, negative thoughts brought about by rumour mongering create chemical reactions that result in depression, failure, sadness and even death.

Keep the brain active. Introduce aggressive marketing strategies to direct the staff's attention away from negativism. An idle mind is the devil's workshop. Try to keep the staff mentally and constructively occupied.

Therefore, squash the rumours with proper communication and action.

Principle No. 39

Dead bodies stink from the head. (Exodus 5-12 – "Then the LORD said to Moses, "Now you will see what I will do to Pharaoh: Because of my mighty hand he will let them go; because of my mighty hand he will drive them out of his country.")

A key reason for companies' downhill slide is undoubtedly the quality of CEO.   Most turnaround situations arise because of the CEO's incompetence, ineptness, carelessness, ego and /or inexperience.   It is simply too much to ask or expect the incumbent management to be objective in evaluating its past performance when the CEO is probably the same person whose mismanagement caused the company's financial health to deteriorate in the first place.   The problem is that some CEOs may lack training even though they may think they know it all.

Sir John Harvey Jones said that the reason many companies always find themselves in trouble is almost always due to the problems right at the top.   Sir John Harvey-Jones is one of Britain's best-known and most respected business leaders. Besides being the Chairman of ICI he won the fame as the star of the BBC TV series 'Troubleshooter.' Harvard's Professor Rosabeth Moss Kanter, whose work focuses on leadership of turnarounds pointed out in the Economic and Social Research Council lecture in London: "Formal structures and process undergird confidence, but what also matters is the willingness of leaders to believe in people and give them opportunities to share.   Behind every winning streak are leaders who care about the team. That is why new leaders are often required to lead turnarounds."   Michael Dell of Dell Computers said, "When a business goes wrong, look only to the people who are running it."

We see a perfect example of how a failure of a leader affected and caused the ruin of a whole country. In the story of the Exodus, the whole downfall of Egypt at that time was mainly due the fault of their "CEO," the pharaoh. Because he is the one making all the decisions that's supposedly for the whole country, – that is, keeping the Israelites to serve as slaves to work for him, he is responsible for all 10 plagues that fell upon Egypt.

Sun Tzu acknowledged the critical role played by generals or CEOs when he said: "When the general is weak and without authority, when his orders are not clear and distinct, when there are no fixed duties assigned to officers and men and the ranks are formed in a slovenly haphazard manner, the result is utter disorganisation.

Many early ventures into China fared miserably as these companies sent the wrong managers to run the operations there. Merely having a local staff or secretary to handle the Chinese relations is insufficient. Companies should send managers with excellent managerial skills as well as those with excellent understanding of China market. Volkswagen and Siemens hired some excellent CEOs who were able to transform their loss-making joint ventures into successful ones. General Motors sent one of its best people to China in the mid-1990s and is now very successful, even being linked to the Shanghai Automotive Industry Corporation. In the early 2000's, Toyota began sending its expatriates for six-month or longer on language courses to prepare them for the China assignments. The crux is to have the best key man in place.

People often confuse the differences between leaders with managers and use those terms interchangeably. Managers do things right, while leaders do the right thing. Managers tend to focus on short-term goals and objectives and administer them. On the other hand, leaders also consider such issues as well as other long-term issues to inspire and motivate their staff. Managers act and think incrementally whilst leaders think and act radically. A leader is someone that will attract other people to follow them voluntarily whereas a manager demands to be obeyed. Whilst the manager uses official and formal communication and procedure, the leader uses passion and stirs up the emotion of the people.

A manager tends to work to benefit the stockholders' short-term gains, sometimes at the expense of the long-term. But a leader should weigh the consequences of both the long and short-term gains and define a path which will lead the stockholders to success in both. For example, CEOs of Parmalat (Italy), Enron (US), Worldcom (US) and CAO (Singapore) went to jail for financial fraud. And now an even greater scandal is being exposed in the late 2008 – that of Bernie Madoff and his hedge funds. At the later part of 2008, it would appear that the corruption of the market allowed Madoff to construct a $50 billion scandal – or that may just be the tip of the iceberg. Because these CEOs were looking only to the short-term and ignoring the fatal consequences of the long-term, both the stockholder and the economy suffered.

Leadership matters. John Maxwell, an author on several books on leadership said: "Everything rises and falls on leadership." And it matters more in times of uncertainty than in times of stability. Leadership is not a fad. It is here today and forever. Leadership is an observable set of skills and abilities. Leadership takes precedence because it is the top management who decides what need to be done and the ones who make things happen. It is true that one person alone cannot change the world, or even a moderate-sized organisation.   It takes the concentrated energy, ideas and enthusiasm of many people. But without a leader, the movement does not get started in the first place, or it quickly fizzles off for lack of direction or momentum. Without leaders, good results are a matter of random chance and therefore unsustainable. Change requires leadership and will not happen by default. Leadership is the backbone around which all the rest of the corporate body takes shape.

Principle No. 40

Board of directors should act like 'T cells' in the body to protect shareholder interest. (1 Peter 4:3, Matthew 6:7 – "For you have spent enough time in the past doing what pagans choose to do—living in debauchery, lust, drunkenness, orgies, carousing and detestable idolatry.")

'T' cells contribute to the immune defences in two major ways. Some help regulate the complex workings of the immune system, similar to the board of directors setting the direction. It is not just the quality of these CEOs that companies have to be mindful of. Undesirable board members are men or women whose sole qualifications are based on their race, gender and social status. However, in the interest of the company, you need to appoint the best people on its board. These are the people who have demonstrated track records as great CEOs and not CEOs who failed and merely filling the board positions as their second jobs. You also need people who have extensive global experience and overseas connections to understand the demands and challenges involved in the marketplace. If you are a listed company, you need people who have good knowledge of the listing mechanism and stock exchange requirements.

These directors should not be serving on too many company boards, otherwise, they would not have enough time to contribute effectively. And tenure of their appointment should be limited to serve on the board. This is a form of check and balance so that long serving board members do not become too comfortable and complacent with the management. Also, it is important that board members remain impartial and not become too chummy that may overlook any misdeeds by the management.

The board of directors has to understand that they are not paid to do the CEO's job. When they get unduly involved with the day-to-day operations such as marketing, hiring and calling for regular meeting, they can create problems for the company. The main role of the board is to hire and fire the CEO and determine his compensation. They should participate in the major issues such as approving the overall strategy, acquisitions and major capital expenditures. Ultimately, the board must understand that they are accountable to the shareholders. They are not there to run the company but ensure that the management does it effectively.

Many board members are just pew warmers. They do not participate actively during the board discussions or attempt to understand the business issues. Hence, they do not contribute and leave the CEO to his devices. The various financial scandals sweeping the major corporations in the worldwide indicate the lack of supervision and close monitoring of the CEOs by the respective boards.

There are what we call "hypocrites" in Jesus' time as well. We know these people as pagans. These so-called religious leaders are only good for show. They say their prayers aloud so that people can hear them, they pray outside the synagogues so that people can see them. People might think that they achieve something with what they do, when in fact they really have nothing. Their ways, written in the book of Matthew, "For you have spent enough time in the past doing what pagans choose to do—living in debauchery, lust, drunkenness, orgies, carousing and detestable idolatry," has given them nothing but shame and condemnation from God. Jesus warns us to keep away from these people; corrupt and hypocrite – we must not follow their ways. We should see how bad these people are as God uses them as a measure for something we ought to not follow. Some board of directors who do not protect the interests of shareholders are also behaving like the religious leaders in Jesus' days. They put out a righteous front in the annual reports and the public, claiming that they are experts in their fields and will contribute for the good of the company that they represent. Unfortunately, they are not spending enough time to know what is happening to the company or worst still, some abusing their legal rights by embezzlement of company's funds. We saw the collapse of the major corporate institutions such as Bear Stearns, Fannie Mae, Freddie Mac and Lehman Brothers. The CEOs were blamed for the collapse, however the board of directors should also be held accountable.

At the other extreme, we see the dichotomy in the board, between the independent and the executive directors. The independent directors often behave like big bosses questioning the executive officers and executive directors only. Whether they are independent or executive directors, all are directors. In the interest of the company each board member must actively contribute and share his know-how and expertise.

It is encouraging to note that the trend in the developed countries is towards stricter corporate governance to ensure that all directors perform their jobs judiciously. The days when directors merely meet to socialise or network and subsequently adjourn for a good meal or game of golf are gone. Directors need to take up a more active role in order to function as 'T' cells in the company, protecting the interests of all stakeholders.

Principle No. 41

Many chief executives pursue the four Ps - pay, power, perks and prestige rather than profits for the company. (Ezekiel 28:1-19, 26:1-21 – To Hiram: "Your heart became proud on account of your beauty, and you corrupted your wisdom because of your splendor. So I threw you to the earth; I made a spectacle of you before kings.")

Every year, there are more and more CEOs falling from grace. In the United States, forced exits accounted for 22% of CEO departures in 2006 up from 11% in 2003, according to Booz Allen Hamilton. In 2002, Enron Chairman Ken Lay, Tyco chief Dennis Kozlowski, Qwest's Joe Nacchio, and WorldCom's Bernie Ebbers. Year 2003 saw the departure of CEOs from Raytheon, Kmart, Spiegel, Scherling Plough, Motorola, Freddie Mac, Boeing, American, etc. Moving forward into 2009, we are going to see more CEOs falling from grace as the economic recession continues to worsen.

Agence France-Presse (AFP) in 13 April 2004 reported that Professor David Yermack of New York University Stern School of Business found that the average shareholder gains underperformed market benchmarks at companies where the chief flies by luxurious corporate jets. In the study, "Flights of Fancy: Corporate Jets, CEO Perquisites and Inferior Shareholder Returns", Professor Yermack said: "The central result of this study is that CEO's personal use of company aircraft is associated with severe and significant under-performance of their employers' stock....Firms' stock prices drop an average of 2 percent around the date of initial disclosure of corporate plane use." We saw the repeat of this in end 2008 when the CEOs of the three troubled automotive companies in US travelled in their private jets to attend the meeting to ask the Congress for financial assistance. It is as one senator put it that these CEOs are dressed in tuxedo together with the poor people to queue up for the government alms.

Some of the CEOs may not be justifiably fired as the economy turns bad through no faults of theirs' but they were held accountable. However, the days of fat cats running corporations are over.

Hiram, the king of the city of Tyre, was of perfection when he was made. God took care of him, catered to his needs. He was special in God's eyes. In the book of Ezekiel, the Lord tells Hiram himself, "You were the model of perfection, full of wisdom and perfect in beauty." "You were anointed as a guardian cherub, for so I ordained you. You were on the holy mount of God; you walked among the fiery stones." However, all this changed when wickedness thrived in him. He became corrupt; he was dishonest in his trade and he became proud because of his beauty.

The Lord declares to Hiram: "All the nations who knew you are appalled at you; you have come to a horrible end and will be no more." And to his kingdom in Tyre, the Lord gave it to ruins. "This is what the Sovereign Lord says: When I make you a desolate city, like cities no longer inhabited, and when I bring the ocean depths over you and its vast waters cover you, then I will bring you down with those who go down to the pit, to the people of long ago. I will make you dwell in the earth below, as in ancient ruins, with those who go down to the pit, and you will not return or take your place in the land of the living. I will bring you to a horrible end and you will be no more. You will be sought, but you will never again be found, declares the Sovereign Lord."

Uncontrolled and unnecessary costs destroy businesses. If your competitor has a limo and you do not, you are already winning. He has a leaky bucket. There are 34 self-made billionaires. And all of them were paragons of simplicity and prudence in self-aggrandisement.

In 1991, Sam Walton founder of Wal-Mart drove an eight-year-old red Ford pickup. He always fetched his own coffee. As President of EDS, Ross Perot paid himself $70,000 a year. However, when Perot sold EDS to General Motors, the President of General Motors, Perot's new boss, made $2.4 million salary plus a bonus. Finally, he paid Perot $2.5 billion to go away because GM executives were embarrassed by the folksy Perot, who did not demand a fat salary or swanky office or specially tuned cars. David Packard never had an enclosed office before he left Hewlett-Packard for government service. Bill Gates of Microsoft often rode coach on planes, until they finally got so big they ran their own fleet of aircraft. Warren Buffet manages Berkshire Hathaway's billions and billions but only pays himself $100,000 a year. When he lunches with his employees, it is McDonald's. Warren still stayed in the same house that he bought thirty years ago which is only appraised at $700.000. Ingvar Kamprad, the founder of Ikea takes the company bus to his stores.

Throughout the past few years, there have been many examples of questionable corporate practices. Even those companies, such as AIG, which are being "bailed-out" by the American government, are also being reported on the news for taking corporate retreats in excess of US$500,000 on a near-monthly basis.

Indeed examples of executive abuses dominated the news even during 2002. Many Enron employees were fired whilst Senior Executives used $200,000 to fund its luxury box at the formerly named Enron Field. Though founded on the innovative idea of instant photography, Polaroid's management failed to save the company from the shift to digital cameras. Polaroid reportedly cancelled health-care benefits for the company's retirees in the wake of its Chapter 11 filing. However, management reportedly petitioned the bankruptcy court for permission to dole out roughly $19 million in bonuses to keep key executives from leaving. Webvan is another example. It failed to compete against the traditional supermarkets with its online shopping services and home delivery. Before it ceased operations, the company reportedly agreed to pay its resigning CEO, George Shaheen, $375,000 per year for life although the Webvan's stock price plunged 99 percent during his tenure.

Kmart in bankruptcy authorised payments of $362,000 per month in retirement benefits to some 242 of its executives. The Kmart's creditors which K mart owed $6 billion protested to a Chicago bankruptcy judge.

In the later 2000's, there was a calling for an uprising against this type of corporate abuse, LA Times writer John Balzar observed that creditors and shareholders are not the only ones enraged at the seemingly arrogant attitudes of America's corporate giants. "Consumers are mad, and some are declaring petty war against the mighty corporation, against shenanigans, the double-dealing, the get-rich-quick schemes, the fraud, the self-serving deals." Those investors felt that they have been robbed as they saw their retirement savings dwindled. And though their behaviour changed in the mid-2000's, that was simply a temporary fix and in the later 2000's, we are seeing more and more evidence of this same greedy behaviour.

In America, CEOs compensation surged 1,000% in three decades, making it to 500 times the pay of the average worker in the later 2000's. Yet, as the decade wore-on, it was evident that they were greedy for more. Martha Stewart of the ImClone System expensed the US$17,000 cost of a holiday party to her company. Dennis Kozlowski spent US$15,000 on a "dog umbrella stand" and US$6000 on shower curtain. John Rigas spent US $20,000 of Adelphia's shareholders' funds on a Christmas tree. The list of corporate excesses goes on and on.

CEOs who live "fat cat" lifestyles using corporate funds should be slaughtered and skinned.

Stage 3: Treatment

Principle No. 42

If you need surgery, call in the surgeon. (Mark 5:21-34, Matthew 11:28-29 – "Come to me, all you who are weary and burdened, and I will give you rest. Take my yoke upon you and learn from me, for I am gentle and humble in heart, and you will find rest for your souls.")

When you need a heart by-pass, you call in a cardiologist rather than a general practitioner. When you are in legal troubles, you consult a lawyer. When you have tax problems, you seek advice of a tax consultant. Yet many troubled companies make the fatal mistake of not approaching the right professional for help. Many try to get out of their conundrum using the internal management. Others rely on their lawyers, auditors, etc. These troubled businesses need to bring in turnaround experts and specialists. In fact, the management of some of these ailing companies behaves like a deer caught in the headlights, petrified and totally clueless on how to move forward.

As chief executives and chief financial officers fall from their grace over accounting irregularities and scandals, turnaround managers, with familiar titles such as chief restructuring officers, turnaround specialists or artists, corporate doctors are taking charge of distressed companies to get them up to speed again. In the US, troubled companies in the early 2000's, such as WorldCom Inc, Enron Corp, and Kmart Corp., appointed turnaround specialists to restructure their businesses. Since the Asian financial crisis in the late 1990s, even Malaysia enlisted the use of professionals, armed with impressive credentials rather than political ties to shake up the government-linked companies. For instance, in 1998, the former premier brought in the first batch of turnaround experts to head the Umno-linked companies and asset management firm Danaharta.

Some of these turnaround experts who generally have a background in business, accounting, finance or operations are called in by the creditors or board of directors who lose faith in the management. In most instances, these specialists have had a significant experience as a CEO, CFO, CIO or COO provide a sense of credibility and glimmer of hope to the board, investors and creditors. . They are a special breed of talent, as they have to be entrepreneurs, visionaries, redesign architects and crisis managers all rolled into one. They have to create resources out of liabilities, find opportunities where none is apparent and travel down

Page 135

uncharted paths to fix "unsolvable" problems. In essence, they have to create value by reinventing the company.

Jesus is very much like these turnaround experts and more. He gave cure when no one else can; faith when no one else believed. In the story found in Mark 5:21-34, there was a sick woman who had been subject to bleeding and was suffering from this illness for 12 years. She had already spent all her money under the care of many doctors, yet instead of getting better, her condition just kept getting worse.

When Jesus was in Capernaum, a large crowd gathered around him, and the sick woman was there too. Having heard of Jesus and the numerous miracles he performed in other towns, the sick woman came up behind him and touched his cloak, thinking that if she did, she would be healed. Upon touching his cloak, her bleeding immediately stopped and she felt her body freed from suffering.

She told Jesus about what had happened and when Jesus heard this, he said to her, "Daughter, your faith has healed you. Go in peace and be freed from your suffering." As for this case, the woman only needed the help of Jesus to end her suffering. Jesus assured her that because of her faith, she has been freed from her suffering, and can now live her life in peace.

Because Jesus knows what we need and is the only one who surely can answer all our problems, he guarantees us with the same promise, as he tells us in Matthew 11:28-29, "Come to me, all of you who are weary and carry heavy burdens, and I will give you rest. Take my yoke upon you. Let me teach you, because I am humble and gentle at heart, and you will find rest for your souls."

Unfortunately, no company seeking to turn around would run an advertisement that says: "Company not making money and need turnaround specialist. Send in your application."

There are many ways of finding quality professionals to enable you to fix your business. The first place to start looking for a turnaround specialist is to contact your banker, lawyer, external auditor, large accounting firms and various business chambers and associations. Through their previous collaborations, these parties may have the contacts of specialist with the requisite skills.

Another way to find the turnaround specialist is to contact those who understand the company's situation such as current employees, company's board of directors and advisors and associates. But one has to exercise care in the selection process. There are many professionals who profess to be turnaround specialists but are actually only financial people who are preoccupied with cost-cutting measures. It takes much more than mere cost cutting to turn around an ailing business. Certainly, such skills and knowledge are important but it is only part of the answer.

Besides having actual turnaround experience, turnaround specialist needs to have a broad understanding of the industry. He or she needs some understanding of the industry. Normally time is not on the side of the turnaround specialists to show results. Therefore if he understands the industry it can facilitate and shorten the learning curve and quickly bring in business through his contacts.

The specialist also needs to have gone through adversity and shows track record of successfully turning around troubled businesses. Successful managers in healthy companies will not cut it as they have not had to work with low-morale employees, creditors screaming for payments and diminishing market share as clients switch to the competitors.

Sadly, most of these restructuring experts are brought in too late, as the restructuring should have been carried out yesterday. Consequently, the success rate of turnaround is very low.

Therefore, when you need surgery, call in the surgeon quickly. Do not delay as it can be fatal.

Principle No. 43

Do not depend solely on the doctor in the house to do the surgery. (Genesis 32:1-21, Ephesians 2:8-9 – Jacob: "Save me, I pray, from the hand of my brother Esau, for I am afraid he will come and attack me, and also the mothers with their children.")

Many business leaders are good at starting a business or maintaining one that has already been well established. However, they are not good at fixing a seriously sick business. They often do not have the experience, skills, temperament or willingness to do a proper turnaround. Sometimes, the business leader himself is the hindrance and obstacle to the entire turnaround process because of past encumbrances and prejudices. An outsider is quite often required to execute the turnaround.

Most of the time, a troubled company cannot be fixed solely from the within. The management may harbour too much prejudices, vested interests and baggage. If the medicine is too bitter, management may not have the guts to swallow it.

Here, Jacob serves as an example for us. He had always relied on himself and was stubborn to ask for help. He wanted to control things and take up matters in his own way. When Jacob was preparing to meet his brother Esau, he sent messengers to tell his brother that he has been staying with Laban and will be remaining there.

Trying to control the situation, he divided the people who were with him and the animals that they had into two groups, that is Esau attacks one group, the other group can escape. Realizing that he cannot fully take control and cannot do it alone, he talked to God and asked God to save him. He prayed "O God of my father Abraham, God of my father Isaac, O Lord, who said to me, 'Go back to your country and your relatives, and I will make you prosper,' I am unworthy of all the kindness and faithfulness you have shown your servant. I had only my staff when I crossed this Jordan, but now I have become two groups. Save me, I pray, from the hand of my brother Esau, for I am afraid he will come and attack me, and also the mothers with their children. But you have said, 'I will surely make you prosper and will make your descendants like the sand of the sea, which cannot be counted.' " Here we can see that as he learns that he cannot handle situation alone, he comes to an outsider, in this case, God, and finally depends on him and asks for his help.

Similarly, God teaches us that we cannot save ourselves. He is that "outsider" we need. We are sinners and we can't possibly do anything to spare us from spiritual death. Nevertheless, because of His son, Jesus, we have a chance to be saved, only if we believe. We see this clearly in the book of Ephesians. The verse reads "For it is by grace you have been saved, through faith—and this not from yourselves, it is the gift of God—not by works, so that no one can boast." It is established here that the expert in this scene, is God. He is of essence to make the necessary turnaround for our lives, and ultimately rid us of eternal damnation.

Likewise, sick companies need somebody from the outside who is able to say "no" firmly when necessary. If the internal management is the cause of the internal woes, then the use of internal management for the turnaround is like using leeches to cure leukaemia. The condition of the patient will not improve and may deteriorate as time passes by.

An outsider brings some unfair advantages to the turnaround game. You have no emotional baggage tied to a new dream or a historically interesting but economically irrelevant service. Nor are you beholden to the big bosses. You can ask dump questions without looking dumb. One or two of those dumb questions will turn out to be brilliant ones.

Contrary to expectations, you will find you are accorded loyalty from employees. Other executives have to work hard to earn this devotion. These employees understand that you represent their last chance, and that you did not create the problem. They knew that the business was wobbling off course before the board or owners understood it. With the right demeanour and without rudeness, the employees will guide you immediately toward the major problems. Few will hold back if you listen hard. They know that if you really quiz them and they will lose their jobs anyway, it is less painful for them, since both of you have tried to salvage the situation.

Turnaround specialists coming from your specific industry are usually quite good. Their names are familiar in the industry and you can check on the reputation of these specialists. They also probably already know something about your company.

These specialists can make objective decisions that the ailing company's management cannot. Some take on full-time positions within the company as the Chief Executive. Others may be engaged as consultants with full authority and access to the company's accounts. They are there to cover the wound, conduct surgery or resuscitation. Once the job is done, they move on as these guys may not be the types suited to running a healthy company. Majority of executives are not suited for a turnaround as this unique situation demands extraordinary leadership. When these turnaround specialists take over the helm of the management, they swiftly proceed do the things that the Chief Executive ought to be doing before the company gets into trouble – restructuring.

When you are afflicted by cancer, see an oncologist and do not rely on your family doctor.
Similarly when you company is not well; seek the services of a corporate turnaround specialist.

Principle No. 44

Accomplish your dream, have a good team. (Matthew 10 – "He called his twelve disciples to him and gave them authority to drive out evil spirits and to heal every disease and sickness.")

Having a good team is fundamental in accomplishing your dreams. In this complex corporate world, no single person can have all the answers. The world is changing so rapidly that even a team comprising internal experts is overwhelmed in trying to follow and monitor the changes. The internal team should also include the use of external consultants and experts to bring in knowledge and skills that are currently not available in the company.

Similar to a surgical operation, a company needs a team to successfully perform a turnaround. Turnaround is seldom a one-person show. Most well-orchestrated corporate comeback teams are fielded with the best talents from within or outside the company including skilled professionals such as insolvency lawyers, auditors and turnaround consultants.

Jesus himself needed a team to perform the duties. He needed them to complete the task while he was away. He needed this team of 12; he trained them, gave them authority over demons, heal the sick and perform miracles themselves. These 12 are as follows: Simon (who is called Peter) and his brother Andrew; James son of Zebedee, and his brother John; Philip and Bartholomew; Thomas and Matthew the tax collector; James son of Alphaeus, and Thaddaeus; Simon the Zealot and Judas Iscariot, who betrayed him. Jesus had instructed the twelve on how to go about the missions he had prepared for them, so that he can send him out to achieve these tasks.

The first step, especially during the surgical stage is to assemble the turnaround team by getting everyone on board. Change is crucial and is characteristic of a turnaround process. Preferably, the team should comprise the turnaround manager, whether appointed from outside the organisation or seconded internally, the financial controller and other key internal staff. The team must work closely with the other stakeholders such as the shareholders, creditors and union.

Whatever the composition, the team must move swiftly like the SWAT unit. Members need to regularly update each other on the status as well as progress of the specific duties of each member. There must be a clear and unchallenged team leader who has the final say in case of dissenting views.

Flexibility is the key and the team may be changed periodically as the situation warrants. For instance, once the company turns around and the financial crisis blows over, the company may need to transform its corporate culture. The team needed at this stage is a change agent. It calls for a more democratic and participative team as opposed to the "surgical" team, which calls for a more autocratic one.

Thus increasingly, human resource management has recognised the importance of good teamwork as an ingredient to the success of the company. Staff appraisal system has recognised one's ability to work as a team and not just individual performance as a key measurement of the staff's performance. Nicor Steel put great emphasis on teamwork in the early 2000's. There are cases whereby staff voluntarily chase out their own colleagues who are poor performers. The staff of Nicor Steel is one of the highest paid employees in the industry.

Companies need to work in teams. No company is an island. Companies also need to team up, share expertise, financial resources and technology. Companies at times too need to consider teaming up with their competitors in strategic alliances when venturing overseas. In today's corporate world, things are no longer cut dried and clean. For instance, there are mega infra-structural projects that require the competitors to pool their financial resources together to clinch mega-projects, which are too big for any single player to handle. In the pharmaceutical industry, R&D development costs for new drug development may be too prohibitive and requiring a few pharmaceutical companies to pool together their resources towards its development. As a matter of fact, pharmaceutical companies are merging and teaming up because of the phenomenal development costs. Some studies indicate that in the years to come, there may only be five major pharmaceutical companies left worldwide as compared to the current few dozens.

Therefore no man or company can be an isolated island. A good team is vital to fulfilling your dream.

Principle No. 45

The surgeon operates on only one patient at a time. Similarly, a sick company needs to concentrate on its core competence. (Hebrews 12; 2 Let us fix our eyes on Jesus, the author and perfecter of our faith...)

During the turnaround phase when the company is on the brink of bankruptcy, there are time and resource constraints. The company needs to concentrate all its resources on doing a few major things right. You should have a laser-sharp focus just as a surgeon focuses on only one operative field during surgery. If you are a patient, you will not allow your surgeon to operate on you and another patient simultaneously.

The Bible in Hebrews 12:2 encourages us to focus on Jesus. Jesus is the source of our strength and energy. If we focus our attention elsewhere, quite often we grow weary and confused because we lose perspective of our long term goals and our purpose in life to please our Lord.

Similarly, an ailing company needs to concentrate only on its core competence and try to rid itself of activities that do not help the bottom-line targets as well as those that do not immediately improve its cash flow. Under such critical circumstances, you can even succeed at far lower cost by ensuring that you do a better job with the businesses and skills you already have.

In order to release resources for its core business, the ailing company has to divest any unprofitable or non-related businesses. Quite often, in their bid to bolster sales performance, troubled companies clinch lots of sales contracts with thin profit margin. This tantamount to buying sales and they often turned into subsequent financial losses. Such a scenario is equivalent to having a lot of sizzle but no steak.

It is better to amputate all loss-making ventures and unprofitable sales whenever possible. According to the standard surgical procedure if there is pus, get it removed. In fact, the famous Chinese military strategist Sun Tzu believed in the principle of concentration in fighting a war. He said: "The strength of an army does not depend on large forces. Do not advance relying on sheer numbers. Rather, one must concentrate one's forces and anticipate correctly the movement of the enemy in order to capture him."

To compete in the global market, it is important to narrow your focus to a specific segment, Olivetti lost its competitiveness in the late 1990's as its product lines proliferated from typewriters to computers. When the market is 58 million people in Italy, a broad line is all right. But when Olivetti went global it could not compete. Hyundai, S. Korea a major conglomerate also lost focus in the quest for expansion. It is involved in all kinds of businesses ranging from chemicals, ship-building, engineering, automotive, pharmaceutical, etc. As a result it confuses the minds of the customers. When the financial crisis hit S. Korea in 1997, Hyundai was one of the first chaebols to fall apart. Marketing will need to be focusing on specific niches for the riches are usually found in niches.

The soft drink giant Coca-Cola tried to venture into the bottled water market in Europe in the early 2000's with the launch of "pure" water Dasani. News broke out that the Coca-Cola's treated tap water contains cancer-causing chemical and it had to withdraw the Dasani from the market, creating a lot of bad taste. Although Coke drinks and "pure" water are in the soft drinks category, the technology and know-how can be quite different. Coca-Cola should have stayed with the " real thing", its core competence.

Remember to have laser sharp focus. The laser is actually a weak source of energy. A laser takes a few watts of energy and focuses them in a coherent stream of light. A few watts of energy are not useful. However, laser is able to drill through diamond, the hardest rock and eradicate cancer cells as well for lasik treatment. Similarly, companies with laser sharp focus can dominate a market. When a company is not focused, its limited energy gets dissipated over too many products or markets.

Principle No. 46

In times of trouble, do not become schizophrenic but let your focus be emphatic. (Philippians 3:14 – "I press on toward the goal to win the prize for which God has called me heavenward in Christ Jesus.")

Schizophrenic patients suffer split personalities, characterised by withdrawal from reality and behavioural disturbances. Management needs to have very sharp and emphatic focus rather than become schizophrenic.

Similarly, God tells us to always be focused on the right things. Israel got side-tracked and lost focus on God. "And I said to them, Each of you, get rid of the vile images you have set your eyes on, and do not defile yourselves with the idols of Egypt. I am the Lord your God." But Israel didn't listen to God. Instead, they rebelled against him and pursued their evil ways; and as a result, God poured his anger among them.

Paul writes in Philippians that we should "press on toward the goal to win the prize for which God has called [us] heavenward in Christ Jesus." He reminds us to set our eyes on the prize and get focused; for he knows very well that each of us can easily lose sight of this which can ultimately lead to our destruction.

Likewise, it does not take very long to mess up a company especially when the focus of the key management is muddled. Just a couple of months should do the job. All it takes is for you to take on some loss-making projects and contracts, neglect collecting your debts and allow excess inventory to build up. You need to remain even more level-headed during problematic times.

The turnaround manager needs to be very focused especially during the surgical stage. The specialist is involved at several organisational levels, both tactical and strategic.

At a tactical level, the specialist needs to focus on cash flow improvements and preservations, establishing open communications with all stakeholders, negotiating with creditors and initiating total financial management.

At the strategic level, the specialist needs to focus his mind on human resources, establishing profitability growth, asset analysis, developing alternative financing strategies and increasing shareholders' values.

Without such focus, the danger is that the turnaround manager is forced to react to problems by focusing on the ramifications of the crisis and passing the buck, blaming others and protecting the culprits.

During the tough times when the share price of the Singapore-based company Creative Technology dropped by 80% from its peak in 2000, its CEO, Sim Wong Hoo said: "This is an exciting time. We have much more energy than we had three years ago." He saw upsides to the dotcom collapse. "It was too easy money and I think things are easy come, easy go," he says. "Now when everybody goes back to basics, the real strong players will surface." This Singapore's icon for creativity and entrepreneurship did not succumb mentally to the tech downturn. In fact, he appeared more energetic and optimistic than ever before. That which does not kill him makes him even stronger.

Bob Woodward has testified in his book, *Bush at War* that Bush has risen to the occasion when confronting the aftermath of the September 11 al-Qaeda attack. According to Woodward, Bush calmed his colleagues' nerves. "You know what? We need to be patient." Bush said. "We have got a good plan. Look, we are entering a difficult phase. The press will seek to find divisions among us. They will try to force on us a strategy that is not consistent with victory. We have been at this only 19 days. Be steady. Do not let the press panic us. Resist the secondary guessing. Be confident but patient. It is all going to work."

Tony Blair the Prime Minister of United Kingdom was able to focus despite his wife Cherie's legal case, the Afghanistan war, the Saddam Hussein, Jacques Chirac. Charged with running the country and playing a significant international role, he remained somehow not distracted by family life and pressing domestic concerns. If you want to be a good turnaround manager, you have to be totally focused and immersed in what you are doing.

Warren Buffet, the second richest man in the world also focused in his investment strategy. He only invested in businesses that he is familiar with. He focuses on a few stocks, know about them and heavily invest in these stocks. To minimise risks, he encouraged investors to focus on a few stocks, there is no need to be an expert of every company, but invest in businesses you know for the long term.

In bad times, all the more you must focus clearly on your goals. You cannot afford to allow your focus be muddled or your energy be dissipated.

Principle No. 47

A sick company needs to undergo surgery, resuscitation and nursing. (Joshua 1:8 – "Do not let this Book of the Law depart from your mouth; meditate on it day and night, so that you may be careful to do everything written in it. Then you will be prosperous and successful.")

Seriously ill companies need to be placed in intensive care unit. As with grave medical crisis, dealing with the business failure quickly becomes extremely exhausting and requiring special care and medical attention. You need a team of specialists to intervene and take the swift control of events. This is akin to the manner that doctors, counsellors and insurance companies step in to sort out the problems in the life of a gravely ill patient.

As in a medical crisis, a company's initial ill health may suddenly deteriorate into a life threatening situation. The ailment appears mild initially and may have already established a foothold in the patient much earlier. Sometimes, it can be a case of bad DNA in its business model or a genetic flaw in its corporate culture. These weaknesses predispose the firm to failure. As with very sick patients, the company's health may spiral quickly downward and eventually become irreversible. It is at this stage that these symptoms of failure become apparent. By the time the management and all the other interested parties are aware of the problem, the crisis has already escalated beyond redemption.

Many companies in the late 2000's are falling sick due to corporate diseases such as global economic recession, competition brought forth by globalization, terrorist attacks and other uncontrollable environmental changes. When a company falls ill, it needs to undergo the three phases of corporate turnaround, namely:

Phase 1: Surgery: This is to restructure the troubled organisation to face the harsh and new reality and quickly improve its cash flow. During this phase, the company may need to downsize, right size, re-engineer or delayer in order to turn the ailing company around. The use of financial control is critical in this phase.

Phase 2: Resuscitation: This is to revitalise the business so as to increase its sales revenues and profits. After obtaining a brief reprieve from cash flow collapse, the company has to grow its business quickly. The use of marketing strategy is important during this phase.

Phase 3: Nursing: This is to nurture and establish a strong and healthy corporate immune system in order to sustain long-term growth. After growing the business, the company needs to be strengthened to prevent a recurrence of the problems while equipping itself to handle future changes in the marketplace. The emphasis here is on innovation.

For complete corporate recovery, it is important to finish the full course of antibiotics prescribed in all the three phases. Some companies may need heavier dosages of surgery while others may require more of resuscitation and nursing. Mere restructuring through surgery alone is not good enough. As a doctor once said: "The surgery was good but the patient died." Without the resuscitation and nursing phases, it is akin to not completing your antibiotics and the bacteria are not completely eradicated from the system. During the next attack, the bacteria may become more virulent as they have built up resistance against the antibiotics. Building a strong and healthy company takes a long time in Phase 3 – it is not a one-time inoculation. It is like taking vitamin pills every day for the rest of your life in order to build a strong corporate culture, which can embrace changes.

Like the three phases, we shouldn't think of our relationship with Jesus as a one-time thing. We ourselves have to take our spiritual vitamins everyday to build a strong relationship with God. This means praying to him and reading his word for the very least, everyday to keep our ties with God healthy and strong, and we can live our lives according to what he approves of. As it is written in the book of Joshua, "Do not let this Book of the Law depart from your mouth; meditate on it day and night, so that you may be careful to do everything written in it. Then you will be prosperous and successful."

There is another medical parallel in the deployment of techniques used in the three phases. Phases 1 and 2 can be compared to the use of Western medical system with its invasive, scientific and chemical approaches. The Western medical approach is very suitable for acute and life threatening situations where time is of essence. Phase 1 and 2 are the science of the corporate turnaround process. In Phase 3, the use of traditional Chinese medicine (TCM) is more applicable, natural, holistic and philosophical. This renders it suitable for chronic and comprehensive cures. Phase 3 is the art of the corporate turnaround process.

To ensure full recovery, remember to finish the full course of antibiotics of surgery, resuscitation and nursing.

Principle No. 48

The right prescription lies in integrative medicine and management that combines the best of Eastern and Western practices. (Exodus 34:5-6, Psalm 86:15, Proverbs 3:3, Proverbs 16:6 – "Through love and faithfulness, sin is atoned for...")

After a century of pill-and-scalpel medicine, doctors have discovered that fighting disease and restoring health are not the same. As medical science examines herbs and acupuncture in traditional Chinese medicine, a new blend of medicine emerges.

In Asia, it is quite common for sick people to turn to traditional medicine for remedies. In the West, the alternative medicine is catching on very rapidly. For example, nearly half of all US adults now go outside the health system for some of their care. In early 2004, some 600 million visits per annum were made to non-conventional healers more than to medical doctors. Complementary and alternative medicine term covers practices ranging from the credible (tui na, acupuncture, chiropractic, natural herbs) to the laughable (coffee enemas) treatments. This new kind of medicine is gaining popular following – an integrative medicine that employs the rigour of modern medical science for fighting diseases and the traditional Eastern medicine for restoring health.

Similarly, the prescription for corporate health can take a leaf from physical health. Managers should adopt the best of Eastern and Western practices. For instance, the Western practice of hiring and firing should be tempered with the Eastern philosophy of treating employees as part of a big corporate family and ensuring that there is communication and harmony throughout the corporate family. The short term Western perspective of corporate performance driven by the stock market indicators can be tempered by the long-term view of profit performance. The hire and fire recruitment policy of the West should be tempered with the long-term employment practices of the East.

For instance Japan's slow economic recovery of the early 2000's was somewhat blamed on its life-long employment policy. On the other hand too, the downsizing and delayering era in the West have created a backlash, as employees are no longer loyal to the companies and will not make sacrifices of themselves for the company. The moderation of both professional management and entrepreneurship is the most appropriate prescription for companies.

Just like how Western and Eastern practices complement each other well in the corporate world, so does love and faithfulness work together harmoniously. In the Bible, we can see how these two describe very well the nature of God. In Exodus we see in verses 5-6 how God used Moses to proclaim his name. The verse reads: "Then the Lord came down in the cloud and stood there with him and proclaimed his name, the Lord. And he passed in front of Moses, proclaiming, 'The Lord, the Lord, the compassionate and gracious God, slow to anger, abounding in love and faithfulness." The same is written by David in the book of Psalm, chapter 86 verse 15. "But you, O Lord, are a compassionate and gracious God, slow to anger, abounding in love and faithfulness."

In several other verses in the Bible, we see how love and faithfulness work well together. Solomon reminds us in the book of Proverbs: "Let love and faithfulness never leave you; bind them around your neck, write them on the tablet of your heart." Love and faithfulness is the best prescription for us, by the loving and faithful God. After all, it is through these that our sins are compensated. "Through love and faithfulness sin is atoned for; through the fear of the LORD a man avoids evil."

There are some criticisms heaped against the practice of family-run businesses, prevalent amongst the Asian businesses. These stem from the Confucian teaching of family filial obedience and loyalty. On the other hand, we are seeing the abuses of professionally run businesses in the West. All the financial scandals and abuses in the West are happening in so-called businesses run by professional management.

There is no such thing as which is the best. The adoption of the best practices of either one or a combination of both is the most appropriate action to take. The Western medicine is the best for curing and treating a disease. The Eastern medicine is more suitable for healing and recovery. The medical science is beginning to understand that the two stages, namely curing and healing are different. The best practices from both Western and Eastern perspectives are the most appropriate prescriptions.

Principle No. 49

Four Cs for restructuring: Communication, Concentration, Cost Cutting and Cash Flow Improvement. (Romans 3:10-12, John 14:6, John 1:12 – "I am the way and the truth and the life. No one comes to the Father except through me.")

Restructuring is not a slash-and-burn exercise, but one that calls for the surgeon's skills. It does not require the use of a parang or long knife but the surgeon's lancet. Like companies, each and every one of us must undergo restructuring as well. Because of our sins, we are bound to death and eternal suffering – which is why we need to be restructured. Paul writes to the Romans: "As it is written: There is no one righteous, not even one; there is no one who understands, no one who seeks God. All have turned away, they have together become worthless; there is no one who does good, not even one."

Jesus, however, is like our surgeon. He is the only one who can completely and successfully restructure us so we can be worthy to be with God. Jesus tells us: "I am the way and the truth and the life. No one comes to the Father except through me." Our restructuring process involves a very important aspect: faith in Jesus. In the book of John, it is written: "Yet to all who received him, to those who believed in his name, he gave the right to become children of God"

In the corporate world, the restructuring process may involve re-engineering, downsizing, rightsizing and delayering. These all require the use of the same basic techniques and approaches.

During the restructuring exercise, remember to use the 4 Cs.

Communication: The manager needs to communicate personally the restructuring plans truthfully to the staff. Similarly, a doctor does not delegate to a nurse the task of briefing the patient about his ailment and treatment. You need to communicate the restructuring plans personally. Regular communication with all the staff, shareholders, board members, customers and business associates is necessary to get their buy-in and support for the restructuring plan. It is also very important that whatever you promise, you need to implement and deliver. There are many anxious and impatient people waiting to know the progress and outcome of the restructuring programme. You need to keep them duly informed. You need to "walk the talk", otherwise it is like shouting at a dead body to leave. The dead body will not leave but your friends may.

Concentration: The surgeon operates on only one patient at a time. Similarly, the sick company needs to concentrate on its core competence. During bad times, you need to concentrate even more as resources are scarce. If possible, sell away all non-core businesses. In desperate turnaround situations, your focus should be as sharp as laser. You cannot afford to be hazy, sloppy or uncertain as these will impinge on your limited resources. Divest away non-core businesses so as to concentrate on the focused areas.

Cost cutting: It is an important antidote or effective remedy to administer especially in desperate situations. Cut costs to the bones without injuring the muscles and organs. If circumstances permit, amputate non-profitable businesses rather than try to bandage and apply stitches. Investigate into cutting your fixed and variable overheads by outsourcing, downsizing, delayering and across-the-board salary cut. Every cent saved or cut goes right into the bottom line.

Cash flow improvement: Cash flow is your lifeblood. Slipping into losses may give you a migraine but a sudden shortfall in cash flow will cause immediate massive heart attack. Try to reduce your inventory, purchases, perks, credits to customers, outstanding debts and related items without hurting the company further. Ensure that your receivables are promptly collected. Negotiate with your creditors for extension of the credit limits or source for more credit lines or more time to pay back the debts. You need to do whatever you can during the financially tight situations to quickly improve the cash flow position.

Typically in a major restructuring exercise, the timing is extremely short for you to deliver the positive results. There are many things to do and remember. However, you need to prioritise and remember these four Cs.

Cash is oxygen during the restructuring process. (Deuteronomy 8:3 – "...man does not live on bread alone but on every word that comes from the mouth of the Lord")

Revenue is vanity, profit is reality and cash is certainty. With God, revenue is water, profit is manna, and cash is His word. Like sheep without a shepherd, the book of Deuteronomy tells us that we cannot survive on bread alone; we need to feed off God's word. "He humbled you, causing you to hunger and then feeding you with manna, which neither you nor your fathers had known, to teach you that man does not live on bread alone but on every word that comes from the mouth of the Lord." In medical analogy, revenue is the food, profit is the water and cash is the oxygen. You cannot pay rent with profit, you can only pay your rent with hard cash. Cash talks, the rest walks.

Just as a critically ill person needs to be administered with fresh oxygen, an ailing company's immediate lifeline is cash, cash and more cash. Fresh fund injections will provide the fillip needed to get the system moving on an even keel as well as to create stable platforms for growth.

In almost every turnaround situation, there is a troubled project that is bleeding or draining cash at an accelerated speed. For a variety of unhealthy reasons such as neglect, denial or mismanagement, these problems remain unresolved. The turnaround team need to apply the tourniquet and immediately stop the continuous haemorrhage and unrelenting outflow of cash. The turnaround team's task is to stomp out the fire and slow down the rate of burnt-out. The West would call this "grabbing the bull by its horns," and the East calls it "catching the tiger by its tail." The managers need to adopt this approach during restructuring. Also they need to promote "corporate catharsis" to purify the system and set the tone of the mode of operation. It is no more business as usual.

Cash flow problem usually arises when the bank recalls its loan or terminate other lines of credit to the company. In Singapore, in the early 2000's, many small and medium size enterprises (SMEs) ran into cash flow problems when the local banks cut or reduced bank loans. In 2003, there was a record high of 4484 individuals who were declared as new bankrupts. In the past there were six major local banks with banking officers who understood the sentiments and businesses of SMEs and had close banking relationships with them. However, the market of the early

2000's, with mergers and restructuring in the local banking scene, only four major banks remained with many of these banking officers retrenched and the bank loans to the SMEs drastically reduced. The banks' understanding and rapport with the SMEs were lost. The new banking officers were stricter and loans were not given to SMEs, which exceed the banking credit facilities and did not provide proper accounting records. Also, the local banks shifted their focus to other low-risk and fee-based services. The Singapore SMEs suffered from "corporate asphyxia", deprived of its vital oxygen supply – cash. In the late 2008, owing to the global credit crunch, we are seeing the same problem repeating itself.

The demands for funds will be there – paying the rental, workers' salaries, bank loan and interests, implementing new technology, upgrading current equipment, reviving R&D, providing advertising support to brands, training people, acquiring competitors to add critical mass to the company, and so on – the list is endless.

Hence it is vital for the turnaround manager to find ways of improving short-term liquidity, cut costs and at the same time, negotiate new loans from the current lenders. Measures to improve cash flow include - reducing inventory and disposal of obsolete ones, tightening stock control, increasing the selling price, divesting ventures that do not add value to the core business, reducing costs, finding refinancing, factoring the receivables, implementing sales and leaseback, exploiting hidden assets, recouping prepaid expense, renting out idle capacities and persuading the customer to pay cash and in advance as well as laying off/downsizing. Fresh funding is critical to jump starting the system.

Every bad debt starts out as a slow repayment, so you need to be vigilant of your collections. Disproportionately high receivables and inventory are trouble signs. The balance sheet calls them assets. They should actually be called liabilities. Cash is an asset, you can buy many things with it. Mounting inventory or receivables is the first warning that the service or product is slipping while your income statement still shows profits. Also do not confuse external borrowing with positive cash flow. Proper accounting says it is, but this is short-term thinking. Only sales collected are the authentic cash flow. All else is temporary or even worse.

Managing cash flow to meet working capital requirements is very important. With insufficient working capital, a business can wind up despite being profitable. On the other hand, an unprofitable business can continue operations if it has sufficient cash to pay its creditors.

The world faces a major credit crunch in late 2008. There is no time for Barack Obama, the newly elected US President to have a honeymoon before taking over the US presidency. He must act immediately – directly or indirectly, during the early 2009 transition period to influence credit flow into the US economy. Even healthy companies quickly asphyxiate without the oxygen of their bloodline – credit. The galloping wanton bankruptcies of 2008, due to the collapse of the US financial system, subsequent collapse of companies and the surge in unemployment must be resolved urgently.

In late 2008, we have seen the declaration from EU that their economy is rapidly approaching recession; Germany and Italy have already issued statements acknowledging a recession of their individual economies; and Japan, one of the strongest economies of the Asian region has declared recession as well. Already we are seeing signs that the US economy's infection has become a global contagion of epidemic proportion and may usher-in a second Great Depression. Because the US is the leader and the highest consumer of goods, Obama must act quickly and decisively in the early days of his tenure to bring revitalize the credit industry and resuscitate the global economy.

Though cash is not everything, its level of importance is the same as oxygen. Without it, you will certainly perish.

Principle No. 51

A troubled company cannot do a quick fix by marrying another problematic one.   (2 Corinthians 6:14-15 – "…what fellowship can light have with darkness?")

Mergers are the equivalent of society weddings in the business world. But the honeymoon is usually over sooner than expected.   Between one half and three quarters of all mergers do not work – they destroy rather than create value.

We can be like troubled companies ourselves. But when we get in trouble or we experience pain and problems, it is best to not approach someone who will just take us down deeper. Just like how sinners would approach fellow sinners – nothing good can come of it. We must surround ourselves with people who can help us to get out of the pit.

Paul tells us in the book of Corinthians that we shouldn't be with people who could just bring us down further. "…what fellowship can light have with darkness?" When we have troubles, we must look for someone who can oversee our pain and transcend it so they can help us. Because being with another troubled person cannot solve anything. Worse, it could lead to more trouble.

Takeovers destroy almost a third of the acquirer's pre-acquisition value, according to studies from the ESRC Centre for Business Research. According to most traditional assessment method, which is to simply compare the pre-bid profitability of the acquirer before and after acquisition, acquisitions result in significant improvement in profitability. However after taking into account the cost of acquisition, the cost of capital and subsequent earnings, then acquisition is starkly found to destroy 30% of the acquirer's pre-acquisition value.

The success rate of mergers and acquisitions is dismal. Research (Gaplin and Hendron) has shown that during the mergers and acquisitions, 70% do not realise their projected synergies, only 30% of the companies acquired their return on the cost of capital and about 50% of executives leave in the first year. The CFO Magazine reported: "75% of Mergers and Acquisitions are disappointing or outright failures. 50% experience a decline in productivity in the first four to eight months. 47% of senior executives in acquired firms leave in the first year, 75% in the first 3 years.

The Economist (1999) reported: "Study after study of past merger waves has shown that two of every three deals have not worked…Look behind any disastrous deal and the same word keeps popping up – culture. Culture permeates a company and differences can poison any collaboration."

A survey conducted by Grant Thornton Business Owners Council across 750 business owners and senior executives in the USA found that some of the major contributing factors for the failure of mergers and acquisitions include a poor integration strategy, a loss of key personnel, the lack of a compelling strategic rationale and inadequate communication.

Yet, mergers happen all the time – more often in bull markets where euphoria propels share prices to giddy heights. In bear markets and hard times, troubled businesses can look like a bargain or teaming up with another anaemic company to escape the doldrums or trouble seems the logical way to go. Managers find turnaround and organic growth to be extremely laborious, boring, slow and difficult. In contrast, a merger is exciting, glamorous and generates publicity and recognition in the media. It offers a quick way to grow in size though not necessary in profits. Weak companies merge to divert the attention away from their domestic problems. Many deals are the result of the merchant bankers' good persuasion.

Another common argument offered in favour of mergers is that a positive synergistic linkup can be achieved. The synergistic sword cuts both ways. When a troubled company merges with another weak one, tantamount to a marriage of two weak persons, each one trying to find solace and strength in the other. Unfortunately, both will eventually discover the true character and incompatibility of the other. Given the high failure rate of mergers, the merger of two weak companies therefore spells the beginning of a bigger set of troubles. You cannot fix a bad computer with another bad one. The viruses residing in each of the partner will spread to one another causing both to be ruined. However, when a weak company merges with a stronger one, the former can tap the benefits of stronger management support, access to financing and a larger customer base. Such a merger has a better chance to succeed as the weaker company benefits from operational efficiencies, marketing and financial advantages.

This is why Henry Ford said: 'Coming together is the beginning, keeping together is progress, working together is success." The yen to merge, acquire or partner is part of the company's natural ambition for growth or to get out of trouble. However, it is the company that can consistently manage the marriage well that will outperform the peers.

Two good companies coming together do not make a great organisation. Two mediocre companies merging do not ensure a good organisation. Two weak companies merging do not solve the problems. You cannot merge yourselves out of trouble.

Principle No. 52

Downsizing is akin to amputation – it creates negative side effects. (Matthew 18:8-9 – "And if your eye causes you to sin, gouge it out and throw it away. It is better for you to enter life with one eye than to have two eyes and be thrown into the fire of hell.")

Downsizing is like an amputation, which removes part of one's body but creates side effects such as low staff morale and bad reputation. If it is badly executed, it can wrench out the innovative spirit and loyalty of the staff. Downsizing and layoffs are part of the price of becoming more competitive. The price for not doing it, however, is much higher later if the issue is not properly resolved. It is not the only remedy available to the managers to improve a company's performance. Other remedies include increasing the sales revenues and other cost control measures. However, the effect of the downsizing is more immediate and impactful.

In the US, when the company is in trouble, it often commits corporate genocide by turning the guns on its own people. Subsequently, after a round of corporate genocide, it suffers from corporate anorexia, that is it trims itself to the core by further cost reduction. Corporate anorexia can make you leaner and thinner but it will also weaken your body. All these are done in the name of maximising shareholders' returns.

There is a problem with one-size-fits-all downsizing. Good people also get fired. The ailing company is unable to attract good calibre staff to replace those who have left since its reputation in the marketplace is tarnished.

Loyalty from the staff makes economic sense. This is because the loyalty of customers cannot be earned without first earning the loyalty of employees. Achieving long-term growth without building a strong loyal base of customers is impossible. Unfortunately with the spate of retrenchments and downsizing, loyalty factor quickly fizzles out amongst the staff. Many employees think that the companies that they work for are not worthy of their loyalty.

There is no problem in removing the corporate fats, dysfunctional personnel or cancerous tumours in the company. In death threatening situations, it is better to amputate the diseased parts than to apply stitches and bandages. In addition, it is better to cut all marginally profitable and loss-making businesses in order to improve cash flow immediately.

Likewise, when we sin, the Lord tells us that it is better to cut off one of our body parts than for our whole body to be thrown to hell. In the book of Matthew, we find in chapter 18 verses 8-9: "If your hand or your foot causes you to sin, cut it off and throw it away. It is better for you to enter life maimed or crippled than to have two hands or two feet and be thrown into eternal fire. And if your eye causes you to sin, gouge it out and throw it away. It is better for you to enter life with one eye than to have two eyes and be thrown into the fire of hell."

Sometimes, downsizing is inevitable. For example, after merging, companies normally experience a duplication of manpower. In other circumstances, companies may need to shed staff after they lost their monopolistic position or major customers. As a result there is a slack in manpower resources that cannot be effectively deployed. Niccolo Machiavelli (1469-1527), an Italian statesman and historian said: "For injuries ought to be done all at a time, so that, being tasted less, their benefits ought to be given little by little, so that the flavour of them may last." This is how downsizing exercise ought to be carried out, all at one time.

One turnaround manager, Randall Wright Patterson of BBK, Ltd, compared rescuing a failing company to saving a row of burning houses. "If you try to fight the fire from the beginning of the row, you will simply follow the fire and you will never put it out. Sometimes you have to let the first three or four houses burn. During that time you design and put in place a plan of action to save the runaway business, a 'fire wall' per se, to save the remaining houses on the block." Similarly, if you do not downsize the 10% of the workforce, you may not save the balance of 90%.

But one has to manage the aftermath of the downsizing exercise with due care. As the saying goes: "Even rats will desert a sinking ship." Haemorrhage or the exodus of good calibre staff may take place and deal a quick and severe blow to the company's vital organs.

All other cost-cutting initiatives must be considered before laying-off employees. These other measures might include implementing pay cuts, putting a freeze on hiring and not replacing staff who leave, using part-time-equivalents instead of full-time staff in order to save costs on medical and paid-leave expenses. Other measures may include scheduling a shorter work week, combining job functions, using 'forced leave', or cutting perks and benefits such as allowances, entertainment or business class travelling, etc.

However, sometimes, the firing of staff is inevitable. In some cases troubled companies that are struggling with excessive costs or companies which have recently merged may not have a choice and may be forced to reduce staff in order to reduce duplicate job functions or keep excessive manpower costs low. Other companies which might necessitate downsizing or resizing may include those previously regulated such as utilities, transportation and telecommunication. If these companies were overly regulated, they might easily have grown too fat and overburdened themselves with employees. In order to compete in a de-regulated market, these companies will have to downsize. Because some companies' core markets will face intense competition, downsizing may also be justified for those companies which depend on patents that may expire such as some pharmaceutical and technology markets. Companies facing the loss of a major agency or customer base without a likely replacement may also be justified in downsizing. Even manufacturers which are relocating for cost reasons to another country are justified in these drastic measures. It is a fait accompli that in many markets, manpower costs are a significant portion a company's overhead.

If you cannot avoid personnel cuts, you must try to quickly re-establish the trust of the existing staff after a downsizing exercise. Silence is not golden here. Communicate to the staff the reasons for this exercise and the plans to resuscitate the company around. Be humane in treating the people to be fired. The golden rule in a downsizing exercise is: "Do not do unto others what you do not want others to do unto you." For one day, you may be the one to be fired, too.

Principle No. 53

Attain the nirvana of low fixed overheads through outsourcing. (Matthew 10:1, Mark 3:14-15 – "He appointed twelve–designating them apostles–that they might be with him and that he might send them out to preach and to have authority to drive out demons.")

The way forward for most organisations is not only to be lean and mean, but to be flexible. In the early 2000's, Dell Computers and Nike have demonstrated the power of flexibility and speed through outsourcing. It is not just the fast that will eat the slow, but the flexible ones will be able to beat the inflexible. One of the most effective ways to stay flexible is to outsource most of the functions. For instance, Dell Computer and Nike were considered pioneers to no longer manufacture most of the parts or components they need. Rather, these are outsourced. These companies do away with the traditional supply chain network and can be very nimble to change parts and components in order to meet customers' specifications without ending up with huge stocks and factory overheads. However, these companies do not outsource everything. For those parts and knowledge that are critical to the companies, they are kept in-house. For example for Nike, the soles of their shoes are still designed in the United States.

Jesus himself outsourced. He had prepared for what God has willed and in doing so, outsourced and appointed 12 disciples. "He called his twelve disciples to him and gave them authority to drive out evil spirits and to heal every disease and sickness." However, for the bigger, more important things, Jesus handled it himself. For example, when Jesus was bound for crucifixion, it was only he who could do it because his life was perfect, his character was perfect. He was the only man who lived without sin. He was God come in the flesh. By contrast, the disciples' lives, as our own, are imperfect - needing the salvation offered by Jesus at the cross.

Organisations are moving towards the virtual organisation concept, using networks linking people, assets and ideas to create and distribute products and services without being limited by ownership of fixed assets and incurring fixed overheads. A virtual organisation is virtually unbeatable and is the nirvana of every accountant for it carries little fixed overheads. This is why outsourcing is becoming very popular, although it may not necessarily translate into lower overall costs but it certainly lowers the fixed overheads and gives the company more flexibility to change with the market dynamics.

Outsourcing is now a hot potato and political issue in the US. The fear is that jobs outsourced to India and China will result in more job losses in the US. Service jobs such as call centres, software development are being outsourced to India and the Philippines, which have a huge pool of well-educated English speaking professionals. Manufacturing jobs are being lost to China, which has become the world's top workshop. Criticisms against offshore outsourcing may force legislations outlawing outsourcing. The US Senate has adopted some interim measures to restrict the export of American jobs and seeks to forbid the outsourcing of work on contracts paid for with federal funds. However, this may work against the US Incorporated.

US can learn from the German and Japanese experience. In the middle 1980s, German industries lost its cost advantage and its high value and production capabilities could not even stop the outflow of jobs to offshore. The same scenario was repeated in the Japanese corporate scene in the 1980s. The rocket high escalation of the Japanese Yen forced many Japanese companies to outsource their manufacturing plants to S E Asia.

The Germans and Japanese have allowed their respective industries to be sharpened by competition by moving out to low cost and efficient offshore operations. This painful transformation took place despite the much less flexible labour law and less performance oriented corporate culture and sluggish economic growth as compared with the United States. Today, the German and Japanese companies are able to remain very competitive without any significant loss in market share as compared to their United States counterpart.

Mr Behravesh, Global Insight chief economist and Lawrence Klein of Nobel Iaureate conducted a study in the early 2000's and found that contrary to conventional belief, 90,000 net jobs were created rather than lost in the United States as a result of moving high-tech work offshore. The report indicated that the lower costs from using offshore resources keeps inflation in check, increases productivity and keeps interest rates low. Furthermore, the benefits of global sourcing added US$ 33.6 billion in 2003 to the real gross domestic product in the United States. The report added that overall GDP is expected to be US $124.2 billion higher than without outsourcing.

Outsourcing is not the only way to create a "virtually unbeatable' organisation. Retaining some key functions in-house may sometimes still offer the organisation the most flexibility. However, a company is trapped when it has a strong bias for doing everything in-house. Laura

Ashley, for example, languished behind competitors in the early 1990's by insisting on manufacturing all products in Wales, long after others had moved their production offshore.

After recognising the benefit of outsourcing, they still took a while to do so. Laura Ashley managers maintained expensive production facilities in Wales out of loyalty or corporate responsibility and protecting the jobs of the staff. As a result, the loss-making Laura Ashley group was bought in 1998 by the Malayan United Industries and since closed the five factories in Wales, pulling out of clothing manufacture altogether.

At this juncture it is too early to tell whether the Obama presidency will be positive for people and businesses in Asia. Historically, the Democrats have been more protectionist and less pro-business than Republicans. Additionally, Obama may not himself have extensive international or business experience, however dependent on the team members he appoints, and their level of Asian savviness, the Obama presidency may affect Asia in a very positive way. As the first American president to be non-white, he will have a stronger affinity with the people of Asia, particularly those in Indonesia where he spent some of his childhood days. However, US protectionist sentiments may increase as US unemployment soars and jobs are continued to be outsourced to the overseas market. However, the US should realize that this is not the time to become protectionist – the US needs a quick recovery of the rest of the world. Corporate America must depend on international markets, particularly during times when the US domestic market is suffering – as during the current economic downturn. The Obama administration must respond quickly to set the tone, and their work is cut out for them.

The advantage when you have no fixed overheads is the flexibility and nimbleness to make swift changes. This is particularly useful in industries plagued with fickle demand. You merely switch and find new contract manufacturers or call centres when the need arises, without being tied down to your in-house resources. This frees up valuable management time and energy that can be better deployed on tactical and strategic planning. Management is not bogged down with non-core and low value activities. It is truly the accountant's nirvana when the company without the fixed costs is able to generate profits.

Principle No. 54

Better health with less fats – do better with less. (Mark 9:35-37 – "If anyone wants to be first, he must be the very last, and the servant of all.")

In today's competitive market, the ones that outlast and survive are those that can do more things and programs with lesser resources. This is why increasingly, we are seeing companies' budget requiring a reduction in overheads and capital expenditures, whilst profits and revenues are expected to increase. Companies have little choice as the marketplace, the shareholders and the investors dictate this. As with eating, in companies less corporate fats really does mean more.

Carl von Clausewitz, a nineteenth-century Austrian officer who fought in the Napoleonic wars and is regarded as the 'father' of western military strategic thought, wrote in his classic book *On War:* "War is not the action of a living force upon lifeless mass, but always the collision of living forces."

And Field Marshal Montgomery said during the Normandy campaign in the Second World War: "Battle is not a one-sided affair. It is a case of action and reciprocal action repeated over and over again as contestants seek to gain position and other advantage by which they may inflict the greatest possible damage upon their respective opponents."

In other words, the enemy fights back! This is the reason that military strategists focus on the enemy. You can only be competitive when you get better whether in product/service quality, delivery, reliability, etc vis-à-vis your competition. You must also be more efficient and effective in deploying your resources.

What the world is facing now is the global situation of excess capacity and oversupply. These excess capacities could last for at least another 20 years until the third world countries develop sufficient middle class demand to absorb the goods and services. We are also facing increasing turbulence and problem as long as the manufacturing sector produces three times more than before. The competition for a shrinking market will continue to intensify and exacerbate daily.

The Chinese can produce computer hard wares and high end electronic products as well as the developed world. In the late 1990's, Singapore lost the electronic segment to Penang, Malaysia, which in turn saw this segment gradually hollowing out to China. This is why American CISCO is tailed by the Chinese telecommunication, Huawei, which became a major threat to it. The Chinese telecommunication company Huawei Technologies teamed up with Siemens Information's mobile division to jumpstart the TD-SCDMA (Time Division – Synchronous Code Division Multiple Access) market in China.

Thus in today's highly competitive marketplace, an underdeveloped country such as China is able to compete head-on with the developed countries in the high-tech industry. This is unseen some forty years ago.

Competing with less applies to us as well. When Jesus heard his disciples arguing over whoever is the greatest, Jesus answered to them that whoever is the last, will be the first, and whoever is the first will be the last. He told them that to be great, they must humble themselves first. "Sitting down, Jesus called the Twelve and said, 'If anyone wants to be first, he must be the very last, and the servant of all." With Jesus, we must humble ourselves first; be the least, and serve others – we ourselves should compete with less.

In the global economy, the modern telecommunication and transportation have made possible for the skilled people in the third world countries to compete against the developed ones. Therefore, one needs to compete more with less.

Principle No. 55

Cut cost to the bones without injuring the muscles and vital organs. (Matthew 19:16-29 - "Peter answered [Jesus], "We have left everything to follow you! What then will there be for us?")

Unless they have an understanding bank or creditor, rigorous cost cutting may be needful for some companies to survive especially during a cash flow crisis. Cutting costs to achieve a turnaround may save the business, but it always leaves behind a demoralised workforce with an acute problem of rebuilding confidence and motivation. Often the key question is whether the company is able to make a comeback with its existing management intact.

Many small and medium size enterprises (SMEs) cannot embark on large-scale cost-cutting measures such as massive retrenchment or large asset disposal to raise cash quickly. The SMEs have difficulty in retaining their staff and do not have a lot of assets to sell off. They may also encounter difficulty to obtaining credit lines from their bankers and creditors. Hence, they have to exercise great care in cutting the costs without injuring the muscles and the organs as any miscalculations can be fatal.

One of Unilever's subsidiaries, a Dutch meat, sauce and soup business was in deep trouble in the late 1990's. Among other challenges, it faced two major problems of shrinking market and a tired organisation. A new chairman was hired to fix the mess. He swiftly acted by replacing those directors who lack the business acumen and enthusiasm to foster business growth. He persuaded sceptical workers to embrace growth and challenges as the new buzz words. A group of younger managers were selected as the team leaders to spearhead new direction for future growth. They created new products and carved out new markets as well as significantly improved production and margins. In addition to growing the existing brands, they were able to strengthen relationships with its retailers and consumers. In all, it took the company five years to rebuild its business and subsequently, it was able to achieve annual double-digit growth.

For Jesus, our earthly possessions – money, house, and all other "treasures" are just extra expenditures which we should be able to easily let go off. In the book of Matthew, Jesus teaches us that to follow him; we must be able to leave everything behind. Like how his disciples left everything they had when Jesus asked them to come and follow them, we must be able to do this as well when Jesus calls us. When the rich young man asked Jesus how he can attain eternal life, Jesus told him "…go, sell your possessions and give to the poor, and you will have treasure in heaven…"

But, unlike cost-cutting in the corporate world that is damaging to the workforce confidence and motivation, Jesus makes sure that when we "cost-cut," we are ensured of ten-times more of greater rewards. "Peter answered him, "We have left everything to follow you! What then will there be for us?" Jesus said to them, "I tell you the truth, at the renewal of all things, when the Son of Man sits on his glorious throne, you who have followed me will also sit on twelve thrones, judging the twelve tribes of Israel. And everyone who has left houses or brothers or sisters or father or mother or children or fields for my sake will receive a hundred times as much and will inherit eternal life."

Management must be diligent and well organised in order to identify any unnecessary expenditure that can be trimmed. These may include magazine subscriptions as nowadays information is readily available on Internet. Telephone and power bills can be trimmed by bidding service providers for lower rates. Furthermore, service contracts are normally not worth the money except for copier service contracts as photocopiers break down frequently. Advertising costs can be reduced by sourcing for the most effective medium and eliminating the advertisements with low responses. Cut back can also be made on entertainments, donations to charity and other worthwhile causes. In turnaround situation even charity has to have a return on investment. Only buy office supplies that are presently needed and cost savings are realised by making purchases that are on sale. To further tighten stationery supplies, it is good to assign a staff to be in charge of the supply closet. Any person must duly sign for any requisitions. Costly overseas trips can be replaced by videoconferences with overseas subsidiaries. Reduce insurance expenses as during very critical period, survival is more important. Reduce professional fees and banking/financial charges.

Downsizing, delayering, outsourcing and business process re-engineering are common prescriptions for cutting fats. But these treatments are only part of the answer.

As staff costs usually form a significant portion of the company's expenditure, it is an obvious place to look for fats. It is important to involve the staff in cost-cutting exercises as they are the ones who know where to locate these fat reserves. The people in the organisation are the producers of business fats or muscles. The activities that people perform and how well they perform them determine the firm's success. Also, it is imperative to instil and preserve the right mindset of cost prevention and cost elimination among the employees after the cost-cutting exercises. The company must not lose out in the long term because of the complacency of the staff.

Many publicly listed companies are infected by the virus of the "quarterlies" performance. The need to show good financial results for every quarter may have become unrealistic. This virus causes companies to forego the long-term business growth for the sake of meeting unrealistic quarterly objectives. This virus can cause cut back on R&D and new product development as well as advertising and promotion expenditures, which may deprive these companies of the vital fuel for future expansion.

Some troubled manufacturing companies may attempt to short change long-term gains for short-term benefits. These short sighted companies may cut back on maintenance or even use the parts from unused equipment as spare parts for other machines. Such shoddy approaches to managing the business is compromising the future prospects as vital muscles and the organs are being cut off, depriving the body of an opportunity to regain strength and energy.

Principle No. 56

Cost control is an important antidote to administer in desperate turnaround situations. (Matthew 4:18-20, Luke 18:22 – "Sell everything you have and give to the poor, and you will have treasure in heaven. Then come, follow me.")

Most firms start out small and lean. Over time, some of them put on fat as they grow and prosper. Corporate fats result from the accumulation of unnecessary and excessive or out-of-date business practices. It also places excessive and opulent perks and benefits of employees and shareholders ahead of customers' interests. Ultimately, it fails to provide sustained value to customers. Corporate fats can also be in the fibre of the culture. "It is not my money but the company's" is a common nonchalant attitude adopted by many in the fat culture that accepts wasteful work styles and attitudes as the norms. Culture becomes fat when they support individual needs at the expense of the firm or when they are no longer suitable for the new environment. A successful firm can become smug and take the easy way out and curtail product innovation and customer satisfaction. A culture is unsuitable for the new environment when it perpetuates hierarchical and top down decision-making when the marketplace requires creativity, flexibility and adaptability.

Any first-year business student will know how to cut costs. The key here is how the costs can be cut to restore financial health in the short term without hurting the ailing company in the long term.

Similarly, cutting costs is like surrendering. When we surrender our lives to Jesus, he not only takes care of the short-term matters but he ensures us of the long-term fixes as well. When the rich young man heard Jesus ask him to do some "cost-control" and give up his possessions, he refused; thereby abolishing his chances for turnaround: heaven.

However, we see the example of how Simon and Andrew, the fishermen, left everything to follow Jesus. Jesus, in turn, took care of their short-term goals – to catch fish, and gave them a boat-full; and by being Jesus' disciple, Simon and Andrew, for the long-term, led lives that served Him. "As Jesus was walking beside the Sea of Galilee, he saw two brothers, Simon called Peter and his brother Andrew. They were casting a net into the lake, for they were fishermen. "Come, follow me," Jesus said, "and I will make you fishers of men." At once they left their nets and followed him." Simon and Andrew knew the key to their greatest gain, and cut down what they could to ultimately save their lives.

Another disciple, Matthew, turned around his life of money-hungry materialism and corruption of his civic duties. He clearly knew that he would no longer be able to dip into the tax monies for his own salaries when he chose to follow the likes of an itinerant Jewish preacher. But he chose to turn away from this life and follow Jesus in order to fulfil the long-term goal of salvation. And only by turning away from the short-term benefits and immediate gratification of monetary rewards was he able to follow the Lord's way and gain the most worthy goal of reaching heaven.

The turnaround manager should discuss the pertinent details with the respective department managers, soliciting their advice early in the exercise as this can improve remarkably the chance for full cooperation and success. Sometimes, staff can offer valuable suggestions that can save time or money or both for the company. Remember, this is not the time to create unnecessary stress by finger pointing. The key is to foster a conducive environment for problem solving, establish solidarity and put everybody's self-interest to work for future gains.

Sometimes, cost reduction can be achieved through streamlining procedures and operations. Through this, duplication and inefficient methodologies can be pared down to a minimum. In some instances, similar or more superior results are achieved through outsourcing. Outsourcing provides you with the advantage of being able to focus on those areas that are vital to the company's operations, instead of being distracted by things that have little impact on the company's success. People-related expenses can be reduced remarkably through cross-fertilisation of multi-disciplinary skills. For instance, the secretary can be trained to perform business analysis and report writing, apart from the normal secretarial duties of typing and organising the boss' activities. Thus, productivity can be improved by deploying staff to perform high value-added duties.

Michael Dell created a formula: Keep prices low through cost controls, not by cutting quality or features. The company uses just-in-time manufacturing techniques, meaning that the systems it sells are basically built to order at the time they have ordered, which keeps inventory costs low. In the late 1990's, its website had some 80,000 support and service items available directly to its customers, cutting down on the number of paid staff needed to handle support issues. And by using the Internet as a direct link to its customers, Dell eliminated the added costs of a manufacturer-distributor-retailer network. These innovative strategies hit the mark. Within a year, Dell's Internet sales had reached $1 million per day. In 1999, Dell opened its own online superstore, Gigabuys, and Internet sales reached $30 million per day. If that is not proof enough of the company's success, Dell's business plan was one of the most copied by up-and-coming e-business companies.

Unnecessary cost is always your Number One enemy. You must attack every cost item, justify and challenge it. Whether your company is in trouble or not, cost is a real threat that can kill you even if you are able to come up with better products. If the cost of your product is your competitor's selling price, you cannot stay in business for long.

Know when to exit, do not be the 'living dead'. (Romans 6:4-7 - "...just as Christ was raised from the dead through the glory of the Father, we too may live a new life.")

Within the corporate world, there are the 'living dead', which are the sick companies that go on a wretched existence, without any hope of turnaround. These companies need a miracle such as a resurrection from the dead. Many of these companies need a change of DNA or business models. They are technically commercially insolvent and the owners will face the fate of bankruptcy if they close down the operations. Therefore, these 'living dead' just hang around, waiting for the death sentence. For some, the death sentence may take years before the owners decided not to throw in good money anymore to chase after bad money. For others, the bubble keeps getting bigger but, eventually, it will explode.

We are as good as the living dead as well. We live our lives in this world, bound to end up in death and eternal damnation. However, there is a perfect and effective turnaround for us: Jesus. Through Jesus we are resurrected from death - we are given a new life in him. "We were therefore buried with him through baptism into death in order that, just as Christ was raised from the dead through the glory of the Father, we too may live a new life. "If we have been united with him like this in his death, we will certainly also be united with him in his resurrection. For we know that our old self was crucified with him so that the body of sin might be done away with, that we should no longer be slaves to sin— because anyone who has died has been freed from sin." Therefore we should exit this old life, stop being the living dead and enter the new life with Christ.

In the corporate world, some of these 'living dead' are large companies with huge amounts of bank debts. However, the banks are unwilling to wind up these companies, as some one said: "When you owe the bank lots of money, you owe the bank." These banks may go under together with these "living dead'. Therefore, these living dead are allowed to survive in the short term. An example is Donald Trump's corporate empire that went into massive financial difficulties in the 1980s. He owed the banks a lot of money then and the banks were unable to press the trigger to stop the flow of credit as they would be dragged down with him

If companies are caught in such situations, the owners have to take some tough decisions to get out of this quandary. It is important to know when to exit. An optimised exit is one of getting out of non-core or under performing businesses, where there is a loss of confidence in the management and further losses and declining profitability are expected. Removing such under-performing assets can free up capital for investments in the core businesses

If you are able to optimise your exit, then it is no longer perceived as organisational failure but rather unlocking of your values. Optimised exits should be made strategically rather than be done out of desperation. This is because when it is done out of desperation and panic, quite often the value of the company is diminished. Successful exits require a lot of planning and can maximise shareholder's value, minimise cost, liability and disruption as well as enhance the value of the enterprise.

Optimised exit is necessary for many 'living dead'. For some it may mean cleaning the "deck" prior to an acquisition or integrating a large acquisition that included non-core or unprofitable assets. For others, the business model needs to be revamped with the market changes. The management needs to be able to bail the company out of the dire situation and scarce resources need to be re-deployed elsewhere for better returns. For some others, it may be a case of the shareholders and owners getting tired of the business and deciding to move on to do something else.

There are various channels to bail the company out. One way is to sell the business as an ongoing concern. Another way is to attempt to turn around the company from financial losses before disposal. If the company has a grim chance of turning around, it is better to close the company immediately, cut losses and move on. There is nothing to be ashamed about with your company going bust. Many successful entrepreneurs suffered failures in their earlier ventures. They are able to make subsequent comebacks. It is better to bite the bullet and recoup the losses and to fight another day than to be totally dragged down to the bottom because of trying to save a hapless situation.

Usually, it is difficult to get a good price or premium when selling a troubled company. Many acquirers try to avoid buying a loss-making enterprise like a plague. They will find it extremely difficult to convince their shareholders to undertake the risks of acquiring a loss-making enterprise. For instance in China, some loss-making and state-owned enterprises are offered for sale at one dollar without acquiring the past liabilities. Yet, there are few takers. You never know the full liabilities that you can be buying into.

In Singapore, many businesses are conducted at a loss. The high rental overheads, expensive manpower staffing, etc, have eroded all the profits. However, many entrepreneurs felt trapped and reluctant to shut down their business as they will have to proceed with bankruptcy procedures immediately. However, any delay in closing down such businesses can dash any hope of recouping the losses.

There are some points to consider before you embark on saving the company. Is it worth the pain and effort? Do you want to keep it going by throwing good money to chase after bad money? Therefore one needs to ask whether one's company is worth more dead than alive. If it is much like a vampire, neither dead nor alive but living on the nutrients and sustenance of the living blood, then it is time to drive a stake through the heart and relieve the misery of the 'living dead'. It is worth more to be dead than alive.

Principle No. 58

Running businesses are like parenting, if you love them you must let them go. (Ecclesiastes 3:1-8 - "There is a time for everything, and a season for every activity under heaven...a time to search and a time to give up, a time to keep and a time to throw away")

When the children grow up, parents will have to learn to let them leave the security of their homes in order to pursue their dreams of studies, careers and marriage. Companies too have to learn to part with their businesses at the appropriate time. Some need to close down, while others sold away or be broken up. Usually, this is a difficult decision as the company do suffer from empty nest syndrome too, similar to doting parents when their children depart from their homes.

However, there comes a time when you have to do things even if it is against your will. Like parents who may be a bit hesitant to let their children go, they know that in due time, they still have to do it. The Bible tells us that there is a time for everything – we have to learn how to hold on or let go of things when the time is right. "There is a time for everything, and a season for every activity under heaven: a time to be born and a time to die, a time to plant and a time to uproot, a time to kill and a time to heal, a time to tear down and a time to build, a time to weep and a time to laugh, a time to mourn and a time to dance, a time to scatter stones and a time to gather them, a time to embrace and a time to refrain, a time to search and a time to give up, a time to keep and a time to throw away, a time to tear and a time to mend, a time to be silent and a time to speak, a time to love and a time to hate, a time for war and a time for peace."

Divestment, demerger or break-up is taking place all the time and will have more impact than downsizing, delayering, etc. AT&T was amongst the first big boys to break up. Luthansia sectioned off its air-freight operations, Sandoz in Switzerland released its chemical division.

A reason for the break up is to obtain better focus. A CEO of the group cannot make the right decision for the subsidiaries as he is not able to know all the details pertaining to its subsidiaries. Therefore such big conglomerates cannot compete against their specialist competitors. People work better when they have some say about their work. The central controllers blame the subsidiaries for serfdoms and empire building. The central head office bureaucracy builds up and bogs down the business.

Getting a fair share price is another cause. Investment bankers actually encouraged this too. The share price of a big group is the average of the group's performance. If the better subsidiary is broken up, it will have a higher share price value. When the group is split up, it is like a share split. Share split is a popular way for listed company to attract more investors to its shares. For instance, a listed company with a US $80/share when split into two of US $40/share each will attract more buyers to its shares as the split share becomes more affordable.

Another reason is to reduce debt. When the subsidiary is geared up, cash is passed to the parent company and the subsidiary sectioned off with the debt. Fear of takeover is another reason. For instance, ICI kept its chemical and pharmaceutical divisions under common ownership until the pharmaceutical division was threatened to be taken over by Hanson in the early 2000's. To ward off a takeover, ICI spun off Zeneca, the bioscience company.

Some do it to separate two parts of the company, which are competitive. While others do it to rid of a troubled unit before it pulled down the whole group. For example, tobacco companies break up for fear of litigation against it.

However, there are exceptions to the rule. GE did not break up to stay competitive. Instead, Jack Welch decided the best course of action for GE in the 1980s was to rid itself of the businesses that GE was not doing well. Those companies that were spun from GE did better than if they had stayed in the GE family. For IBM, Lou Gerstner was not convinced to break up IBM in order to turn it around. Instead Lou moved the organisation to focus on services. Lou was proven right not to break up IBM, which his predecessor John Akers had wanted to do.

Like a woman giving birth to the child, it is difficult to let the child go. You must enjoy and be able to manage it. You must earn what you are worth. Do not let the ego and emotions get in the way, stop if it is not working well.

Evaluate your businesses; some may fare better if they are spun off. For others, which are terminally ill, it may be better to close them down and bury them.

Principle No. 59

Two types of dysfunctional personnel - benign and malignant tumours. (James 2:19-20, Jeremiah 14:14-16 – "Then the Lord said to [Jeremiah], "The prophets are prophesying lies in my name. I have not sent them or appointed them or spoken to them.")

Similar to the human body, the corporate body has two types of dysfunctional tumours – the benign or inactive ones, which are often dormant as well as the malignant or harmful types which are very dangerous. Both types of dysfunctional cannot be left to their own devices for they can cause damage to the company.

The benign tumour group consists of the demotivated staff which are not contributing productively to the company. Some are unable to find alternative employment so they just hang on, waiting for payout during the retrenchment. Many comprise the "dead woods" in the company leftover after their better colleagues have all left for greener pastures. The situation is unhealthy and counter-productive as some of these individuals may complain excessively, spread rumours and even sabotage the operations through poor productivity. In the handling of such benign cases, one should fire them up first rather than firing them. If possible, one should try motivation and training/development to elicit peak performance. These dysfunctional personnel are like weeds. If you do not manage them, they will quickly spread. Also some of these benign tumours may have turned malignant and harmful, requiring careful monitoring.

The malignant tumour cases are the more harmful ones. Just like in the case of malignant carcinoma or cancer cells, such staff are working against the company all the time. Therefore, attempts must be made to eliminate this group as soon as possible.

An example of malignant tumour is staff with integrity problems taking bribes from suppliers, distributors or competitors. Malignant tumours are not only a physical disease, they also involve a negative state of mind. Other malignant tumour cases include staff with bad attitudes or incompetence. These staff have a negative mindset which are difficult to change and can become detrimental to the company impeding its progress. The malignant tumours also include incompetent management staff, who perpetuate the "incompetency vicious cycle" through the recruitment of other incompetent staff. Just like cancer cells, such tumours will proliferate if they are not eliminated quickly.

Just as there are two types of dysfunctional personnel in the corporate world, so are there two types of "followers" in the Bible: people who say they believe but not do anything about it; these are what we'll call the benign tumours, and the malignant ones are those who are hypocrites and false prophets, who preach and practice erroneous ways – ones who can be very destructive.

Benign tumours in the Bible are those who proclaim they have faith in Jesus, yet they do not back this up with deeds. These people are deemed foolish and are criticized in the Bible. "You believe that there is one God. Good! Even the demons believe that — and shudder. You foolish man, do you want evidence that faith without deeds is useless?" On the other hand, malignant tumours are those like of false prophets. They go out and preach false prophecies against the Lord's teachings. Jesus highly detests this kind of people and has set out punishment for them. "Then the Lord said to [Jeremiah], "The prophets are prophesying lies in my name. I have not sent them or appointed them or spoken to them. They are prophesying to you false visions, divinations, idolatries and the delusions of their own minds. Therefore, this is what the Lord says about the prophets who are prophesying in my name: I did not send them, yet they are saying, 'No sword or famine will touch this land.' Those same prophets will perish by sword and famine. And the people they are prophesying to will be thrown out into the streets of Jerusalem because of the famine and sword. There will be no one to bury them or their wives, their sons or their daughters. I will pour out on them the calamity they deserve."

Some companies are slow to take action against these malignant tumours because they believe in life-long employment. As they do not want to fire such non-performing employees, they are instead put in "SLEEP" department, which stands for Segregation for Least Effective and Efficient Personnel. In such "cold storage" or "SLEEP" departments, these staff are still kept on the payroll but they are not assigned any duties. It is hoped that these dysfunctional staff will be under pressure to resign rather than to be fired. However, nowadays, companies cannot afford to support such non-performers. In the early 2000's the Japanese learnt that life-long employment does not work in the recessionary market. It is better to suffer briefly with the initial pain of removing the malignant tumour quickly than to incur lingering pain and irreversible damage by allowing the cancer to spread uncontrollably through the entire system.

Principle No. 60

Bureaucracy is the parasite to productivity. (Matthew 6:7, Luke 11:2-4 – "And when you pray, do not keep on babbling like pagans")

A parasite is medically defined as an organism that lives on within another organism at the expense of the host. Bureaucracy is an administrative system, which places undue emphasis on adherence to complex procedures and inflexible rules of operation. It is an administration characterised by excessive red tape and routine. This impedes effective action, slows down decision-making and adds unnecessary layers of costs. Bureaucracy is sometimes described as the tail wagging the dog and is a parasite to productivity. It is also like the millstone around one's neck, limiting mobility.

In the Bible, a form of bureaucracy can be seen in pagans, who only memorize their prayers and repeat it countless times, thinking that this would be the best way to do it. However, the Bible tells us that this is not how it should be. "And when you pray, do not keep on babbling like pagans, for they think they will be heard because of their many words." We can read in the Bible how David, Solomon, or King Hezekiah prayed – always personal and direct, never memorized. Memorized prayers only restricts you from what you need to tell God – it robs you of creativity and freedom to tell God what you want to tell him; after all, prayer is the place where we can build our relationship with God, and how will we be able to do that if it is "scripted?"

Jesus tells us a structure of how we should pray. When a disciple asked him, this is what Jesus said: "When you pray, say: "Father, your name is holy, your kingdom come. Give us each day our daily bread. Forgive us our sins, for we also forgive everyone who sins against us. And lead us not into temptation. ""

Most of the large organisations have some form of bureaucracy. It is a given, inherent structure created largely by Alfred P. Sloan, who became president and CEO of General Motors (GM) in 1923. He recognised the need for coherence and unifying order when he confronted GM, a sprawling corporation that was in dire need of organisation. It was Sloan who transformed GM's loosely configured, far-flung divisions into a coherent corporation. But while that organising form worked well for many years, it had begun to become too restrictive as business became more demanding and more global in the 1980s.

Jack Welch told his people to "fight it, kick it." Welch fought a two-decade war against bureaucracy with initiatives like "boundaryless" and "Work-Out". GE's list of values specifically addressed the company's intolerance for bureaucracy and it was at the top of this list for many years. Welch recognised the adverse effects of bureaucracy and knew that unless he rid the organisation of the worst of it, GE would never become a legitimate global competitor. He called bureaucracy "the Dracula of institutional behaviour," meaning that it kept rising from the dead after being driven with a stake into it. He was concerned that bureaucracy was creeping back into the organisation. He hated bureaucracy, knowing that layers slow down decision-making. He delayered the organisation and removed the use of headquarters in order to help GE become more nimble and competitive. By waging "war" on bureaucracy and the old ways one movement at a time, Welch established a solid foundation on which he eventually built GE's famed learning organisation

Margaret Thatcher, the former Prime Minister of United Kingdom (1979 – 1990) who privatised Britain Inc, the state-owned enterprises, did not support bureaucracy and consensus. She said: "To me consensus seems to be: the process of abandoning all beliefs, principles, values and policies in search of something in which no one believes, but to which no one objects; the process of avoiding the very issues that have to be solved, merely because you cannot get agreement on the way ahead. What great cause would have been fought and won under the 'I stand for consensus' banner?"

With privatisation, Britain Inc. was able to cut back on bureaucracy and re-gain its natural corporate wellness. Many countries have followed Britain's footsteps to privatise its government sector thereby minimising bureaucracy and boosting productivity.

If you desire speed and quick response to market changes, then the command-and-control bureaucracy is not the best way to run a business. It is more important to get everyone involved than adhering to a rigid hierarchy. Many companies are cutting down on headquarters' bureaucracy as they are bogging companies down, stifling the units' ability to reason and quickly decide. Business was moving too quickly and bureaucracy was strangling creativity and innovation. Gun down bureaucracy as it is the enemy of productivity.

Principle No. 61

Pregnancy takes nine months, gestation of leading-edge technology is equally time consuming. (Romans 12:6-8, Ecclesiastes 3:1-2 – "There is a time for everything, and a season for every activity under heaven: a time to be born and a time to die, a time to plant and a time to uproot.")

Many healthy companies fall into the trap of their success. They tend to be more 'technology' driven mode rather than being 'market' driven. Many companies develop the product first then start out looking for the market. Successful companies look at the market first then start developing the products.

Exxon Chemicals was the first largest fax machine supplier in the world. But Exxon Chemicals was ahead of its time and after making horrendous financial losses decided to give up. Instead the late entrants, Japanese companies such as Canon, made a success of the fax technology. In the 1980s, many videotext services such as the Singapore Telecoms Teletext made losses. The technology of videotext appeared very promising, with each household being able to access electronic data and information from the television screens. The only problem was that the market application and services were not widespread enough to create a critical mass. It took time for the wide acceptance of videotext services to kick in. Internet technology took over the top spot of online services instead although the Internet is a much less sophisticated technology and an earlier head-start than videotext. Also, notwithstanding the more powerful colour picture quality and technology of the videotext as compared to the Internet, the Internet has the advantage of wider market acceptance. As a result, videotext applications were dwarfed by the Internet ones.

The following shows that the other gestation period between a technological invention and commercial production is shortening.

Invention	Invention Date	Production Date	Waiting Time
Fluorescent lighting	1852	1934	82 years
Radar	1887	1933	46 years
Ballpoint pen	1888	1938	50 years
Zipper	1891	1923	32 years
Diesel locomotive	1895	1934	39 years
Power steering	1900	1930	30 years
Helicopter	1904	1936	32 years
Television	1907	1936	29 years

It takes a long time for the technology to pick up. However, the lapse of timing between invention and production is speeding up and narrowing.

In technology, there is a trigger point when the price gets low enough, the application gets widened and people think that they want to have it. The technology can stay latent for a long time before hitting the trigger point as the market is not quite ready to embrace the applications of the technology. The key is to prepare for the trigger point and ride with the wave and revolution when it arrives.

When the technology is triggered off and embraced it will permanently change the way we do business. Just as fax technology phased out the telex, email technology is slowly phasing out faxes. CD phased out VHS years ago. Now, CDs have been virtually phased out by DVDs. Tomorrow, such optical disk technologies will be succeeded by BlueRay discs. And this change happens quickly. We may wake-up the day after tomorrow and find this "new" technology gone with the winds of change as well.

In the late 1990's, people would buy computers and not ask for a DVD drive, now they expect to have it only ten years later. Not so long ago, wireless phones were not common, today even students must have it as part of their school kits. In the 1980s, Internet was not popular. Today any business which is not registered on the web is not in business.

However, it was foolhardy for many dotcom companies that thought that the New Economy revolution would radically change the consumers' habits within months of the introduction of a new product or service. An example is the telecommunications market, where start-up after start-up promised new technology to bring data, voice and video together. They failed to deliver not because the technology was not ready, but rather the market was not yet ripe. Their debt loads finally killed many of these start-ups.

To gain competitive edge, you want to position your company in the leading edge. You want to leverage on technology advancements and be prepared for the flashpoint. Pioneers do face arrows and the leading edge all too often translates into the bleeding edge. If you are a small company, you do not have the resources to develop lead-edge technology. You position your organisation ready for the trigger point by finding tools to apply with existing technology.

This is why Rosabeth Moss Kanter said: "The problem before us is not to invent more tools but to use the ones we have."

Likewise, our God who created us, knows that there is a waiting period for every outcome. Ecclesiastes 3:1-2 – "There is a time for everything, and a season for every activity under heaven: a time to be born and a time   to   die, a time to plant and a time to uproot. Certain things cannot be rushed as there is a gestation period.

Principle No. 62

There is a time to be born and a time to die. Correct timing is everything. (John 7:1-9, Romans 5:6-8, Ecclesiastes 3:1-8 - "There is a time for everything, and a season for every activity under heaven")

The right timing is absolutely important. There is an old Chinese saying that for a business to flourish, you need to have the correct timing.

If a company ventures into a particular market too early in the product life cycle, perhaps at the introduction stage, it may not be able to reap the full benefits. The grounds may be hard and it has to invest substantial resources into developing the market. In the process, the early entrants may end up paying the high "tuition" fees as they will make all the mistakes. A case in point is the early pioneers of companies into China as most of them lost money because China's business infrastructure was very backward then.

However, if the company enters the market too late, for instance at the saturation or decline stage in the product life cycle, it runs the risk of curtailing its future growth potential as competition will be very intense. Examples include the many dotcoms and telecom start-up companies. They seemed to make a lot of sense then – proven leaders with real assets and business plans. The timing was bad as the high tech stock collapsed in the early 2000's.

The best time to enter the market is during its growth stage. The ability to recognise this opportunity and take timely action is also important. Both IBM and Digital Equipment Corporation had better access to the technology than Bill Gates and Paul Allen. These giants recognised the opportunity but limited their scope of their technology to serving their existing corporate customers with their existing and constantly upgraded products. Consequently, both companies did not recognise the timing to take the actions and missed the PCs precursors – the dedicated electronic word processors that made Wang Computers successful. The latter missed the timing and did not see that personal computers could replace word processors by executing far more functions than word-processing. Microsoft saw the timing and opportunity.

No one at IBM, DEC or Wang Computers took much notice of the MITS Altair 8800: the "World's First Microcomputer Kit to Rival Commercial Models". That headline in Popular Electronics magazine in January 1974 inspired Gates and Allen to write a version of the well-known BASIC computer knowledge for the machine to run on. The rest is history. In the book, *The Road Ahead,* Bill Gates remarked: "Getting in on the first stages of the PC revolution looked like the opportunity of a lifetime, and we seized it."

Since He knew all things, including the plans of his enemies, Jesus was also able to clearly see that timing was crucial to all choices. It is a fact that Jesus is all about finding the right timing for each act. When he knew about his death, he didn't want to go to the places where they would capture him and harm him, instead, he waits for the perfect time. "After this, Jesus went around in Galilee, purposely staying away from Judea because the Jews there were waiting to take his life..." "Therefore Jesus told them, "The right time for me has not yet come; for you any time is right. The world cannot hate you, but it hates me because I testify that what it does is evil. You go to the Feast. I am not yet going up to this Feast, because for me the right time has not yet come." Having said this, he stayed in Galilee."

What's more, Jesus' death came at the right time. It wasn't a coincidence – it was in the perfect time that he can save us sinners. "You see, at just the right time, when we were still powerless, Christ died for the ungodly. Very rarely will anyone die for a righteous man, though for a good man someone might possibly dare to die. But God demonstrates his own love for us in this: While we were still sinners, Christ died for us."

The Bible reminds us as well that there is a time for everything. In Ecclesiastes chapter 3, we are reminded that everything has its own time. "There is a time for everything, and a season for every activity under heaven: a time to be born and a time to die, a time to plant and a time to uproot, a time to kill and a time to heal, a time to tear down and a time to build, a time to weep and a time to laugh, a time to mourn and a time to dance, a time to scatter stones and a time to gather them, a time to embrace and a time to refrain, a time to search and a time to give up, a time to keep and a time to throw away, a time to tear and a time to mend, a time to be silent and a time to speak, a time to love and a time to hate, a time for war and a time for peace."

It is therefore important to identify the right timing and trend. One must however not mistake fad for trend. Trends are unstoppable and last much longer than fads. In the 1970s, it was the microwave technology, in the 1980s, the VCR and the 1990s, the PCs and the Internet. In the 2000s it was hand-held mobile devices. The "corporate wellness" as well as "physical wellness" has also become the trendsetters. Therefore be prepared as Neil Peart said: "Luck comes when preparation meets opportunity."

There is a season for everything. Timing is everything.

Principle No. 63

Customer's loyalty is the very fibre of your business. (Psalm 33:4, Psalm 18:25, Psalm 25:10, Romans 3:3, 2 Timothy 2:13 – "For the word of the Lord is right and true; he is faithful in all he does.")

Customers do not measure you on your earnings per share. They have their own measurement. The important thing to have from customers is their loyalty. Companies that ignore this important element face dismal future of low growth, weak profits and shortened corporate life span.

Frederick Reichheld, a customer-loyalty guru and author of bestselling books, *The Loyalty Effect* and *Loyalty Rules*! argued that loyalty is the guarantee of your competitive advantage and survival. Based on his study, 5% increase in customer retention will be translated into growth of between 25 and 95 percent in profitability.

When you set aside your own interests and do something extra for a client – when the client perceives that you have helped him in some out-of-ordinary way and gone the extra mile – the result is often loyalty. The extra mile can be represented by many different gestures and acts. Sometimes, they have little to do with your formal contract. This may include helping your client to get his children to school. Going that extra mile builds client loyalty because it enhances trust. It shows that you are focused on your client's interest rather than your own agenda. There is something else behind going the extra mile and it is called reciprocity.

Just as customer's loyalty is the fibre of one's business, so are the loyalty and the faithfulness of God the fibre of our faith. For how can we believe in a God who is not faithful? "For the word of the Lord is right and true; he is faithful in all he does."

However, there is also a call for reciprocity. The Bible tells us in Psalm 18:25 shows to us how Jesus values reciprocity: "To the faithful you show yourself faithful, to the blameless you show yourself blameless…" In chapter 25, "All the ways of the Lord are loving and faithful for those who keep the demands of his covenant." However, we must not forget that even though we are not faithful, he still remains faithful. Romans 3:3-4 reads: "What if some did not have faith? Will their lack of faith nullify God's faithfulness? Not at all! Let God be true, and every man a liar." Likewise, in 2 Timothy 2:13 it is written: "if we are faithless, he will remain faithful, for he cannot disown himself."

The problem in business today is that loyalty is not measured or evaluated. Accountants have devised sophisticated measurements for assets, costs, revenues and inventory. However, they do not make distinctions between sales revenues from new with old customers. Investments in old customers and acquisition of new customers are considered as costs, instead of amortizing it over the life of the customer relationship. Thus the full value of loyal customers is hidden.

The most effective CEOs start with a view of the market, then work back to create an organization focused on satisfying customer needs. The best example is Dell Computer, a company that puts the customer at the center of virtually everything it does. Michael Dell said that he did not create what became known as the direct model out of any great vision. That model though is what makes the company unique and has helped it to expand. "The direct model has a number of attributes," Michael Dell stated. "Of course, being in touch with the customers' needs is one of its most fundamental principles." It is difficult to imagine a more customer-centric organization than Dell's since each product is custom-ordered, and the company is structured around customer or customer groups.

Wal-Mart's success against all odds was due to the founder Sam Walton's fierce commitment to offering his customers the lowest prices, regardless of where they lived.

Sam Walton once said: "Every time Wal-Mart spends one dollar foolishly, it comes out of our customers' pockets." He also said: "There is only one boss. The customer. And he can fire everybody in the company from the Chairman on down, simply by spending his money somewhere else." That sentiment is still deeply embedded in the psyche of the company, more than a decade after Walton's death. In 2003, Wal-Mart was voted by the Fortune Magazine as the most admired corporation in the United States.

In his book: *Who Says Elephants Can't Dance?* the former turnaround CEO of IBM, Lou Gerstner said that in 1990, IBM had lost touch with the marketplace and its customers. When the company failed to grasp the microcomputer revolution and other important changes within its industry, the company almost went under. Lou Gerstner got IBM to refocus on the marketplace as the only valid measure of success. He started by telling virtually every audience in the first couple of months that there was a customer running IBM. He wanted to rebuild the company from the customer back.

Perhaps Jack Welch, GE's former chairman gave the penultimate word on the importance of customers when he said, "Companies can't give job security. Only customers can." In other words, succeed in the marketplace or you're out of a job.

Herb Kelleher, CEO of Southwest Airlines was quoted in Fortune February 1994 on a pilot's decision to return to a gate to pick up a passenger who arrived late: " Rules are great, but the bottom line is to do the right thing."   Sally Price of PepsiCo, quoted in Business Week, March 21, 1994: We are taking customer service from the must-have necessary evil it was in the past and turning it into a competitive advantage." The customer is not king anymore. The customer is dictator.

Principle No. 64

Ensure a cure, don't just take the medicine. Establish a relationship with the customer, don't just take an order. (Psalm 139:13-16 – "All the days ordained for me were written in your book before one of them came to be.")

Superficial actions will not do in this competitive market. All of us can take the medicine for our ailments, but the objective is to be cured. Every company can take an order, but at the end of the day, it aims to secure a loyal customer. This is why there is a Chinese saying, "You can change the soup without changing the medicine." The effect will not be efficacious. Sadly, sometimes we spend a lot of money on marketing, but know very little about our customers.

In the past, the target was to satisfy the customer. Today the ante has been raised and merely satisfying the customer is not good enough. The target is to gain loyal customers who will not switch to your competitors because of lower prices, rather, buy your products and services on a regular basis and even recommend you to other customers.

Consider research done by the Forum Corporation, which analyzes commercial customers lost by 14 major manufacturing and service companies. Some 15 percent of those who switched suppliers did so because they found a better product – based on technical measure of product quality, such as a greater mean time between failures or a lower defects rate. Another 15 percent took off because they found a "cheaper product" somewhere else. Twenty percent of the lost customers hightailed it because of the "lack of contact and individual attention" from the prior supplier; and 49 percent left because "contact from old supplier's personnel was poor in quality." It seems fair to collapse the last two categories into one, after which we could say: 15 percent left because of quality problems, 15 percent scooted because of price and 70 percent hit the road because they did not like the human side of doing business with the provider of the product or service. In other words, there was a problem with the relationship. Recent finding indicated that due to the dog-fight-dog competition, 65-85% of customers who leave for another supplier claim to have been satisfied. Thus merely satisfying customers is not good enough.

Relationships evolve through three distinct phases, and in each phase your role changes. You start as an expert for hire, this is how your client sees you when he first gets to know you. The crux is how to break out and develop a longer-term relationship. Next you become a steady supplier and get rewarded with a steady repeat business. However, you are still a vendor and certainly not part of your client's inner circle. You should target to be your client's extraordinary advisor and then possibly develop into a broad-based business advisor.

Successful companies also tend to create personal relationships with their customers. High-end hotels take copious notes about their frequent guests' preferences, from the specific rooms they desire, to the items stocked in the mini-bar. Successful online companies such as Amazon have used technology to create the same sort of personalized relationships. When you visit the Amazon website, you are greeted by name, reminded of your last transaction and presented with new recommendations that your profile suggests you might be interested in. Likewise, personal computers have increasingly become more personalised, even though the word-processing and Web-browsing programs are necessarily standardised. Users can download more options from free sites on the Internet. They can customise their computers with macro programs, sounds and other options.

Jesus very well knows the principle of "gaining customer loyalty." While we know he's faithful, the things he has done for us are more than enough for us to be drawn faithful to him. Jesus knows what's best for us, and that's why he gives it to us; things happen for our good, although we may not see it. Jesus tailor-makes his will for us to what best suits us. He can do this because it is he who created and therefore knows our inmost being, even from when we were in our mother's womb, he already knows us. "For you created my inmost being; you knit me together in my mother's womb. I praise you because I am fearfully and wonderfully made; your works are wonderful, I know that full well. My frame was not hidden from you when I was made in the secret place. When I was woven together in the depths of the earth, your eyes saw my unformed body. All the days ordained for me were written in your book before one of them came to be." Talk about knowing the customers.

Call centres are the rage today because companies recognise the need for customers to have front-line sales and support contacts. When the client perceives that you have helped him in some extraordinary way, the result is often loyalty.

Involve the customers in the decision-making. What better way to build customer loyalty than to have customers create an entire life around your product – whether virtual or real? Unfortunately, many companies fail to achieve this extreme differentiation from their competitors' products.

In fact, they move to quite the opposite direction, turning their product into a commodity. All too often, the result is that they become locked in a competitive price battle to the death. In such an environment, innovation is often stifled because it is either too costly as margins become razor thin or too risky because a wrong bet will surely sink the company.

The customer is profit, everything else is overhead.

Principle No. 65

Dream, do and devote in marketing and selling. (Matthew 28:19-20 Therefore go and make disciples of all nations, baptizing them in the name of the Father and of the Son and of the Holy Spirit.)

What do Bill Gates (Microsoft), Sam Walton (Wal-Mart), Roger Smith (General Motors), Robert Goizueta (Coca-Cola), Ross Perot (Perot Systems) have in common? These men are some of the most celebrated chief executives of the past. They are, according to Advertising Age magazine, "Marketers of the Year" from 1985 to 1994. David Packard, co-founder of Hewlett-Packard once said too: "Marketing is too important for the marketing department." Lou Gerstner of IBM said about Bill Gates and his company Microsoft, which is the most successful company of the past decade, "Our biggest competitor in software is not a very good technical company. But it is one of the best marketing companies I have ever seen, and I have spent twenty years in marketing."

A good way to illustrate and describe marketing and sales is like going fishing. Marketing is throwing all the fish food and baits to attract the fishes. When the fishes come to feed the baits and fish food, selling is casting the net so that the fishes can be hauled in.

How did McDonalds make a success of the hamburgers? The same question also applies to Starbucks for coffee beans and Nike and Reebok for sports shoes? These are very mundane and so-called commodity products. This is because McDonalds and Starbucks market their products that go beyond supplying fresh concepts and stimulating experiences; they actually influence our lifestyles. Nike and Reebok market their products that indulge people's hunger for an association with sports heroes, the rich and famous or peer recognition, in the same way that Revlon sells hope, not cosmetics. For instance, Nike uses Michael Jordon and Tiger Woods to attract yuppie customers.

David Packard, co-founder of Hewlett Packard also said: "Marketing is too important for a marketing department." In his book, "Your Company depends on it, "Al Ries said that a good chief executive officer should also be a Chief Marketing Officer.

Some of the best examples of marketing of the late 2000's have been focused on specific events. For example, the Formula 1 racing event in Singapore and the Olympics held in China. Formula 1 racing has been a staple of world competition for over 20 years, however, with the inaugural Singapore night race the enthusiasm for a new location was evident with the uptick in marketing. This branding effort brought 40,000 spectators – most of which were not natives. The same effort was applied by the Chinese regarding the Olympics. The significant effort put into marketing the event was the impetus which drew 300 million spectators, compared to a quarter of a million who attended the Sydney games.

Many successful entrepreneurs started their careers as marketing and sales persons. The founder of Microsoft, Mr Bill Gates, the founder of Dell Computers, Michael Dell etc are all outstanding examples.

The Bible also stresses the importance of marketing the Christian faith. Jesus commanded his followers to evangelize and market the faith all over the world – the Great Commission. His last words before he ascended to heavens as in Matthew 28:19-20, "Therefore go and make disciples of all nations, baptizing them in the name of the Father and of the Son and of the Holy Spirit, and teaching them to obey everything I have commanded you."

In the corporate world, there is some form of marketing and selling going on every time you talk or interact with customers. In fact, successful entrepreneurs have one thing in common: the ability to market and sell. For example, every successful courtship and marriage has one thing in common: the ability to market and sell yourselves to attract the other party.

Principle No. 66

A reputable doctor, like a good brand name commands a premium. (1 Timothy 3:1-7, Romans 2:21-23, Proverbs 22:1 – "A good name is more desirable than great riches; to be esteemed is better than silver or gold.")

In the long term, the ailing organisation needs to build a strong brand name as it will help to strengthen the company's future prosperity. The American Marketing Association defines a brand as a name, term, sign, symbol or design or a combination of them, intended to identify the goods or services of one seller or group of sellers and to differentiate them from those of competitors.

Customers can only remember a limited a number of brands in their minds. Brands help the customers to remember the products. Thus, when you think of Mercedes, it suggests luxury, success, prestige, fast speed, well-engineered, customer service par excellence and good resale value in Singapore. When you think of Volvo, you think of safety, thanks to the solid-as-a-tank bodywork. When you think of Nike, you might think of Michael Jordon or "Just Do It". When you think of hamburgers, you may recall McDonalds; soft drinks, you think of Coke; and fried chicken, Kentucky Fried Chicken. Customers are attached to the loyalty of the brand rather than the company's name.

A brand is merely an idea and the only place that it exists is the mind. Logos, tag lines, designs etc are only the physical expression of a brand. Companies with powerful brands can command a price premium and have a competitive advantage. To build the brand name, you need to define an idea that is relevant to your target audience and next develop programs to best communicate the brand message to your target audience.

In very competitive markets such as consumer packaged goods companies, Nabisco, Quaker Oats, Gatorade are losing their lustre. Consumers are no longer willing to pay a premium for branded goods. Companies with big brands should also focus on building better relationships with suppliers and retailers to improve the supply chain and maximize profits. You just cannot think of selling products. You have to think about selling solutions. This may include ready meals for working mothers, ready to go breakfast bars, events and ambience.

Brand name is the only asset that your competition cannot destroy without your help. Yet, many companies lost their customers not because of product, quality, features or even price. As a matter of fact, their products were well made, up-to-date and reasonably priced. However, customers find it difficult to do business with these companies. There were errors in delivery, billing system was complicated and customer service was atrocious.

You need to deliver what you promise and say so in your brand. This means a variety of conveniences for customers to do business with you. It means that you can accept customers' order when it is convenient for them and easy for them to check the status. It means that orders are worded in customer terminology and billing is easy to understand. It also means that the customers can call upon you whenever they need help without going through the hassle and different levels of approval. It also means that there are no hidden costs to the customers.

There is a high price to pay for loss of reputation due to products that created health risks, Consumers will be reluctant to continue to buy for a long time. For instance, the tainted milk incident and the poor safety measures of toys manufactured in China caused the loss of many years of good will and reputation. Trust is gone.

We have seen the same with mini bonds (Lehman Brothers) in Singapore – the bad press had eroded many good years of reputation built up by the financial institutions. This time, the customers lost money in the investments and were angry that the financial institutions that sold them these investments were mis-selling a risky product. Good reputation once lost will take a long time to return.

Likewise, "men and women of God" bear God's name – like their own brand name. And when they carry around his name, they themselves have to live out what it means to be carrying God's name. In the book of 1Timothy, we see an example of a man for God and how he should live. "If anyone sets his heart on being an overseer, he desires a noble task. Now the overseer must be above reproach, the husband of but one wife, temperate, self-controlled, respectable, hospitable, able to teach, not given to drunkenness, not violent but gentle, not quarrelsome, not a lover of money. He must manage his own family well and see that his children obey him with proper respect. (If anyone does not know how to manage his own family, how can he take care of God's church?) He must not be a recent convert, or he may become conceited and fall under the same judgment as the devil. He must also have a good reputation with outsiders, so that he will not fall into disgrace and into the devil's trap."

This is what we fondly called "practicing what we preach." It is not good enough that people call themselves men and women for God, but in their lifestyles, they must be able to show and back that brand up. "…you, then, who teach others, do you not teach yourself? You who preach against stealing, do you steal? You who say that people should not commit adultery, do you commit adultery? You who abhor idols, do you rob temples? You who brag about the law, do you dishonor God by breaking the law?"

It is therefore not enough to tell people how great your brand is, you need to live out the brand and deliver what you promise.

Ineffective publicity campaigns are like taking Viagra – short-term thrill but long term remains impotent. (Matthew 7:24 Therefore everyone who hears these words of mine and puts them into practice is like a wise man who built his house on the rock.)

Some companies spend millions of dollars annually on advertisement and publicity without knowing the returns of those investments. With limited financial resources, it is important that the company understands whether it is getting maximum mileage out of their advertising dollar.

Companies send out thousands of "no-brainer" publicity mailings, not worth their time, energy and money. Some spend thousands of dollars in newspapers and television publicity campaigns, which confuse the consumers. Others launch telemarketing programs but instead irritate the customers with nuisance calls.

Your advertisement needs to stand out and make an impression. Better yet, it should be designed such that the reader or viewer can clearly grasp the central theme or idea behind the advertisement, and also take note of the call to action.

An ineffective advertising campaign is like taking Viagra, it gives you short-term thrill and excitement but does not cure your long term impotence.

Depending on the nature of the business, companies should consider deploying a mix of public relations, direct marketing and advertising programmes to convey their key messages to their target audience, rather than just depend on the advertising vehicle alone.

For a person, a healthy and balanced diet, regular exercise and a happy family life are vital to staying in the pink of health. Just as a person should adopt a holistic approach to staying healthy, likewise, a company should employ an integrated, multi-pronged communications strategy as part of its marketing approach.

All publicity campaigns should have clearly identified objectives and target market groups. The strategies and tactics used should also incorporate some form of measurement for the results achieved. After all, an increase in awareness of the company or products is surely a good sign, but ultimately, if these do not impact on the top and bottom line, these campaigns would be hard to justify and sustain.

Another way to get the maximum punch out of the publicity campaign is to benefit others. For instance, the information should help the viewers in lifestyle, body, mind and spirit. Target the publicity campaigns to educate, fill a need and change the quality of life. They should be selfless rather than selfish, offer benefits rather than features and give rather than take.

Matthew 7:24-27 advises the importance of building a strong foundation: "Therefore everyone who hears these words of mine and puts them into practice is like a wise man who built his house on the rock. The rain came down, the streams rose, and the winds blew and beat against that house; yet it did not fall, because it had its foundation on the rock. But everyone who hears these words of mine and does not put them into practice is like a foolish man who built his house on sand. The rain came down, the streams rose, and the winds blew and beat against that house, and it fell with a great crash."

In a crisis, the communication and public campaigns play a crucial role and can make or break of the company's reputation. Both in good and bad times, company needs to effectively communicate to their target audience. A crisis merely increases the intensity of the communication and accentuates the need to communicate the organisations' publics about those decisions and any subsequent corrective actions that are taken. The organization also needs to keep all the key business associates and staff apprised of its various publics' reactions. In some instances, such as the well-known Tylenol tamper-proof case, effective public campaigns can actually enhance an organisation's reputation.

Thus you may have a better mousetrap, but if you do not effectively promote your mousetrap, how are your customers going to beat a path to your door?

Principle No. 68

Corporate suicide – getting bigger instead of better. (1 Samuel 17:1-51 – "So David triumphed over the Philistine with a sling and a stone; without a sword in his hand he struck down the Philistine and killed him.")

Work on becoming better and guess what, you naturally grow bigger. But pushing for size by itself makes you fatter, not bigger, less specialized and easier to succumb to the vagaries of internal and external forces. Often you lose what made you viable in the first place. A chicken that has wings does not mean it can fly, similarly the big companies are not necessarily the better ones.

In the Bible, bigger doesn't mean better as well. We know of the story of David and Goliath. Goliath, the 9 foot tall Philistine who challenged Israel for battle, that if anyone defeats him, the Philistines will be subject under the Israelites. Surely enough, a young shepherd named David, slung a stone over the giant's forehead and defeated him. "So David triumphed over the Philistine with a sling and a stone; without a sword in his hand he struck down the Philistine and killed him. David ran and stood over him. He took hold of the Philistine's sword and drew it from the scabbard. After he killed him, he cut off his head with the sword."

Many Asian conglomerates learned this to their despair in the 1997 financial crisis - there is no safety net in being big. As a matter of fact, the bigger they were, the harder they fell. The list includes many of the Asian "giants" and conglomerates such as the Korean banks, the Hanbo Steel, Sammi Steel, Jinro Ltd and Kia group, the Indonesian state-owned banks Bank Dagang Negara, Bank Bumi Daya, Bank Negara, Bank Rakyat and Bank Exim and other banks as well as major corporations in Thailand, Malaysia, the list goes on. All these so-called large major corporations and banks were mauled badly by the financial crisis in Asia. On the other hand, the smaller enterprises in Taiwan were largely being spared because of their nimbleness. In 2008, we also saw a similar phenomenon with the collapse of major financial institutions first. In addition, the big automotive companies such as General Motors, Chrysler and Ford in the US are on the brink of bankruptcy. Even mighty Toyota Motor Corp, the world's biggest automaker, is likely to report its first annual parent-only operating loss in 71 years, hit by plunging sales and the soaring yen. Big companies have high overheads and quite often over leveraged financially. When the demand drops big time, the big boys are always to take the hit first as it cannot sustain its high fixed overheads and they are less flexible to change.

Small companies are able to be more nimble and make changes more swiftly than large ones. This is because small companies do not have to persuade many people and the communication channels are shorter. Thus the small businesses are more sensitive to changes. However, the answer to getting better does not lie entirely on being small as such companies face financial and resource constraints.

Many construction companies in Singapore in the mid-2000's were expanding their top lines, however, clinching sales contracts and projects at a loss. The government tenders were awarded to the lowest price bidder. As a result, it was quite easy to increase the sales contracts by dumping the tender price. Owing to the risky nature of construction contracts, which are fraught with many unexpected costs, projects were delayed and costs overrun. In addition, many contractors ran into problems with liquidated damages because of delay in completion as well as the payments being delayed. Some even land up in expensive and protracted litigations, which brought further financial burden to the cash-strapped construction companies. Getting bigger without any regard for profitability spelled the death knell for many contractors.

Research firm Bain & Company reported that over a 10-year period, the five largest drug makers in the United States had grown fivefold to $16.8 billion dollar, in the late 1990's. However, their operating margins paled by comparison, increasing only a minuscule one percent. The major setback for profits was the limited return on research and development (R&D) efforts. Despite the four-fold increase in the R&D expenditure, there was no increase in new drugs' approval from the Food and Drug Administration during the same period. Whilst hopes of profits from the introduction of new drugs dwindled, the pharmaceutical industry resorted to mergers to bolster their revenues.

However, such strategy to get bigger led to the dilemma of larger drug companies having to launch three or more new drugs per year just to bring in a moderate annual sales growth of ten percent. These pharmaceutical companies compounded their problems by pursuing a strategy of number games – the more drugs to be developed the more chances of hitting success. As a result, there was little differentiation amongst all the large drug companies in their drug development. Such strategy is not only costly but also gives the company a bad name when the much-publicised wonder drugs failed in their trials.

When asked about the design of Virgin's organisational architecture, Branson replied: "My philosophy was always that if there were fifty people in a building I would go there and ask to see the deputy managing director, his deputy sales manager, his deputy marketing manager, the deputy press officer". Branson continued: "You are now the managing director, the sales manager, the marketing manager, and the press officer of a new company I would put them in a new building. Then again, when that company got to a certain size – fifty people – I would do the same thing again. Also, if you are given a card by somebody who says he is the managing director you might, I am afraid take him more seriously than if you were given a card saying that the person was the deputy to the deputy to the deputy managing director."

And although it would appear that there are ample examples, companies which have heretofore been nimble and strong are learning the hard way that bigger does not equal better in the recent economic downturn of the late 2000's. Things are real bad for the entire world economy, but injuries are felt worse if you have lost your nimbleness and flexibility while you grew. There is nothing wrong with getting bigger, but one has to make sure that it is getting better.

Principle No. 69

Good posture strengthens one's stature, good organisational structure enhances one's infrastructure. (Acts 14:23, Acts 16:5 – "So the churches were strengthened in the faith and grew daily in numbers.")

A person who has a lazy, slow-moving gait tends to look less commanding than someone who walks with a good posture that exudes confidence. Likewise, the way the company is organised can help it position for future growth.

The world has changed dramatically. These days, being internationally competitive is the name of the game. With the dissolution of the international trade barriers and the evolution of a new global economy, many companies have gone through a continuum of transition from being international (stressing an export-import orientation), to being multinational (having major operations abroad that are concentrated on specific, relatively protected markets) to being global (looking at the entire world as a market). The new and total global economy has come of age.

There are three organisational structures:

Multi-local
The overseas affiliates are given full autonomy with little interference from the headquarters. This structure is suitable for organisations that require high customisation, flexibility and speed to respond to the market place. Examples of industries requiring such structures include the retailing, auditing and consulting businesses etc. The downside is that there are wasteful duplications and low cost efficiency. However, in industries that require ground knowledge, the trade-off for economy of scale and duplications is speed and flexibility.

Global
The overseas affiliates are given little autonomy. The headquarters make all the major decisions. The organisational structure is by functions, with each function such as the sales and marketing, financial heads of the subsidiaries reporting to the headquarters' functional heads. In some companies, the functions are grouped by product lines and major customer accounts reporting back to the heads for the product lines and multi-national accounts. If worldwide efficiency is required, then this structure is more appropriate. Examples of industries requiring such structure include electronic chips, consumer electronics etc. The

disadvantage of this structure is the erosion of local responsiveness as it entails very centralized control.

Transnational
In some cases of both local and global know-how are important, the transnational structure may be appropriate. The organisational structure is based on a matrix with dual reporting and the achievement of consensus as the key driver.

Depending on the nature of your business, you should adopt an organisational structure that enables you to meet with your business objectives, and which will provide flexibility and room for future growth. The common thread in the above three structures is the concept of 'flat organisation'.

The phrase 'flat organisation' is now overworked and misunderstood. It is an oxymoron, a contradiction in terms. Any organisation that exists for a purpose needs a spine of decision-making accountability. This applies to private corporations, public institutions, voluntary organisations and cooperatives.

A good organisation structure is one with the optimal number of layers of leadership, which demonstrably add value to the work of the others. This includes the design and delivery of mission and strategy. It provides space and challenge for individuals to achieve, continue to learn, grow and enjoy their work and be duly rewarded for their performance.

Likewise, building the church and its leaders in Jesus' time was just as crucial, for reasons that its structure mattered to its very core, as it was designed and targeted to help the apostles preach the Good News to the nations. The apostles had to make important decisions; organizing churches and its body, to prepare, unite and establish it.

For instance, Paul and Barnabas appointed elders, those whose foundations of faith are strong and established, to lead the churches in Syria. Recognizing that this task and its success is yet beyond their capabilities, they committed the churches and elders to God by praying and fasting, that God may bless his church and its leaders. "Paul and Barnabas appointed elders for them in each church and, with prayer and fasting, committed them to the Lord, in whom they had put their trust."

The apostles went around cities and to its churches to strengthen them, that it may be able to preach God's word effectively, withstanding troubles and oppositions it may encounter. The apostles were successful in doing this and in turn drawn it to grow. "So the churches were strengthened in the faith and grew daily in numbers."

The theory is clear. The problem for managers is how to design it in practice. How many vertebrae should there be in this spine of accountability? What are the key functions? How are they identified? What is the impact of removing a function from this spine? What impact will this have on the development and motivation of the incumbents? Surprisingly, at the beginning of the 21st century this is still an area of guesswork and fashion in most organisations

Principle No. 70

Be paranoid about healthy growth. (1 Samuel 2:26, 1 Samuel 3 – "And the boy Samuel continued to grow in stature and in favor with the Lord and with men.")

John Chambers, CEO of Cisco Systems said that he possesses a "healthy paranoia". He was paranoid that Cisco may grow too far from its customers, partners and employees. Andy Grove of Intel first wrote about paranoia in the book, "Only the Paranoid Will Survive." Companies should not just be paranoid about survival, it should also be paranoid about healthy growth.

John Chambers grew Cisco from 1995 to become a super growth engine, which fuelled the burgeoning demand for computer networking. Its sales revenues grew from $2.2 billion in 1995 to $18.9 billion in 2000. The profits grew from $0.84 billion in 1998 to $4.3 billion in 2000. Without Cisco routers, there would be no World Wide Web. By year 2000, over 75 percent of all Internet traffic travelled over Cisco products and the future appeared bright and expected to grow from 275 million to 1 billion by 2005.

However late in 2000, the US economy went sour and by early 2001, the high-growth Cisco System was in trouble. It was forced to write off billions of stocks and laid off 7,900 employees. The stock fell and Cisco Systems fell from its pedestal of growth.

Chambers was always mindful that Cisco's bubble might burst, although he was taken by surprise too by the sudden turn in Cisco's fortunes. Faster than most other CEOs under similar circumstances, Chambers restructured Cisco by putting stress on profit and cash flow performance. He put emphasis on focus, execution, productivity and taking only calculated risks. The company did subsequently show signs of improvements.

Another example is Donald Trump's corporate empire. He was acquiring and growing very rapidly from real estate, hotel, casino and airlines. When the real estate market crashed in New Year in the late 1980s, Trump was almost bankrupt. Like the proverbial Phoenix, he emerged from the ashes and became a comeback kid in the 1990s. Both John Chambers and Donald Trump had learnt a bitter lesson that a company must emphasise on getting healthy first before growth and expansion.

The 1980s and 1990s were decades of growth by merger and acquisition. However, the successes had been far and few. Also, companies that went through growth by merger and acquisition were highly geared and paid dearly for their overburdened debt situation. As a result many were a long time in digesting their acquisition or prevented from further acquisitions. In the 2000s, growth became more organic rather than through pure acquisitions. Companies planned more for real growth through internal development and expansion. Branson rose to this challenge by building his businesses through organic growth rather than acquisition. Growing and starting new companies enabled him to stretch his people and he has stated that he enjoys providing opportunity for his employees. At the risk of overplaying his image, this strategy fits his concept of the organisational family, one that grows by progeny rather than by adoption.

We as individuals should be paranoid about our own growth as well. We should be sure to grow by Christ, that we may be sustained and find favour in him. We see the great example of Samuel, who, even when he was just a young boy, he had already walked with the Lord. As he grew, he still ministered before the Lord. "And the boy Samuel continued to grow in stature and in favor with the Lord and with men." Because of this, the Lord found favour in Samuel, and he stayed with him until he grew older. This is the kind of growth we want - a growth in Jesus Christ that we may grow in Spirit; that God uses us, makes us his prophet; that God be with us all the days of our lives.

However, in the corporate world, one also ought to be paranoid if the company is not growing. The market, the staff, the creditors and the shareholders demand growth. The bank interests, inflation, wage increase, returns on investments are all expected to grow and therefore the company must also grow correspondingly. Chances are that if you are not growing, your competitors are growing at your expense. Companies need to have sustainable growth, otherwise they are dying. Similarly, a person who totally retires is heading for the grave and need to grow mentally in order not to become senile.

Even in so-called mature and competitive industries, companies are growing. For instance, Dell Computers is still growing despite the very tough and mature personal computer market. Many old companies such as Coke, Proctor and Gamble and Gillette are still growing in the markets with hundreds of similar brands. Growth is always possible no matter what the age is. Thomas Alva Edison deemed mentally slow by his teachers patented a total of 1,033 inventions! His work spanned a lifetime and grew with age, with the first patent issued at age twenty-one, his last at age eighty-one. For both corporate and individual, the lesson is never to stop growing.

However, top line growth per se is useless, as evidenced in the demise of many dotcom companies in the world and construction companies in Singapore. If the growth is not accompanied by attention to costs, productivity and efficient use of resources then the growth is not sustainable and can spell more troubles.

However, companies need to have a healthy and balanced view of growth. If growth is done artificially to please the stock market and shareholders, then it cannot sustain. This happens to companies that go on an acquisition binge and they get indigestion. Therefore, one should target for healthy growth, which is based on a solid foundation.

Principle No. 71

Unlock corporate energy. (2 Corinthians 12:10, Isaiah 40:31, Revelation 2:3 – "You have persevered and have endured hardships for my name, and have not grown weary.")

Physicists tell us that energy cannot be created or destroyed and that all masses already have large quantities of energy stored in them. Vast amounts of energy exist in any organisation. However, the organisation's energy is dormant waiting to be harnessed and released by the correct stimulus.

Organisations also have the potential to tap a special kind of energy that is released when the staff takes on risks and challenges. People experience this energy in the form of exhilaration, enthusiasm, vitality and a sense of urgency. This charged-up one's entire being creating the desire to excel, to win, and to belong.

Similarly, we must find and unlock the desire to live for and serve the Lord, that is just like Paul, we may unleash the energy to find "delight in weaknesses, in insults, in hardships, in persecutions, in difficulties." For example, we may think like Isaiah, who said that: "those who hope in the Lord will renew their strength. They will soar on wings like eagles; they will run and not grow weary, they will walk and not be faint." And ultimately, we may lead lives pleasing to the Lord, striving and persevering and not growing tired until the very end. "You have persevered and have endured hardships for my name, and have not grown weary."

The creation of corporate energy involves everyone in the organisation. Every employee has a part to play regardless of location and division. It springs from something deep inside each person, which causes them to work enthusiastically, with their hearts and heads as well as their hands. Corporate energy drives employee commitment to rendering superb service. They must be empowered to change the course of events for the better if necessary. When the vitality of an organisation's people is focused and applied collectively, almost anything can be accomplished.

Corporate energy not only fuels organisations to grow spectacularly during good times but also grants them the inner strength to endure and survive the bad. It is garnered and unleashed when a few people at the top echelon demonstrate consistent leadership that are visible to their people. Today, in most large companies, half the available energy remains untapped. Effective leaders act as the catalysts when they provide the proper stimuli. But the catalytic role in high-performance organisations is not restricted to those in the top management. The real magic happens when leaders ensure that the catalytic agents are dispersed throughout the organisation. However, if the initial impetus is missing from the top, it will be prevented from generating energy in the organisation. A chain reaction can start in a single division, branch or work team.

What organisations need most to triumph in today's fast-paced marketplace is people who possess skills that empower others; leaders who know how to inspire workers to aggressively seek out and seize opportunities that will enable their organisation to surpass the competition; leaders who can help others visualise potential solutions, not just problems; people who motivate others to rise above the status quo, envision greater possibilities and constantly propel the organisation toward a preferred future.

Senior managers often unwittingly diffuse instead of aspire, confuse rather than inspire. Successful organisational performance seems to go hand in hand with people being active and having fun at work. Many managers genuinely believe that when employees are having fun at the job, they are goofing off. Unfortunately, they believe that their role is to keep everyone tightened up.

An interesting measure of corporate enthusiasm is the parking lot. In an organisation where there is a lot of energy, the parking lots are full even on weekends. The employees are so charged up that they continue to come in even on the weekends and stay up late and come in early on the weekdays.

Eventually, we do not need to have the knowledge of Albert Einstein's quantum physics knowledge to understand how to unlock the atomic energy in the corporate world. Each one of us can in our own little way be the catalyst to ignite the corporate energy.

Principle No. 72

A sick company's internal energy "qi" is usually blocked or obstructed. (Acts 14:21, Acts 8:4, Acts 13:24 – "Those who had been scattered preached the word wherever they went.")

In traditional Chinese medicine, ill health is often associated with the blockage of one's internal energy, "qi". If one is ill, clearance of the obstructed "qi" will result in the normalisation and re-establishment of the optimal functioning of one's body and most diseases should disappear. If one is not ill, the free flow of "qi" will further enhance the existing sense of wellness and wellbeing. Incidentally, the concept of the internal energy is prevalent in most Asian cultures. The Japanese called it "reiki". Even the Koreans and Indians have their beliefs in internal energy.

In the corporate context, "qi" is the passion, drive, ambition and human spirit. It is the same "qi" that keeps you awake when you are watching the World Cup matches and Olympics games. It is also the same "qi" that impelled Walt Disney to risk his reputation by creating Disneyland and the Epcot Centre without any market data on their viability. It is the same passion and drive that caused Bill Gates to give up his Harvard University study in pursuit of his dream of establishing Microsoft. You do not create Disneyland or build personal computers because the outside environment demands it. These things arose out of the inner urge for progress: the drive to go further and do better as well as create new possibilities without any external justification.

Peter and all the other apostles may not have built themselves their own Epcot Centre in Jesus' time, but they did create multitudes of disciples and followers after Jesus had died. "They preached the good news in that city and won a large number of disciples." They in them had the passion and the drive, the "qi" to act themselves, even without Jesus by their side telling them to do so. The apostles had the ambition, the love Jesus was talking about while he was still with them, which was a force within them that drove them to move. "Those who had been scattered preached the word wherever they went." "…John preached repentance and baptism to all the people of Israel."

Jack Welch, the former chairman of General Electric US recognised the power of energy in his later part of his career. In early 1980, when he first took over the helm, his emphasis was on maximising market share. His directive was for all GE's affiliates to be number 1 or 2. Subsequently, it was a case of maximising market value through productivity programmes such as the 6 sigma, Workout, etc. In the later years, Welch indicated that he would hire people with the two types of energies: those who are energetic and able to energise others.

Philip Morris was the leading manufacturer and marketer of tobacco products in the mid-2000's whose brands include Marlboro, Virgina Slims, Benson & Hedges, Merit and Parliament. Philip Morris' executives were both charged up with passion and passionate consumers of its products. They saw themselves as independent and maverick 'cow boys', depicted in the Marlboro billboards. Philip Morris at that time had 45% of the US market and 12% of the world market and Malboro name is the world's best selling brand. On the other hand, besieged R J Reynolds diversified away from the core business of cigarettes without a care for the staff's passion for its products. Later in the 2000's, R J Reynolds Tobacco has lost market shares and announced in September to retreat from stiff discount-brand competition and planned for massive retrenchment.

To compete effectively in the future, companies need to maximise the energy of their staff as well as to exploit and tap the energy of their customers. The unblocking of the internal energy is like releasing the creative juices and energies of the staff. In the modern day corporation, the ideas and creative juices are the raw materials that can be packaged into blockbusters. You can also unleash the internal energy of your customers too. Once the customers are all charged up for you, they can become the channels for your products and services by "word of mouth" and reference selling. When you win them over, they can become loyal long-term customers as well as evangelists who will win converts for your products instead of becoming the terrorists who bad mouth your products. The "word-of-mouth" selling is one of the most effective channels of selling as the customers can speak volume about the strength of your products much better than your own promotional/advertising efforts. The best part of it is that all these benefits are for free! This is the power of unleashing the internal energy of your customers.

Today, it is possible to release the internal energy of your customers through technology and one-to-one marketing. With the use of Internet and other online services, the vendors can literally know the individual's spending pattern, consumer lifestyle, preferences and other demographic information. They can draw much closer to each customer individually and have the unlimited opportunity to energise them

Stay healthy and do not allow your corporate internal energy to be blocked.

Page 213

Principle No. 73

Adopt the spiritual paradigm for re-inspiration. (Isaiah 11:2-5 – "The Spirit of the Lord will rest on him")

Spirituality is a therapeutic form that is often ignored, but yet plays an important part in healing. Many religions believe that the body and spirit are inseparable until death. Complementary medicine recognises this importance. Although rejected from traditional science and medicine, it is still recognised that the mind or spirit of an individual can determine life or death, sickness or health. It is observed that when a patient is denied his expression of belief and faith, healing stagnates and often deteriorates. Spirituality is often used synonymously with religion. Religion is an outward expression and response encased in traditional beliefs and practices.

The world's seven great religions – namely, Christianity, Judaism, Hinduism, Confucianism, Taoism, Buddhism and Islam - amongst them account for a following of over 75% of the world's population in one or other of their many manifestations. They have all endured in a form not far removed in essence from their original manifestation for an average of over 1500 years, although in their societal role they have evolved, sometimes quite dramatically. That survival rate favourably compares to an average Fortune 100 life span of 42 years. It also favourably compares to the average age of the sovereign state of around 200 years.

The reason for their long-term success is that, as institutions, they satisfy a set of universal and psychological needs. All of the great religions evolved over at least 1000-year period in response to fundamental needs, adapting to the changing environmental until they hit on a formula that worked. They have therefore had plenty of time to empirically discover what their customers need. Most corporations, by contrast, have achieved a collective history of no more than 50 years. Corporations can take a leaf out of the book of the great religions.

Religions provide a context of moral authority and a framework, which offers the chance for personal redemption. Every party to it feels infused with a virtuous ambition to propagate the religion's way of doing things. They emphasise looking beyond self-interests and working towards a common good. They are essentially optimistic in their outlook and their view of the competitive universe is positive. It confirms at every turn that the future is worth fighting for. There is an intense level of enquiry and debate about objectives and goals that dispels the status quo and keeps the process of re-invention moving ahead of the industry. Millions of people have sacrificed their lives in providing full-time services for their beliefs in their religions and paid a pittance. Some have even died as martyrs for their beliefs in their religions through the centuries. That's the power of the spiritual paradigm.

Like the other Biblical principles written in this book, for instance, we see the power and love of God, his favour, pouring on his children, on the faithful. If individuals would learn to devote themselves to God, the rewards will be great – not just spiritually but on every aspect of the man; an experience, a re-inspiration, a renewal of our spirits. "The Spirit of the Lord will rest on him — the Spirit of wisdom and of understanding, the Spirit of counsel and of power, the Spirit of knowledge and of the fear of the Lord - and he will delight in the fear of the Lord. He will not judge by what he sees with his eyes, or decide by what he hears with his ears; but with righteousness he will judge the needy, with justice he will give decisions for the poor of the earth. He will strike the earth with the rod of his mouth; with the breath of his lips he will slay the wicked. Righteousness will be his belt and faithfulness the sash around his waist."

If a human soul buys into an idea like a faith or religion with a passion, with total commitment, the bounds of what we are collectively capable are quite simply astounding. The last fifteen years of change, downsizing and restructuring have left many employees feeling weary and demoralized. The right way forward is to re-inspire them with the fervour like the great religions.

Principle No. 74

Spread positive infection – enthusiasm. (1 Thessalonians 2:7-8, Mark 16:15 – "Go into all the world and preach the good news to all creation...Whoever believes and is baptized will be saved")

Never underestimate the power of enthusiasm. If you are feeling unenthusiastic and bored in life, the people around you fall asleep too. True enthusiasm is very contagious. You have it and others will soon have it too. Nothing great is achieved without enthusiasm. Enthusiasm is even more important in some cases than intelligence and hard work. This is because projects will face obstacles, companies will face challenges of all sorts and disappointments will come in many proportions. If you are hardworking, work smart and have full of enthusiasm, nothing will be able to stop you.

The Bible talks about spreading a positive infection as well – the Good News. The Gospel of the Lord is probably the best infection we can ever spread; with this, people are blessed, renewed and saved. "Go into all the world and preach the good news to all creation. Whoever believes and is baptized will be saved." Jesus, his apostles and their disciples know the power of the Gospel which is why they choose to live their lives dedicated to sharing and proclaiming it. "As apostles of Christ we could have been a burden to you, but we were gentle among you, like a mother caring for her little children. We loved you so much that we were delighted to share with you not only the gospel of God but our lives as well, because you had become so dear to us."

Jeffrey A Krames says his subjects of CEOs including Microsoft's Bill Gates, Southwest's Herb Kelleher and Intel's Andy Grove displayed an ardent enthusiasm for what they do, which arouses a similar response in others. He said that each had a fire-in-the belly excitement that helped to arouse enthusiasm in others. They felt strongly about a particular idea, product or process, and were able to use the bully pulpit of their office effectively to spread their 'gospel'.

The enthusiastic trait has little to do with the personal magnetism and everything to do with devotion or commitment to a cause or idea. With the turn of the millennium, a new kind of leader emerged, one who can enthuse others. Microsoft's Bill Gates is a good example. He enthusiastically drives the market and the market in return respects him and believes in his reasons for enthusiasm. He is able to express himself on the subject of the future.

Louis Gerstner at IBM did just that. He was able to enthuse his company. In his book, 'One Voice', Gerstner relates how he saw the situation when he took charge as CEO in 1993. He emphasized IBM's strengths; how he viewed the future; and how he thought the employees should handle it. Every IBM employee received a copy of the book from him.

Another very enthusiastic leader who has become equivalent of a brand is Richard Branson. He personifies both his brand and the brand value in Virgin. The company markets a lot of different products from air travel and bank services to fizzy drinks and cosmetics. Branson, like Gates and Gerstner spreads positive infection from the top.

Good business fitness means more than the absence of crisis and negative symptoms. It needs to have enthusiasm. According to a UK-based study carried out by the Department of Trade and Industry Management Best Practice Directorate, which interviewed 121 top companies, healthy company needs to have visionary and enthusiastic leaders who can unlock the potential of their people. They must be able to deliver products that exceed their customers' expectations and continuously introduce differentiated products and services. This means keeping the enthusiasm of the customers high for your company.

If you are lukewarm, you will never be able to get others all boiled up. Think enthusiasm and act enthusiastically.

Principle No. 75

Rest and rejuvenate. (Matthew 11:28-31 – "Come to me, all you who are weary and burdened, and I will give you rest.")

One of the most effective ways to improve mental and physical health is rest. People also produce their best results when they are relaxed and comfortable at their workplace. The first concept of rest in the corporate context is stability. Therein, lies an apparent paradox. To cope with the rapid changes, the company needs to change. Yet, in the quest for growth-inducing changes, the company needs to have rest and stability. It is the same with the human body. A company needs some amount of organizational slack or thinking time. Many companies focus on changes after changes except they forgot that the things that they are currently doing are just as important. As a result these companies went through fruitless diversifications and divestments. Finally they ended up losing focus or neglecting their core businesses because they did not protect their fortresses back home.

Rest is indeed imperative in the life of every individual. In the Bible, it says that if it is rest that we seek, we must turn to the Lord. This is because it is only in God that our burdens will be lifted from our shoulders and our minds relaxed. "Come to me, all you who are weary and burdened, and I will give you rest. Take my yoke upon you and learn from me, for I am gentle and humble in heart, and you will find rest for your souls. For my yoke is easy and my burden is light." Anyone seeking the highest form of rest and rejuvenation in order to recharge from the hustle and bustle of everyday life should come to the Lord, for only He has the power and grace to free us from all of our earthly troubles. Only God can give us the rest we need to achieve the renewed strength that will arm us for the stressful battles we face in our daily lives.

Times of stillness during rest facilitate a shift of focus from being immersion in one's stressful environment to a more tranquil state of mind. This will not only allow one to cope with the onslaught of stress but also enable the mind to be energized and rejuvenated while emptying the negative emotions accumulated throughout the day, week etc. The body needs rest in order for it to re-charge and repair itself. It needs time to relax, think and reflect back. But at the same time, the body needs to remain active in order to achieve optimal body functions and good health. One cannot remain inactive or passive indefinitely. Otherwise, prolonged periods of inactivity can result in the loss of mental lucidness and thereafter a steady decline in one's body functions and health. It is found that people who retire and do not keep active, often die shortly.

This is why the turnaround manager has to master the art of preserving stability amidst change as well as spurring change during stability

Managers think that if the staff take things easy and relaxed, they are goofing off. This is not true. Most creative ideas and innovations come about when the person is relaxed. When he is tense and over-crowded in his mind, he has no time to truly think. How can then the creative juices be generated?

Change can create workload and stress to the staff. If the change is well managed to bring in better processes and increased efficiency, then it is justifiable. However, if the changes come frequently and constantly with little respite, then the workload can bring stress and detriment to the individual as well as the organization. Prolonged stress can result in high employee attrition and customer service deteriorates.

It is therefore abhorrent to hear a manager say: "Firing shall continue till morale improves." Some companies hire and fire whenever they like. This is binge-and-purge staffing or corporate bulimia, an illness in which there is a great and uncontrollable desire to eat, usually followed by vomiting in order not to gain weight. Such frequent changes in management and staff not only breed suspicion and disloyalty among the staff but also rip off the innovative heart and fabric of corporate cohesion. Frequent changes through downsizing exercises have proven to be a corporate cultural disaster. Self-interest will replace corporate interest, as loyalty and trust are lost.

This is why Lewis Platt, the former Chairman and CEO of Hewlett-Packard said: "There are times when the right strategy is probably to back off on current growth in order to have the company better positioned for the future." Rest, you cannot afford not to. The time to rest is when you do not have time for it.

This is why there is a saying: "God grant me the serenity to accept the things I cannot change, courage to change things I can, and wisdom to know the difference." This is why you need R&R – Rest and Rejuvenate.

Principle No. 76

Laughter and fun are the best medicine for companies. (Deuteronomy 12:7, 1 Chronicles 16:10, Job 8:21 – "He will yet fill your mouth with laughter and your lips with shouts of joy.")

The immune system is the body's defence mechanism to handle viruses. Laughter and fun have been held for a long time to be the best medicine. Science has now found that every cell in the body has a receptor for the substances produced when we are laughing and having fun. Thus our first line of defence against viruses is laughter and fun.

The correct use of laughter and fun in the workplace facilitates learning, and changes people's behaviour as it helps them feel less threatened by the prospect of change. Laughter and fun have been found to be the best tools for giving the corporate identity a human face. Laughter and fun have been recognised for centuries to be the best medicine. When people are having fun and laughter, work is no longer a chore or something to get over quickly. They will gladly take on extra work as it gives them joy.

People like doing business with people who are fun. Look at Disney World, the fun place for kids and many adults who want to be kids. It attracted millions of visitors. Many of them have patronised the place several times. Another example is McDonald's. Its philosophy is that going to McDonald's is fun. The McDonald's clown is the comic icon representing fun and laughter, the kind of place where you go to enjoy yourself.

Also a fun working environment is more productive than a routine one. People who enjoy their work will come up with more and better ideas. Fun is contagious.

God is one who enjoys fun and happiness. Many accounts in the Bible ask of men and women that they rejoice before the Lord for their blessings. "There, in the presence of the Lord your God, you and your families shall eat and shall rejoice in everything you have put your hand to, because the Lord your God has blessed you." "Glory in his holy name; let the hearts of those who seek the Lord rejoice." When Job was sorrowful because of what had happened to his life, Bildad comforts him by saying that God will make him happy again. "He will yet fill your mouth with laughter and your lips with shouts of joy."

In excellent companies, employees seem to enjoy themselves. If fun is the meta-value in an organization, the distinction between work and play disappears. Excellent companies acutely aware of the link between fun and creativity encourage the playful potential of their people. The leaders recognize that if people have fun, they not only work harder, but have more creativity, which is the ingredient for global competitiveness. In bad times, when the company can afford little, the key is how to take out the frills and yet keep the thrills.

In organizations that fail to recognize fun as a value, work is merely a chore. The staff behave just mechanically, going to work everyday listlessly, whiling away the time and waiting to be released at the end of the day so that they can have fun outside organization. Richard Branson is a prime example of turning work into an exciting adventure. Branson said of Virgin, "We have done things differently, and that has made life more fun and enjoyable than if we have taken a slightly more conservative approach. I have been determined to have a good time."

Therefore, to have a really happy workforce, you got to do more than pass out bonuses and *angpaos*. You need to make work fun. Science opens to us the book of nature, while laughter and fun open the doors to human creativity.

Principle No. 77

The Hippocratic Oath for a manager is "walk the talk." (James 1:22-24, Romans 2:21-23 – "Do not merely listen to the word, and so deceive yourselves. Do what it says.")

Every professional body has its code of conduct, which ethically guides the practice and direction of the profession. The young, budding doctors have to take the Hippocratic Oath, which basically stipulates that every doctor has to give treatment to anyone who needs it, whether rich or poor.

The turnaround manager is guided by a code of conduct too. The most fundamental is that the turnaround manager has to practise what he preaches. He has to "walk the talk." This is particularly important during hard times. People are watching your behaviour much more than your messages. If you do not practise what you preach, you will be seen as hypocritical.

Oftentimes, we are misled that if we only listen to the Word, we already are doing everything. We forget that this is just but one step. We need to back this step up with action. We need to walk the talk. In the book of James, we are commanded to not just hear about what is right, but to actually do it. "Do not merely listen to the word, and so deceive yourselves. Do what it says. Anyone who listens to the word but does not do what it says is like a man, who looks at his face in a mirror and, after looking at himself, goes away and immediately forgets what he looks like." In Romans, Paul confronts us of hypocrisy. "...you, then, who teach others, do you not teach yourself? You who preach against stealing, do you steal? You who say that people should not commit adultery, do you commit adultery? You who abhor idols, do you rob temples? You who brag about the law, do you dishonor God by breaking the law?" To these questions Paul presents, are all our answers "NO?"

During bad times, everyone is expected to chip in and make sacrifices. If the top gun does not practise what he preaches by making personal sacrifices as well, then he will lose his credibility and thus will jeopardize his future turnaround endeavours. "Walk the talk" is an ethical code for the turnaround manager as its non-compliance is perceived as deception by the other team members. Furthermore, you also deceive yourself as you are lying to yourself, as you do not firmly believe enough to practise what you have preached.

You also need to lead by example if you withdraw the perks and corporate benefits of the managers,. For instance, you will lose credibility if you continue to fly business class when you have decided that all the staff must downgrade to economy class ticket or you continue to wine and dine in expensive restaurants when your staff are retrenched to save costs. Once you don't walk the talk, you become inconsistent and you will lose respect from your team members.

The non-verbal aspects of business communication are often more important than the verbal ones. If you want to promote flat and informal management style, you cannot work behind closed door all the time. If you tell your people to come in punctually, you must ensure that you come in punctual too. If you want your people to be customer oriented, you must set the example by meeting up with the customers. What you do speaks so loudly that others cannot hear what you say.

The message here is "We are in difficult times and it must start with me." Leadership by example is the guiding motto for the top management, especially during difficult times. If you want others to take a salary cut, volunteer to cut your own salary first. If you want your staff to work long hours, you must be prepared to work even longer hours. This is why it is abhorrent to hear the manager who said that "do what I preach, but do not practise what I do."

People are very receptive and take the cue quickly. They are able to fathom the sincerity of the senior management. To be successful, you need to solicit their co-operation. They are watching whether your actions are consistent with your words. No amount of preaching and communication will be as effective as practising what you preach and communicate. No amount of threats can even change behaviour unless the leader is perceived as being serious in his actions.

The behaviour of the leaders sets the tone for the organisation. Be aware that you must "walk the talk" and set the example for others to emulate.

Principle No. 78

Without ethics, the company has lost its soul. (1 Kings 9:4-5, Job 2:3,9, Job 41:10-16 – "As for you, if you walk before me in integrity of heart and uprightness, as David your father did, and do all I command and observe my decrees and laws, I will establish your royal throne over Israel forever...")

"In the end, integrity is all you've got..." this statement succinctly encapsulates the importance of ethics in the corporate scheme of things, and underscores its role as the corner stone of business practices today.

Integrity is of great value even in Jesus' time. We see in the account of King Solomon how Jesus had advised him regarding his integrity and its rewards: "As for you, if you walk before me in integrity of heart and uprightness, as David your father did, and do all I command and observe my decrees and laws, I will establish your royal throne over Israel forever..."

Job was the perfect example of a man of integrity. When God was talking to Satan, God presented Job to be tested by Satan, for he knows Job is blameless in his ways. "Then the Lord said to Satan, "Have you considered my servant Job? There is no one on earth like him; he is blameless and upright, a man who fears God and shuns evil. And he still maintains his integrity, though you incited me against him to ruin him without any reason." Even though he had suffered the loss of his animals, his house and all his family, he kept his integrity and never cursed God until the end. Though his wife may have been against it, "Are you still holding on to your integrity? Curse God and die!" he remained righteous in God's eyes.

In the end, God restored everything Job had twice more than what he previously had. "The Lord blessed the latter part of Job's life more than the first. He had fourteen thousand sheep, six thousand camels, a thousand yoke of oxen and a thousand donkeys. And he also had seven sons and three daughters. The first daughter he named Jemimah, the second Keziah and the third Keren-Happuch. Nowhere in all the land was there found women as beautiful as Job's daughters, and their father granted them an inheritance along with their brothers. After this, Job lived a hundred and forty years; he saw his children and their children to the fourth generation. And so he died, old and full of years."

Jack Welch, former chairman of GE is a major champion of the supremacy of ethics in business. Whenever an employee's actions have put GE on the wrong side of the law, he has hastened to co-operate with investigators, admit guilt and take prompt corrective action. Such corporate *mea culpa* has served the company well.

The time-card scandal in 1985 was the first significant ethical challenge of Welch's 25-year GE career. GE Re-entry Systems, a GE subsidiary, was making a new nose cone for the Air Force's Minuteman missile. Federal prosecutors in Philadelphia charged it with 108 counts of criminal fraud. The indictment alleged that GE managers had altered workers' time cards with improper charges totalling $800,000. Welch's response and damage control were brilliant, thereby winning the trust of government officials. Welch personally called on Secretary Orr, presenting a comprehensive proposal for cleaning up the mess and preventing such mess from recurring. He created a top-level review board within GE to oversee compliance.

In this time-card case and other similar instances, candor and a determination to ally GE with the forces of law have enabled GE to emerge with more vitality and systematic approaches to ethics. The experiences also underscore the challenge of having to raise employees' awareness of the need for high ethical standards.

"You can't audit integrity into a system any more than you can inspect quality into a machine. Where you can make a difference is by changing the culture, by tireless, forceful leadership that won't tolerate winking, rule-bending or looking the other way." Welch was quoted as saying. His favourite question to GE employees was: "Can you look in the mirror every day and feel proud of what you are doing." According to Welch, "In a global business, you can win without bribes. But you better have technology. That's why we win in business like turbines, because we have the best gas turbine. You have got to be the low-priced supplier, but in almost all cases, if you have quality, price and technology, you win."

Even the comeback kid, Donald Trump has this advice for businessmen: "Be honest, even if there are others around you who are not." In the 1999, he almost wanted to run as a candidate for the Presidential election but eventually did not. Apparently, he had received good support of popular votes in the unofficial poll on his chances of running for Presidency. You can go bankrupt and fail in your business, but as long as your reputation of strong ethics stay intact, people will always remember that and you can make a comeback again.

Companies spend a lot of money in selecting its candidates. This is normally based on competence and achievements, which are easier to measure. However, it is equally important to select candidates with high levels of integrity and ethics. Strong ethical practices should pervade across the whole corporate spectrum. It is important that board members need to be more independent. Analysts too need to provide independent views and assessments in their reports on companies. Shareholders and investors need to focus and do their homework rather than merely relying on earnings per share and short term profits. Looking to the short-term can lead to long-term disaster. Take Bernie Madoff for instance. The retirees and innocent investors were happy to give Madhoff funds in order to invest in the short-term. However, when the market began to unravel, those same investors have had to pay a price as their investments became zero the moment the government realized the scandal. The larger society has also paid a price, losing further confidence in already troubled times of the late 2000's. All of these issues have to do with integrity as it is necessary to do what is right and ethical.

Principle No. 79

Core values are invaluable. (Proverbs 31:10-45 – "A wife of noble character who can find? She is worth far more than rubies.")

Turnaround managers have to operate under very tough environment. In some instances, he or she has to make bold decisions based on very little information.   All decisions will result in consequences, whether these are positive or negative. His decisions are based on his value system that is his personal beliefs, connections and other influences. You are where you are because of the various decisions taken in your life.

For instance, a manager who is heavily in debt will be fearful of losing his job. As such, he may not take decisions that take too much risks and therefore risking his job. Thus he may just go along till the whole ship sinks together with him in it.

For others, it may be a case of being a very democratic and caring personality. As such he may not be the right person to make tough decisions on cost-cutting or downsizing matters. Therefore, he may not be the appropriate person to exercise the restructuring. However, his temperament and values would place him in good stead to grow the company's business.

In Proverbs 31, King Solomon writes to us about the wife of noble character. He describes the "perfect" wife; able in mind, spirit and body to establish and live a comfortable, glorious life for herself, her husband and their children. "A wife of noble character who can find? She is worth far more than rubies. Her husband has full confidence in her and lacks nothing of value. She brings him good, not harm, all the days of her life." "She gets up while it is still dark; she provides food for her family and portions for her servant girls. She considers a field and buys it; out of her earnings she plants a vineyard. She sets about her work vigorously; her arms are strong for her tasks. She sees that her trading is profitable, and her lamp does not go out at night." "She is clothed with strength and dignity; she can laugh at the days to come. She speaks with wisdom, and faithful instruction is on her tongue. She watches over the affairs of her household and does not eat the bread of idleness."

People's ethical inclinations are governed by their value systems. If they are easily tempted by small things, chances are that they will be succumbed by bigger temptations. For example, some dishonest executives may inflate their expense claims. They claim more on taxi fares, entertainment and tips than the actual. Such dishonest behaviour is rather stupid as amounts incurred for the claim can easily be validated. Most supervisors will not reject the claims unless the discrepancies are substantial. The conduct of such executives will leave behind a very bad impression. Such dishonest conduct may even jeopardise the future promotional prospects for these executives. If they cannot be trusted with small sums of money, chances are that they will not be trustworthy for handling larger portfolio involving big dollars and bucks.

It is believed that a political leader in Singapore determines the leadership of his young colleagues by inviting all their family members to have dinner with him. During the dinner, he will observe silently and closely how these young leaders handle their wives and children. This political leader believes that if these young and budding leaders cannot even manage their families, then chances are that they will not have the ability to manage national matters. It is rumoured that this leader does not take lightly to any of these political fledglings if they are divorced.

Normally, most people make decisions based on their own value and belief systems, rather than what they ought to decide. Companies too have their value systems. This is why many successful companies have enshrined their corporate values as part of their corporate culture. When the company's value is right, it can maximise shareholder's returns and delight the staff and the customers. It appears that the types of values that a company subscribes to are not as important as long as the values are ethical, honourable and acceptable. For example, 3M's value has been an emphasis on innovation, IBM on customers, Singapore Airlines on customer service, CISCO on technology. Right values can make the Fortune 500 companies not only stay within the 500 list but will also make them fortunate companies.

The truth will set the turnaround manager free. (Exodus 20:16, Proverbs 12:22, Revelation 21:8, 1 John 2:22 – "The Lord detests lying lips, but he delights in men who are truthful.")

The doctor faces the same problem as the turnaround manager in whether he should tell the patient truthfully about the state of his ailment. Oftentimes, it is better to tell the patient the truth so that the he can prepare himself or herself mentally, psychologically and physically. There are exceptions when it may be better to conceal the truth from the patient. In such cases, the patients may not be mentally strong enough to cope with the ramifications of their ailments.

Nowadays, downsizing, delayering and outsourcing are the normal regime of corporate life. It is important to communicate honestly to the staff throughout these trying events. When dealing with difficult matters, 'honesty is the best policy'. It is unethical to sugar coat, mislead or lie to the staff concerned. They will eventually come to learn the real situation. Any mishandling of the outcome can create distrust, sense of betrayal and loss of confidence in the management.

Thus, in the case of a sick company, it is better to recognise this fact, tell the truth and relevant matters relating to the turnaround plans. By concealing the truth and going about business as usual, one falls into the denial trap. Be truthful and do not hide the truth as people are not against bad news per se. Some of the staff would have already sensed that something is amiss, just as a sick person is aware that all is not well with his body. Most staff only want to see quick results in the turnaround and the uncertainty to be cleared so that they can move on with their lives. Hence, after communicating the truth, the turnaround manager must ensure that he has a plan to rectify the problem and implement some tough measures and unpopular actions. The idea is to acknowledge the truth and quickly work with the employees to administer the right medicine. Usually, the staff are the first ones to realise that the ailing company needs drastic actions to fix a difficult situation and there is often no necessity to do much convincing of the need for tough turnaround measures. Many executives are actually looking for a saviour to resuscitate the organisation.

As a corollary to this, it is also important to let the bank know the financial health of the company. Some ailing businesses try to hide their financial predicaments from the bankers. Most bankers are sympathetic and will try to help those debtors if they can show concrete rescue plans.

The bankers will lose total confidence in their debtors if the bankers have to learn it from other secondary sources about their borrower's financial difficulties. In such situations, the bankers may not be very sympathetic as it is deemed that their borrowers are trying to hide the truth from them.

In the Bible it is written: "The truth will set you free." Indeed this is true and realistic. When you are lying, you have to remember what was said earlier in order to remain consistent. You lose credibility immediately with your staff when they learn that you have been lying to them. This is the quickest and surest way to lose your staff's confidence.

One of the gravest commandments in the Bible is to be honest with whatever matter you are dealing with. In Exodus we find the commandment: "You shall not give false testimony against your neighbor." In Proverbs, "The Lord detests lying lips, but he delights in men who are truthful."

We may think lying is only a small sin, but we can see in the Bible that God treats liars as how he would treat a murderer, or an idolater. "But the cowardly, the unbelieving, the vile, the murderers, the sexually immoral, those who practice magic arts, the idolaters and all liars — their place will be in the fiery lake of burning sulfur." "Who is the liar? It is the man who denies that Jesus is the Christ. Such a man is the antichrist — he denies the Father and the Son."

People are prepared to forgive you for your mistakes, they can overlook your weaknesses or incompetence and some will even support your stupidity. However, when you are caught lying to them, they will lose trust and respect for you. Trust and support are pre-requisites in a turnaround situation. And you need a team to do a turnaround and transformation.

The corporate world punishes companies for telling untruths. In Singapore, Informatics Holding, the once darling of the Singapore Stock Exchange fell from grace because it had overstated its actual $5.5 million profit by $8.6 million for the nine months ended December 2003. Its share fell by more than half. Accounting and legal problems have also affected the Tyco, Enron, WorldCom, Global Crossing as well as Martha Stewart's company because of accounting irregularities.

Therefore, being truthful is always the best policy.

Principle No. 81

Your future view will determine the future you. (Jeremiah 29:11, Romans 8:23, Lamentations 1:9 – "For I know the plans I have for you," declares the Lord, "plans to prosper you and not to harm you, plans to give you hope and a future.")

How you view the future shapes your actions. Technology has changed the future. The future is not what it is. Anticipation of the future is the key to the success of corporations.

It is good to step back to look at the big picture at times, hence the need for rest and relaxation. Your worst enemy is relying on past successes. You need to reinvent your cash cow. Your views and perceptions of the future will determine the new you.

Even Jesus used this principle. He had planned a great future for us "For I know the plans I have for you," declares the Lord, "plans to prosper you and not to harm you, plans to give you hope and a future."

However, we need to learn to set our eyes on it. We must patiently wait in hope for the coming of our Lord, for our redemption. "...but we ourselves, who have the first fruits of the Spirit, groan inwardly as we wait eagerly for our adoption as sons, the redemption of our bodies. For in this hope we were saved." When we set our eyes on the future, we modify our lifestyles and change the way we live, in accordance to the future. We must prepare for the future and focus our view on it; else we pay the price, and ultimately be unable to reach that future. "Her filthiness clung to her skirts; she did not consider her future. Her fall was astounding; there was none to comfort her."

Many things are shifting and future views have to be changed. We have shifted from the information age to communication age, from passive data to interactive media, from computerization to intelligent network, from local access to universal access.

Human resource management has shifted its focus from upgrading technology to upgrading people, job security to job employability, job titles to job skills. We need to become migrant professionals instead of corporate men, and change from single-skill specialists to multi-skilled generalists, and institute reward and promotion based on performance rather than seniority.

Page 231

Corporate culture has also changed from status quo to rapid change, incremental innovation to fundamental change. . The nature of management is undergoing a paradigm shift – from management to leadership, from process to strategy, from management by control to management by commitment, from managing today's crises to managing future opportunities.

Today, the focus is on teamwork versus individual action, giving acknowledgement rather than taking credit, empowering rather than controlling others, and continuous rather than periodic improvements.

Even the dynamics of manufacturing is changing - from sell what you make to make what you sell, mass production to lean production, long cycle times to short cycle times, quality manufacturing to flexible manufacturing, mass production to customized mass production.

The realities of the global competition compel firms to view their opportunity differently. Business opportunities are no longer to be viewed in local terms or on an individual country basis. Companies and individuals need to view the entire world as the economic opportunity. However, it is not about the old or the new economy, it is about fundamental principles.

It is the ability to open up your future view where the limitless wonders are discovered.

Principle No. 82

To survive, you need to teach old dogs new tricks. (John 13:34-35, 1 John 2:7-11 – "A new command I give you: Love one another.")

The sea change that most businesses face today is increasingly becoming the norm rather than the exception. The change is driven by globalisation, technological and social dynamics. Hovering around the status quo is like a cancer-stricken person waiting for his condition to get better. If you continue doing the same, things are not going to get better. There is a saying that you cannot teach old dogs new tricks. To survive in today's competitive market, old dogs need to be taught new tricks.

Likewise, for the disciples to survive the troubles they go through carrying out what Jesus had tasked them to do, these "old dogs" had to be taught new tricks. Jesus gives them a new command apart from what he had already given them. Jesus states: "A new command I give you: Love one another. As I have loved you, so you must love one another. By this all men will know that you are my disciples, if you love one another." Further in the Bible we see the apostle John reaffirm this new command as he knows it is crucial for their survival: "This old command is the message you have heard. Yet I am writing to you a new command; its truth is seen in him and you, because the darkness is passing and the true light is already shining. Anyone who claims to be in the light but hates his brother is still in the darkness. Whoever loves his brother lives in the light, and there is nothing in him to make him stumble. But whoever hates his brother is in the darkness and walks around in the darkness; he does not know where he is going, because the darkness has blinded him."

Organisations fail to change because of old ways of doing things. There is unclear vision as most CEOs are unable to communicate their visions in three minutes so that other people can understand and embrace it. Also, oftentimes, the vision is not communicated and obstacles such as bureaucracies are allowed to block the vision.

Management also fails to plant the new behaviour and vision in the company's values. They fail to show employees that the new behaviours and approaches can result in improved performance. Top management fails to develop a shared commitment to the renewal. The future corporation ought to be less bureaucratic, with fewer levels, more performance oriented and risk-taking.

Shareholders are increasingly becoming impatient with Chairman and CEOs who are set in their old ways. If the old dogs do not mend their ways, the shareholders and investors will speak with their feet and be quick to voice their protest. In March 2004, Sir Philip Watts, the embattled chairman of Royal Dutch/Shell was forced to resign after an audit. He was due for retirement the following spring. One of the largest investors remarked that they wanted more independent executives rather than lifers. Michael Eisner of Walt Disney was stripped of his chairman position but remained as the CEO. He has been the head of the Walt Disney Company since 1984. It was popularly believed that shareholders voted against him to register their rebuke against Michael Eisner's leadership.

In contrast in the late 1990's, Well Fargo forewent their 150 year of history by eliminating all waste – sold away the corporate jet, cars, free drinks to staff etc. Conversely, another 150-year bank, Bank of America did not respond as rapidly with the banking deregulations. Subsequently, BOA did learn to reduce waste; however, it had already lost valuable time to Well Fargo.

In the area of marketing, companies still continue to think that marketing is selling. They focus on selling the products to customers and neglected maintaining a relationship with them. They are only interested in selling to new customers and neglected the existing and old ones. It is perhaps more glamorous and exciting to chase for the new accounts, when studies have found that it is cheaper to keep old customers than acquire new ones.

For instance, many companies see the potential of the Internet but never make the change. The bookshops continue with expensive brochures and advertisements in the media, when more and more customers are using online purchases. One day, these bookshops woke up to the fact that Amazon.com overtook them because Amazon.com does not have expensive warehouses to stock their books and people are purchasing online.

The acceptance of the Internet as a tool for business has saved many companies from going out of business. It helps small companies compete against the big companies as on the website, there is little differentiation. It is probably the best and most cost-effective medium to promote a company's products and services and generate new sales. Nicholas Negroponte, an American writer and director, MIT media laboratory said: "The Net is a 10.5 on the Richter scale of economic change."

Some moderations are required in throwing out all old things. One must not always equate 'old' with obsolete and 'new' with best. It is also not wise to hastily throw away any old and workable traditions and conventions. They may require modification, but they are the result of the experience of many generations. Also, the decades of downsizing have eliminated many staff with many years of rich experience and expertise which new staff will take many years to learn. Therefore, old staff have a lot of value to the company.

Employees go through several stages during a change and re-orientation process. They are namely, denial, frustration, confusion, acceptance and finally commitment. There may be some resistance at the beginning through denial, frustration and confusion. But once they see the value of the changes, they will accept them and be committed to them.

However, one has to be aware that if you leave old things alone, you leave them as they are. But you do not. If you leave an old thing alone you leave it to a torrent of change.

The key is that the champions of tomorrow see an opportunity, which their competitors too can see. The difference is that champions take action to make the change.

Principle No. 83

Don't act your age, act the present age you are in and the future age that you will be. (1 Timothy 4:6-12 – "Don't let anyone look down on you because you are young, but set an example for the believers in speech, in life, in love, in faith and in purity.")

Many people give the excuses that they are too old or young to accomplish anything. Their hopes and ambitions are dashed and hampered because they only act in their physical age. But do you know that one of the richest men in the world started his business at age 19? Bill Gate founded Microsoft when most people would say is too young. Another young successful entrepreneur is Steven Spielberg who created and directed the movie, "Jaws" at the age of 27. If you think that you are too old, look at several so-called old entrepreneurs. Sam Walton got tired of corporate life at age 44 and founded Wal-Mart. Ray Crock founded McDonalds at the retirement age of 52. These successful businessmen did not act in their present ages and went beyond.

In the Bible, Timothy, even though he was young, was already given tasks and entrusted with big responsibilities – to preach, teach and command the peoples, by his father, Paul. Paul didn't think that Timothy was incapable because he was still young, rather, he taught him well; encouraging him and instructing him to train his self to be godly. He gives this message to Timothy: "Don't let anyone look down on you because you are young, but set an example for the believers in speech, in life, in love, in faith and in purity." In the end, Timothy emerges strong, regardless of his age; he transcends that, remaining faithful and blameless in his ways, pursuing what his father Paul had commanded him.

Success can numb an organisation's responses. The executives who presided over the near collapse of some of the world's greatest corporations were mostly leaders of proven ability. Their failures stemmed from reliance on ideas and practices that had worked splendidly in earlier times. The times changed and they didn't.

Jack Welch admits that at first he did not see the Internet as a great transformer of businesses. "It did not grab me with the intensity it should have." He also said that "two years from my retirement I was a Neanderthal about the Internet, and I am a gonzo." But once he saw its power, he quickly became a convert. "I just saw the power of it, " he said, "It will change every company's culture." In 2001, Welch said that e-business represented the largest opportunity the company has ever seen.

He became a full-fledged fanatic and declared that, "e-Business is the elixir that came along and changed the DNA of GE forever."

The problem as Welch saw it, was that 'the knowledge of Internet was inversely proportional to the age". In order to make sure that GE's e-Business initiative would take hold, Welch turned hierarchy on its head once again. Managers at GE needed to learn the Internet quickly. He paired the 1,000 most senior GE executives with younger, junior people in the organisation. This way the young would teach the old while the two cultures had a chance to interact. "We got the bottom of the organisation, the young talking to the top of the organisation who are the older ones. It had an enormous impact." Welch says that, "the Internet truly makes the old young and the slow fast."

And yes, Welch had a younger colleague and spent three hours per week with her. Eventually, he promoted her to head GE's corporate website. Welch took great pride in the fact that he had learnt the idea from another younger GE colleague. It was "the best idea I ever heard", he declared.

Organisations that have been operating for a while tend to become unwieldy with their 'age'. Very often, they become blinkered by their own past success, and tend to behave like geriatrics with their own ossified thinking about the business and the marketplace. What they should do is to inject fresh talent, and tailor their entire management philosophies and strategies to suit the changing market dynamics. Similarly, the entire corporate culture needs to be reviewed to ensure that it is in sync with the times.

Principle No. 84

Turnaround is near death experience, transformation is revival experience. (Acts 3:19, Romans 12:2 – "Repent, then, and turn to God, so that your sins may be wiped out, that times of refreshing may come from the Lord.")

Turnaround refers to the two phases described earlier as surgery and resuscitation. It is more of a science rather than an art as it follows a ruthless formula of cost cutting, staff layoffs, divesting etc. These quick fixes although at times necessary, do not address the issues of long-term and holistic recovery and the company may fall sick again in the future. You cannot go through too many episodes of near death experiences as one day you may not be lucky enough to survive one.

On the other hand, transformation is the revival experience and the nursing phase, which is more of an art than science. Transformation seeks long-term and sustainable foundation that can enable the company to grow. Transformation takes nurturing and time to build a strong healthy corporate culture that can handle the vagaries of changes in the marketplace. Companies should welcome numerous transformations to revive their fitness.

We go through the same processes in our lives. Our turnaround experiences take the form of repentance. We ask for forgiveness whenever we sin. However, this is not the complete change. This is just a quick fix and is only but one part of the whole changing process, as it is highly probable that we'll sin again. The Bible tells us that we need the transformation part as well. In the book of Acts, it is written that we should not only repent, but we must completely turn to God: "Repent, then, and turn to God, so that your sins may be wiped out, that times of refreshing may come from the Lord." Transformation is essential that we may not just turn away from sin time and time again, but be able to completely turn our backs from the world and set our eyes Jesus. "Do not conform any longer to the pattern of this world, but be transformed by the renewing of your mind. Then you will be able to test and approve what God's will is — his good, pleasing and perfect will."

There are a few great turnaround and transformational leaders. Gilbert F. Amelio took over the as the President and Chief Executive Officer of National Semiconductor Corp in mid 1991. The company was on the brink of bankruptcy with three days worth of operating capital and reeling from years of financial losses. He successfully not only turned around the fate of National Semiconductor Corp, but also transformed the organisation. In 1995, National made approximately $330 million in

Page 238

pre-tax income and had the highest sales and net earnings in its history. The company had a low debt-to-equity and more than $450 million in cash. Shareholders' equity had increased to $1.4 billion from $540 million in 1991.

Gilbert F Amelio introduced the transformation process of people and business leadership. In the people leadership, he charted the course of action with the clear vision and values. Under business leadership, he fixed the timeframe and financial targets. For operational excellence, National adopted the McKinsey 7 S model: strategy, structure, systems, staff, style, skills and shared values.

He led the transformation by promoting the five essential elements of: Leadership, the Soft Skills, Promoting the Vision, Building Cross-Company Connections and Tapping the Right Brain. These were taught in a formal training program. Every National employee went through some kind of training to engage them in the transformation process.

Jack Welch is another example of a turnaround and transformational leader. It is not just the excellent performance at GE, but the fact that Jack is continually reinventing himself. In the early 1980s, when he first took over the helm of management, he was known as neutron Jack. He subsequently fired 150,000 GE staffers to turn it around. Towards the end of the 1990s Jack is known more as a 'Transformational Jack'. He is known for emphasizing on coaching his younger colleagues at the GE's training centre at Crontonville. Welch was also famous for introducing transformational programmes such as Six-Sigma, Work-Out, etc to GE.

Lou Gertsner of IBM and Larry Bossidy of AlliedSignal and later Honeywell International understood that both their companies did not require major turnaround and restructuring of neither products nor personnel. What they needed was transformation. They needed proper management to get things done in an efficient, speedy and effective way.

Another example is Bill Gates. At first, he did not take the threat of Internet seriously. But through the system of allowing for free flow of ideas and criticisms, Bill quickly took cognizance of the threat of Internet and immediately transformed Microsoft. James R. Houghton of Corning Company is another example. He has engaged a human resource person who, before he retired to become Houghton's personal coach. This retiree also used to work for his father and Houghton wanted to tap this retiree's wisdom. He was willing to be transformed by a more experienced colleague and later transformed Corning Company to be a great company.

Turnaround and transformation are the business equivalences of strong medicine. They can work wonders but also have serious side effects. Prudent managers should not embark on such treatments lightly. Many factors have to be considered such as management's ability to lead such processes or perhaps there more appropriate financial cushions or alternative treatments.

Principle No. 85

Be a creator of change, rather than a creature of change. (Daniel 1:1-15 – "Please test your servants for ten days: Give us nothing but vegetables to eat and water to drink.")

We are going through a period of history of 'creative destruction', which entails incessant changes both in the structure and our economy. Leaders need to consistently re-invent, redesign and recompose the organisation to meet these challenges. Harvey Golub, CEO of American Express in 1993 said: "To succeed, I believe an organisation has to change and adjust before it is forced to do so by external forces. It must reinvent itself and become the very business that could put it out of business before someone else does."

Bill Smithburg, CEO of Quaker Oats in 1996 said: "Competition is a way of life. If you don't have a really tough competitor, you ought to invent one." Lewis Platt, CEO of Hewlett-Packard said in 1994: "It is counter to human nature, but you have to kill your business while it is still working." John Chambers of CISCO said: "We have a philosophy that we will eat our own young before someone else does."

When you compete against yourself and recreate yourself, you cannot lose. This is why there is a popular saying in Silicon Valley: "Either we obsolete ourselves or the competition will."

Daniel and his friends, Shadrach, Meshach and Abednego did just that. They created their own change, and set themselves apart, even when there were no competitions yet to rise over them. When King Nebuchadnezzar had to pick the finest young men in Jerusalem these four were among those chosen. "...young men without any physical defect, handsome, showing aptitude for every kind of learning, well informed, quick to understand, and qualified to serve in the king's palace."

However, these four learned to transcend the already grand status they had. Though the king offered them fine wine and food, they refused and instead challenged themselves to only eat vegetables and water. The king agreed to test them, and in the end, the four came out strong. "At the end of the ten days they looked healthier and better nourished than any of the young men who ate the royal food."

Some companies even manufacture a 'crisis' in order to produce a sense of urgency in the organisation. Motorola created an awareness-building program called 'Rise to the Challenge', which confronted employees with the early warning signs of impending doom and described the competitive challenge confronting the company. Boeing created a video for its employees depicting the demise of this great company. It helps the employees understand the need to change.

In order to recreate themselves for the future, organisations must be prepared to let go of the past. Otherwise, they will be trapped and hindered by their past successes. The trick is not to let go of the past all at once; for a time, the past and future have to coexist in the present. According to Charles Handy, "The way to make sense of the future in organisations and in societies and your own life is by taking charge of the future. Not by responding to it." Charles Handy also said: "I wrote a book called The Age of Unreason. The reason I chose that particular title was because George Bernard Shaw once wrote that the reasonable man responds to the world, while the unreasonable man tries to make the world respond to him. All progress and disasters too, comes from the unreasonable person; the person who actually tries to change the world. What that means is that we cannot wait for people to offer us secure jobs and long careers. We have to decide what kind of life we want to lead and go out and make it happen."

We cannot drive into the future in a leisurely manner any longer. Many market leaders fell asleep while driving and were overtaken by smaller competitors, which come out of the blue. Today, there is no certainty at all about where we are going. We have approached the age of uncertainty. Past successes will not see us through the future. We need to unlearn and re-visit all the old assumptions. Peter Drucker called it 'every organisation has to prepare for the abandonment of everything it does.' The future will no longer be an extrapolation of the past.

The future winners will be trailblazers rather than slow coaches. They are creators of change rather than becoming creatures of the change. The way into the future is to take charge of the future and not by responding to it immediately. The challenge of running the modern day corporations is to manage the process of creative destruction. Yet, few corporate leaders have the foresight or energy to do so as demanded by the market dynamics.

Manage yourself with the head, manage others with your heart. (1 Chronicles 28:9, Philippians 4:7 – "And the peace of God, which transcends all understanding, will guard your hearts and your minds in Christ Jesus.")

It is the head that helps to analyse and strategise, but it is the heart that fosters understanding and commitment so critical for long-term corporate success. To increase the corporate life span and longevity, you need to manage the head or hard issues as well as the heart or soft issues. Therefore, make decision from the top of your head and from the bottom of your heart. Good companies have the peoples' heart in their business and the business in their hearts. The heart of the matter is the matter of the heart.

To create your vision, you need your head and heart. Your head supplies you with all the basic facts and figures of the business issues, strengths and weaknesses of your company and competitors, the market environment, etc. It is the heart that tells you the intangibles. The desire to succeed, the fear that cripples the mindset of you and your team, the spirit and passion to get up again when things are going awry etc. To achieve your vision, you need both the soul-searching and fact-finding.

In dealing with Jesus, we have to remember that we need both heart and mind to serve him. Jesus checks our hearts and heads, to make sure that our ways are true. It is not enough for Jesus to check our hearts or our minds alone, he keeps both in check to keep us in check, "...serve him with wholehearted devotion and with a willing mind, for the Lord searches every heart and understands every motive behind the thoughts" and helps us to maintain these things on our own as well. "And the peace of God, which transcends all understanding, will guard your hearts and your minds in Christ Jesus."

In the corporate setting, strategies and hardware will come to naught if the people's hearts are not with the company. The implementation will go wrong if your people's support and commitment are not there. In turbulent times, one needs also to deal with the soft or hard issues especially those relating to people. You should be hard on performance but soft on people.

An example of winning the hearts and minds is the second Iraqi-USA war. The Iraqi regime collapsed very quickly and all the Saddam's soldiers fled with little resistance when the American forces arrived.

Iraqis who have been for many years living under the fear and threats under Saddam Hussein were won over. Saddam was himself subsequently arrested and sabotaged by his closest aides who gave him away to the American forces. All the years of strategies and plans to coerce the Iraqi populace under the Saddam regime did not work. This is because Saddam did not win his people's hearts and minds,

Corporations have for centuries searched for that elusive fountain of corporate youth through all kinds of different management theories, technologies and programmes. We invest millions of dollars in the quest for corporate excellence, but we forget the basics. It is the people who make the products and the people who buy them that ultimately determine the corporate longevity.

Just like a human being, the corporate body needs strong cells to fight corporate ailments. Often, it is the people that fail not the business. At the end of the day, you have to remember that all the work is done by your people. This is why an old proverb says: "If you are planning for one year, plant trees, if you planning for 100 years, cultivate people." You want to win their hearts and minds.

Principle No. 87

Building up your cash reserves is like eating calcium-rich food. It fortifies your bones later in life. (Proverbs 21:20, 2 Corinthians 9:6 – "In the house of the wise are stores of choice food and oil, but a foolish man devours all he has.")

Sick companies have difficulties generating cash or are consuming cash or burnt rate at a much faster rate than what they can earn. This is because they do not have enough reserves for a rainy day.

Jesus places importance in saving too. In the Bible, a man is identified foolish if he doesn't save: "In the house of the wise are stores of choice food and oil, but a foolish man devours all he has." Paul reminds us that we only reap what we sow. If we save a little money, then expect to amass a little. Likewise if we plant a few crops, expect to harvest a few also. "Remember this: Whoever sows sparingly will also reap sparingly, and whoever sows generously will also reap generously."

The financial crisis in Asia in 1997 has taught companies the importance of saving. Those countries with huge financial reserves such as Singapore and Taiwan were spared. Countries with low reserves such as Indonesia, Thailand, Malaysia and Korea suffered economic devastation as there was a big run of money out of these countries. Many of these afflicted countries have banks with huge non-performing loans. A huge amount of money was spent on major prestigious construction projects that did not contribute to the bottom-line and led to gangrenous inefficiency. For several years, many of these buildings and construction projects remained uncompleted or unoccupied. The companies borrowed heavily in US dollars and when their local currencies depreciated, these borrowers were not able to service their loans as these have increased in value. Although, these companies may still have strong fundamentals, overnight they became technically insolvent. This further created a systemic collapse of the investors' confidence in the region.

Any country or region is subjected to such major disruptions when there is a massive out flow of funds. Many of these funds are purely speculative in nature and do not have any productivity or backing behind it. The outflow of such funds has hit US in the 1980s, Asia in 1997 and Latin America in the late 1990s and now hitting the whole world in the 2008. If companies are borrowing beyond their means without savings, when such speculative outflows of funds happen to the region, it will be like a rug pull under you.

In Singapore, a publicly listed company, Ferro China went under not because of the financial tsunami of the late 2008; they collapsed well before the financial tsunami hit them. Ferro China had negative reserves but was making profit. Their 2007 financial results were showing positive profits but operating in a negative. Cash flow because they had borrowed too much, they were already on the path to destruction before the economy ever faltered.

Indeed, many individuals have become bankrupt when credit is suddenly taken away from them or when their sources of income dried up. Many companies are highly geared to sustain their businesses; few are financing their operations from their own cash flow. When the high interest rate hit them or the onslaught of hedge funds and currency speculators hit the country, all these borrowers are unable to service their loans.

The same problem of poor saving hits individuals just as it adversely affects companies. In Singapore, many individuals are heavily committed in housing and car loans and have very little savings. When the economy went into topsy-turvy in the late 1990s and early 2000s, many individuals lost their jobs or their businesses went bust. Having little savings, these individuals were declared bankrupts. More recently, we can see the same trend in the US. Many people bought homes on loans which had adjustable rate mortgages. However, these people oftentimes bought a house beyond their means. By over-buying, these people were not able to make payments when the adjustable rate increased and, subsequently, sweeping foreclosures occurred across the nation. It was this poor planning and the unscrupulous loan practices that led the US to the economic collapse of the late 2000's.

The lesson here is: Always live within your means. The problem is that this bad habit of living beyond their means is prevalent in companies, many of them taking on projects and contracts beyond their means. When the economy collapsed, many of these companies went down the tubes with the economy.

Building up your calcium content for your body takes time and cannot be done overnight. Similarly, building up a strong reserve takes a long time and a lot of patience and hard work. With the current low interest rate situation, it is even less convincing for companies and individuals to save. However, it is necessary in these days to prevent funds from being dispersed haphazardly.

Saving for cash is a learned practice. It involves reprioritizing projects, altering inventory and in-stock positions, making arrangements with suppliers and some modifications of the processes.

This is why there are some truths in the saying: "Save for a rainy day." These days, it rains more often than usual.

Principle No. 88

There are three certainties in life: deaths, taxes and changes. (Genesis 12:1-7 "The Lord had said to Abram, "Leave your country, your people and your father's household and go to the land I will show you.")

Nobody likes death and taxes. Many people also do not like changes either. They are quite reluctant to make changes once they are well settled into their "comfort zones".

Abraham, however, freely accepted the changes God was about to implement in his life. God asked him to leave his country – his friends, his home, his comfort zone, his whole life and go off to an unfamiliar, strange land that he doesn't know about. He only brought his wife, Sarah and his nephew, Lot, everything else he left behind. "The Lord had said to Abram, "Leave your country, your people and your father's household and go to the land I will show you."

Abraham didn't hesitate when God asked him to leave his home; instead, Abraham followed him without thinking twice. Abraham never reached his destination. As long as he lived, he kept travelling from places to places. However, the Lord was with him. Because he obeyed God, God guided him all the way, and in the end, kept his promise to Abraham: to give his descendants Canaan, the promised land.

In today's world, change is a certainty and it brings forth tremendous threat and yet abundant opportunity to businesses. Author and psychiatrist Dr James Gordon once said in reference to the mindset change, "It is not that some people have will power and some don't. It is that some people are ready to change and others are not." Goethe said: "We must always change, renew, rejuvenate ourselves; otherwise we harden."

In business, the ability to embrace changes is the prerequisite for future survival. This is because of disruptive technologies that cause upheavals in product development and the manner which business is being conducted. The online airline reservation has rendered it as the mandatory requirement for airlines to be in business. New comers to the industries have caused upsets to existing players. The emergence of China and India economies has created drastically low price competition. Multi-national companies in the US in order to stay competitive in the global market are out-sourcing their manufacturing to China and services to India. Life in modern organisations is no longer what it was during our parents' generation. Today, companies' business models ought to be reviewed at least every two to three years.

Change is all around us and moves at a dizzying pace. In the late 2000's oil prices slipped from 150 USD/gallon to less than 40 USD in a period of about six months. The Dow Jones has shown in this same time period that it can swing by 1,000 points in a day, leaving many investors in the red. Over the past few years, the world order has also been disrupted by terrorism, which has become a very real threat to global peace and stability after the Sept 11 attack. Even India an emerging economy was not spared with the Mumbai terrorist attack in November 2008 on the guests of luxurious hotels. Companies cannot take security and safety for granted. Change is the order of the day.

Thanks to the Internet, we also live in an immensely interconnected world. Customers become more sophisticated as they can access the Internet for information and choices with one click of the button.

One of Welch's great contributions is the way he approached the topic of change. From his first days in the CEO's office, he recognised that change was not only inevitable, but also sorely needed. In the late 1970s and early 1980s, most business leaders had little appetite for change. Even a weak economy and the threat of new global competitors were not enough to shake up most CEOs. Welch not only recognised the need for change, he saw the need for radical change, and then set out to turn the company and its century-old traditions upside down. For example, Welch knew that manufacturing alone would not deliver the growth he sought. As a result, he embarked on an ambitious plan to make service the centrepiece of GE's growth engine. In 2000, service accounted for more than 70 percent of GE's revenues.

At GE, employees are urged to think of change as an opportunity and not a threat. In the last year at the helm, Welch explained that, "predicting is not what it is all about. It is being adaptive. It is not about the precision." Welch also said that change is in the genes of every GE employee: "We breathe in our blood every day, now is the time to change the game." Welch preached on change at Crotonville and used other parts of the operating system to drive change throughout the company.

Changes also bring about opportunities. More millionaires are made during bad times than good. If you keep doing the same thing, nothing changes. This is why it is found that 66% of the companies that retain the same board of directors in a crisis failed.

Principle No. 89

The business that considers itself immune to changes will soon find itself immune to business. (Romans 12:3 Do not think of yourself more highly than you ought.)

Managers should never fall into the common mindset trap that their business is immobile and immune to changes. They often extrapolate past trends to forecast future growth. Changes in the competitive context can render these forecasts irrelevant, but managers are often slow to see this disparity. The staff may lapse in complacency adopting lethal attitudes of ignorance and sloppiness – we do not know and do not care. Firestone's managers knew radials lasted twice as long as the existing tires, but still forecast growth for its obsolete products. Its executives also delayed restructuring redundant factories to protect the interests of its employees and host communities. Consequently, Firestone collapsed in year 2000, as it could not withstand worldwide lawsuits on its tire recall.

Wang Computers' corporate DNA was word processing and could not switch to personal computers. Wang Computers' death knell was sounded by Lotus 123 and subsequently by Microsoft. Many of the dotcom companies with their non-viable business models also met their demise when the NASDAQ collapsed in 2000.

High-tech leaders such as Cisco and Siebel may have fallen into the same trap when demand for information technology slowed. Subsequently, CISCO had no choice but to downsize. In the early 1980s, Management Science America (MSA) thought that being the undisputed leader in financial application software in the mainframe, it could venture into Peachtree, the personal computer software. Unfortunately, MSA was badly hurt by this venture, which was subsequently sold out to Dun & Bradstreet.

A clear focus on only a single competitor can distort and limit the management's peripheral vision. Compaq's focus on IBM kept its managers from quickly recognising the enormous threat posed by low-cost clone makers such as Dell. The National Westminster executives' focus on Barclays reinforced the bank's ill-fated strategy of global diversification.

A single-minded focus on market share can also give a false sense of security. For example, Swedish manufacturer SKF led the global ball-bearing industry in market share for much of the twentieth century. However, its dominance was threatened by Japanese competitors, SKF's management responded with aggressive capital spending and marketing in a bid to win share. Its managers' strict focus on market share sidetracked its attention on profits and led them to undertake marginal and unprofitable businesses. A fundamental rethinking of its strategy to pursue profitable segments might have proved to be a better option.

Many construction companies in Singapore fell into the same trap of preoccupation with market share and landed in trouble. The listed group Van Der Horst secured many power generation jobs and contracts but was unable to make a profit out of them. In the early 1980s, some fire protection companies, like United Kingdom's Thorn Emi as well as the Australian based company Wormald International got into financial difficulties when they pursued a wrong market strategy. They were under the erroneous notion that they could push for greater market shares through the acquisition of more projects at low margins. Subsequently, Tyco Laboratory, US acquired Thorn Emi and Wormald International when they were unable to deliver their contractual obligations.

The difficulties posed by changes are even more challenging for small businesses as they have inadequate financial resources, limited pool of professional managers and experience to call upon. Many dare not take risks or deviate from their past practices for fear of making mistakes or facing adverse financial consequences. Therefore, companies are unwilling to face up to change until it is inevitable. By then it is often too late. Instead of willingly embracing change with enthusiasm, it is forced upon them. This is usually less palatable and more detrimental as there is no other option available.

The Bible also advised against the proud who refuse to change. In Romans 12:3, ..Do not think of yourself more highly than you ought, but rather think of yourself with sober judgment, in accordance with the measure of faith God has given you.

Most of the long-lived companies displayed anticipation and desire for change at least once during their lives. Frequently, this opportunity was born out of a crisis and other challenges in the market environment such as trade restrictions, emergence of new competitor, consumer changes in demands and technology. These successful and long-lived companies seemed to have an uncanny ability to be able to anticipate changes, identify crises and benefit from them.

Principle No. 90

A healthy culture is the immunity of a healthy organisation. (1 Corinthians 16:15, Isaiah 7:9, Roman 10:9, Colossians 1:21-23 – "If you do not stand firm in your faith, you will not stand at all.")

When used as a long-term basis, surgery, antibiotics and vaccinations used to combat diseases may actually depress the immune system. And with increased concerns about the perils of vaccination and antibiotic resistant organisms, the boosting of the immune system is the ultimate solution.

On the other end of the spectrum, consumption of natural foods and nutrients such as fruits, vegetables as well as exercising do serve to strengthen the immune system and restoring health. In the corporate context, its immune system is the corporate culture. This is a natural healing system for companies. The corporate equivalence of surgery and drugs administration is downsizing and restructuring. These measures are not only unnatural but they also create negative side effects such as low morale. Hence, they cannot sustain the long-term health of companies. Only a strong corporate culture can ensure their long-term health.

In the spiritual context, faith is our immune system. A strong, unshakeable faith is our immunity to false prophecies, lies, and the devil himself. Paul tells us in the book of 1 Corinthians: "Be on your guard; stand firm in the faith; be men of courage; be strong." Our faith is our foundation. We need to make sure we strengthen our faith, because if we don't, it is as good as having no faith at all. "If you do not stand firm in your faith, you will not stand at all." Our faith is crucial in our lives as it is our way to heaven. Romans 10:9 reads: "That if you confess with your mouth, "Jesus is Lord," and believe in your heart that God raised him from the dead, you will be saved." This is our ultimate solution: to believe in Jesus, whom God sent. "Once you were alienated from God and were enemies in your minds because of your evil behavior. But now he has reconciled you by Christ's physical body through death to present you holy in his sight, without blemish and free from accusation—if you continue in your faith, established and firm, not moved from the hope held out in the gospel."

In the foreword to Arie de Geus's The Living Company, Peter Senge (1997) commented: "Most large, apparently successful corporations are profoundly unhealthy." It appears that we are all still learning how to build a healthy company. Corporate culture has a big impact on the state of the health of the company.

Corporate culture is the behavioural pattern and group norm of a set of people developed over time. These group norms are not just merely endeared as repetitive group behavioural patterns but also embrace those actions, which are unconsciously reinforced by everybody in the organisation. Corporate culture is about implicit shared values among a group of people – it is about what is important, what is good and what is right. Usually, these values are consistent with the group norms. The culture can be thought of as the genes of the company. The culture guides the firm's people as they continuously encounter familiar or new situations. In this very competitive era, companies need to re-wire their corporate brains quickly to generate new neurons to effectively handle the rapid changes in the marketplace. The strong corporate culture acts as an immune system for the company, pre-empting and killing off viruses that try to attack the corporate body.

A dysfunctional corporate culture can severely damage even a strong company. That is what happened at Xerox. It was very successful in the 1960s and 1970s. The office copier became the most profitable product in US business history. However it became arrogant and insular. It centralised decision making, discouraged experimentation and displayed little tolerance for initiative. The market landscape changed dramatically in the late 1970s and 1980s, with changes in the copier business brought forth by the Japanese manufacturers. Within a short span of six years, Xerox's market share dwindled from 82 percent to 40 percent. Having first developed the personal computer at Palo Alto Research Centre, it also failed to exploit this remarkable invention. Instead companies like Apple Computer were able to capitalise on its best ideas.

According to one school of thought, getting rid of 10 to 20 percent of the worst performing employees automatically refreshes the survivors who become healthier. This is the flying geese fallacy. If 100 geese are flying against the oncoming wind, culling 20 will not enable the remaining 80 to fly any faster. The problem is the prevailing wind and not the efforts and abilities of the geese. Talented individuals cannot contribute to their full potential in a dysfunctional corporate culture. It will only stifle initiative and limit achievement. No amount of training to improve skills and competencies will overcome this barrier. Just as 100 geese will all fly faster with the aid of the favourable wind direction, so individuals will perform best in a culturally healthy organisation. The organisational setting and climate have critical impact on individual and group performance. The healthy culture facilitates the nurturing of healthy organisation. In an unhygienic environment, it is very difficult to stay clinically clean. In other words, geese fly better when they are headed in the same direction as the wind.

If you have a healthy corporate culture in place, its acts like a vaccination or booster shot during bad times. It triggers off a positive reaction in the corporate immune system and people in the company bond together in an effective manner to combat the viral threat.

Principle No. 91

Everybody wants to go to heaven, nobody wants to die. Everybody wants to succeed, nobody wants to fail. (Romans 5:3-5, Hebrews 10:36, James 1:12 – "Blessed is the man who perseveres under trial, because when he has stood the test, he will receive the crown of life that God has promised to those who love him.")

Today's business environment is very competitive and fraught with many challenges. Nonetheless, failure is an inevitable step to success. The key to corporate success is learning to fail faster than your competitor and not to repeat the failures. Failure is not the worst thing in the world. The worst is not trying.

The famous inventor Thomas Edison is a classic illustration of the need to fail in order to succeed. He performed several thousand experiments before finally discovering the right filament to be used in the light bulb. He was ridiculed by a university professor who said: "Thomas, don't be a fool, light does not come from wire, it comes from fire." Fire was the norm of providing light in those days. Nevertheless, Edison persevered and continued relentlessly with his experiments using wires. He ultimately found the right filament shortly after. Many of life's failures were men who did not realise how close they were to success at the point when they gave up.

When Edison was interviewed by a reporter on his success, he was asked: "Sir, how did you persevere despite thousands of failure? Edison's reply was that it was not a few thousand times of failure but rather a few thousand steps to the right solution. Edison taught us that genius was 1 percent inspiration and 99 percent perspiration. He later became the founder of modern day General Electric (US).

It is a given that, as sinners, we fail...a lot. But we cannot let our sins stand between us and our God. God already provided us a way, didn't he? What we have to do for ourselves is walk in that way. If we stumble, we get back on our feet and keep walking. In our walk with Jesus, we need to persevere, despite our sins. Our failures, sufferings, and sins, are what builds our character. "Not only so, but we also rejoice in our sufferings, because we know that suffering produces perseverance; perseverance, character; and character, hope. And hope does not disappoint us, because God has poured out his love into our hearts by the Holy Spirit, whom he has given us."

Perseverance amidst suffering is what keeps our faith strong. In the book of Hebrews, it is written: "You need to persevere so that when you have done the will of God, you will receive what he has promised." James tells us: "Blessed is the man who perseveres under trial, because when he has stood the test, he will receive the crown of life that God has promised to those who love him."

Henry Ford went bankrupt a few times trying to automate the motor vehicle. Walt Disney went bankrupt in his first business endeavour, but died one of the richest men in the United States. Sadly, the corporate culture of many modern corporations does not permit failure, not to mention embracing or even tolerating it.

Roberto Goizueta, the former CEO of Coca-Cola in 1995 said: "We became uncompetitive by not being tolerant of mistakes. The moment you let avoiding failure become your motivator, you are down the path of inactivity. You can stumble only if you are moving." Robert Goizueta was credited with the transformation of Coca-Cola into a soft drink giant.

Yet, many founders of modern day successful corporations went through numerous failures. Bill Gates was frank in his admission of mistakes. He said: "Believe me, we know a lot about failures at Microsoft. The first Microsoft spreadsheet flopped. So did the first database. So did the OS/2 operating system. Other failures included an office machine product and TV-style Internet shows." But Gates claimed that the lessons from many of the failures paid off in later years as product winners.

Henry Ford (1863 – 1947) suffered five bankruptcies before succeeding with the Model T cars. He was the founder of Ford Motor Company and he said: "One who fears failure limits his worth." Singapore's distinguished entrepreneur, Sim Wong Hoo's business idea of Sound Blaster failed in Singapore but subsequently succeeded in the United States. The previous king of computing, Thomas Watson of IBM remarked: "That's where success is – on the far side of failure." Stan Shih, CEO of Taiwan-based Acer said that he was prepared to write off the loss as tuition fees for the manager if he has taken an intelligent risk and made a costly mistake. The presence of thoughtful mistakes suggests that people are experimenting and trying new ideas.

This is why somebody said "Failure is the mother of success."

Principle No. 92

Egotism is the anaesthesia that dulls the business sense. (Proverbs 16:5, Isaiah 13:11, Psalm 25:9, Psalm 149:4 – "The Lord detests all the proud of heart. Be sure of this: They will not go unpunished.")

In the Bible it is written: "Pride goeth before destruction and a haughty spirit before a fall." Pride can lead to a sense of complacency with the status quo and dull the management's motivation to change. It also gives them a false sense of superiority that they have "arrived," that is they have found the effective formula for competing, and winning. Hence, there is no need for better alternatives, and they remain haughty even when the environment shifts. For most sick companies, the disease is not technical competence but egotism or arrogance.

On January 12 1998, a beaming Eckhard Pfeiffer graced the cover of Forbes magazine as the CEO of Compaq, which Forbes editors had named Company of the Year. One year and four months later, he was asked to resign by Compaq's board of directors.

The Compaq's case is not an isolated example. Of the seven companies that Forbes has chosen for the honour since 1996, four have under performed the relevant industry stock index by at least 10 percent, three replaced their CEO before their retirement age, and another three have either been acquired by or merged with others.

Successes can lead to an ego trap if companies are not careful. As soon as any company had been praised in the popular magazine or literature as excellent or exemplary, it began to deteriorate. The long period of prosperity, coupled with low inflation during the Asian miracle era, lulled and drugged businesses and consumers into a false sense of security and euphoria. As credit was readily available, then businesses and consumers borrowed to the hilt to feed the frenzy of business activities, as investments, assets and stock prices soared. When the Asian currencies crashed in 1997/98, these businesses and consumers were caught in ballooning debts and unable to extricate themselves. We are seeing the same old scenario happening now the whole world in 2008 with one major institution after another start to collapse. Yet, barely a year ago, all these institutions were boasting of its strong financial status.

Many big companies let success go to their head. They have the illusion that they are invincible, still being number one when actually they have already lost that position. These successful companies began to pride themselves as the "Know-all", and have the right answers to everything.

Ultimately, this is always because there is no right answer for everything and no one knows all. If you deal with contemporary art, you will learn that there are many answers and some of them are right and wrong at the same time. WorldCom's founder Bernie Ebbers once remarked: "The thing that has helped me personally is that I don't understand a lot of what goes on in this industry." This is a symbol of corporate arrogance. Former President of US, Bill Clinton called Bernie Ebbers 'the symbol of 21st century America.' Bernie was disgraced in the financial scandal. Some people called Iaccoca, the arrogant turnaround Chairman of Chrysler: "I Am Chairman Of Chrysler Always". Lee Iaccoca who turned around Chrysler in the 1980s was also blamed for the company's downfall and eventual sale to the German company Daimler in the 1990s.

"The Lord detests all the proud of heart. Be sure of this: They will not go unpunished." It is clear in the Bible that pride and arrogance have no room in Jesus' Kingdom. "He does not answer when men cry out because of the arrogance of the wicked. Indeed, God does not listen to their empty plea; the Almighty pays no attention to it." The Lord declares: "I will punish the world for its evil, the wicked for their sins. I will put an end to the arrogance of the haughty and will humble the pride of the ruthless." The proud and the arrogant will be brought and struck down by the Lord. It is in this light that we should be embraced in nothing but humility; humble ourselves even in our successes. It is the humble that God favours and blesses. "He guides the humble in what is right and teaches them his way." "For the LORD takes delight in his people; he crowns the humble with salvation."

Good times often make us forget the fundamentals. Warm flesh covers and conceals the bones underneath. Today, when the intensity of competition is cutting us to the bone, we need to wake up to the cold realities of the real world.

Thus, when euphoria soars, the company must exercise even more care and not to fall into the ego trap. This can cause the companies to become over-zealous in accomplishing its corporate expansionary objectives and impair their independence. The CEO's ego-driven acquisition was justified with fanciful labelling such as "Synergy" and "Growth". These can degenerate into corporate bulimia through over-leveraging, resulting in massive losses and bruised egos. This is why somebody said, "Ego equals time to go." The very instance that you think you are good, you are dead.

Principle No. 93

Quickly cull the infected birds to rid of bird flu. Quickly admit your mistakes to avert their impact. (Proverbs 28:13 – "He who conceals his sins does not prosper, but whoever confesses and renounces them finds mercy.")

When the bird flu hit Asian poultry farms in 2004, some authorities try to deny and cover up the problem. The result was disastrous as the bird flu quickly spread across the whole world. The aftermath was bad publicity and criticisms of the authorities concerned. Similarly for CEOs, the handling of damage control is crucial. They need to admit they have made mistakes so that the situations can be quickly rectified, thereby limiting the damage. It takes a lot of humility, boldness and guts to admit that one is wrong. Many CEOs have the tendency to behave like gods and do not wish to admit their human fallibility. After all to err is human.

We sometimes overlook the fact that our God is an all-loving, forgiving and just God. We try to justify and cover up for our sins in vain, worse, commit even bigger sins - when all he asks from us is to admit to our faults, come to Him and repent. It is written in the Bible that we shouldn't cover up for our sins, rather, we should just tell God about it and ask for his forgiveness. "He who conceals his sins does not prosper, but whoever confesses and renounces them finds mercy."

Many businesses also fail because the founders, CEOs or senior management are too proud to take the advice, feedback or suggestion of the customers and staff. They do not admit their errors and behave in deity-like manners. They would rather that their companies sink than to lose face.

When a CEO admits a mistake, apologises and takes steps to correct the mistakes, it is a demonstration of maturity and respect for his staff and customers. His staff will reverse the CEO as only human, capable of making failures and mistakes like everyone else. People can see clearly that there is justice and the mistakes are not swept under the carpet and will not be repeated. The healing process, reconciliation and corrective actions can only take place when the mistake is admitted. The CEO who admits his mistake will command more respect and trust from his people.

Making mistakes should be a normal part of corporate dynamics. CEOs have to frequently make decisions based on limited information or wrong feedback. We may overlook the threats of competition or underestimate the risks of the projects. If you have not made any mistakes, it is indicative that you are not trying hard enough. By admitting your mistakes, it can limit their potential damage or adverse consequences.

People are far more forgiving than we can imagine. The admission of a mistake also seems to humanise the relationship. However, people are less forgiving if the mistakes are repeated and there is a lack of competency on the part of the management.

Michael Dell, the founder of Dell Computer was a student of business history and knew the danger of some of tech's legendary figures, which lost their way by refusing to admit mistakes. He cites Digital Equipment Corp's Ken Olsen as one who stuck with his strategy until the market passed him by. Unlike its rivals, Dell is quick to pull the plug on disappointing new ventures. In the mid-2000's, despite a year of work and extensive news coverage, Michael Dell stopped a plan to put e-commerce kiosks in Sears stores after just four were installed. Instead, the kiosks were placed in public areas like the malls.

He also scrapped a plan to enter the mobile phone market just six months after hiring a top executive from Motorola Inc. to head it. He decided the prospects were not bright enough to mitigate the high costs of entry. In year 2000, Dell also wrote off its only major acquisition, a storage-technology company which was bought in a year earlier for $340 million. Dell backed out of the high-end storage business because it decided its technology was not ready for the market.

It is a humble attitude, not just a business model. At other industry giants, the CEO might have shrugged off personal criticisms. Not at Dell. Michael Dell focused on the complaints against him personally. Within a week, Michael Dell faced his top managers and offered a frank self-critique, acknowledging that he is very shy and that made him appear aloof and unapproachable. Days later, he began showing a videotape of this talk to several thousand of his staff, admitting his mistakes and promising to be less detached.

It is not possible to avoid mistakes. Contrary to the poor leader, a good leader will admit his mistakes, apologise and take corrective actions. A great leader will not only admit the mistake, apologise, and take corrective actions but will never make the same mistake again.

Worry about saving money rather than saving the face.

Principle No. 94

Turnaround CEOs need to learn to eat humble pie too. (Deuteronomy 8:2-3,5 - "Remember how the Lord your God led you all the way in the desert these forty years, to humble you and to test you in order to know what was in your heart, whether or not you would keep his commands.")

In the 1980s and 1990s, CEOs such as Jack Welch, Percy Bernevik and Lee Iaccocoa were household corporate names for corporate turnaround. Jack Welch created the modern General Electric (US) while Percy Bernevik created the Swiss-Swedish engineering conglomerate ABB Group. Lee Iacocca turned around Chrysler in 1980s. All were strong and articulate leaders who demonstrated their abilities to revitalise businesses.

However, these CEOs were also vulnerable mortal beings and were subsequently brought down from their pedestals. Welch went through a messy divorce. The press has revealed a list of Welch's retirement perks from GE, which are deemed to be extravagant. In addition, GE has been scrutinised for its accounting methods and its share price slumped at peak of US $60 in year 2000 to less than half during the investigation. Mr. Bernevik was forced to return some of his retirement pay and ABB was on the brink of collapse.

While Lee Iacocca did the fabled turnaround of Chrysler, there were some questions as to how much was due to being fixed operationally and how much was the taxpayer's gift. Later, with fanfare, Mr. Iacocca took over Koo Koo Roo, a small and troubled chain of chicken restaurants, but did not stay long. The company went belly up. Furthermore, Chrysler under Lee Iaccoca got into financial trouble again in early 1990s.

Other turnaround CEOs had to be humbled too. Al Dunlap pulled a dramatic financial improvement for Scott Paper, partly due to cost cutting and partly due to a lucky upward swing in commodity prices. Unfortunately, he destroyed Sunbeam in his next assignment. Sanford Sigiloff nicknamed himself "Ming the Merciless". He took over Wickes after its record-setting bankruptcy, shuffled off assets, sacked some people and pronounced victory. Wickes was primarily a lumber and home supplies company. Two of the incompetent executives Sanford eliminated started a new business, Home Depot.

The people of Israel experienced the same thing when they were humbled by God. After being brought out of Egypt, God had to make sure that all of them will remain faithful and obedient to him. God did a preventive measure and humbled them before they can even boast of their successes. "Remember how the Lord your God led you all the way in the desert these forty years, to humble you and to test you in order to know what was in your heart, whether or not you would keep his commands. He humbled you, causing you to hunger and then feeding you with manna, which neither you nor your fathers had known, to teach you that man does not live on bread alone but on every word that comes from the mouth of the Lord."

Through facing humility, we are disciplined. Just like the many turnaround CEOs, they needed to be disciplined and pulled back down to earth. But we must not take this as a bad thing, rather an act of concern and love. The verse from the book of Deuteronomy continues: "Know then in your heart that as a man disciplines his son, so the Lord your God disciplines you."

The truth about being humble is evident throughout the world. Hillary Clinton was appointed to Secretary of State in the Obama administration. This would not have been an opportunity for her if she had been unable to accept that Obama was the clear leader during the primary race. If she had not stepped down and turned to support her previous rival, he would not have been able to consider her for this esteemed position in American government. That she was humble and changed her position from one of opponent to ally allowed her to be open to the beneficial change that came later with her invitation to this prestigious appointment

All personalities thrive on change. Change is great when things are bad but lethal when times are better. They are unable to sustain changes when success gets into their heads. This is why a Chinese entrepreneur who owns a huge conglomerate arrogantly once said: "I treat the turnaround managers like chickens, for one day, when the companies turn around, I would have to chop off their heads like chickens." This Chinese entrepreneur is ruthless and turnaround managers will find it difficult working for him. However, he found that many of these turnaround managers were unsuccessful in growing the business as they continued to adopt the same management style and approach, after the initial turnaround. Hence, the entrepreneur discovered that after successful turnaround, he needed to engage managers with relevant temperament and management style for growing the business. In this way, he will avoid dysfunctionality from setting in.

Studies also indicated that most turnaround situations do not succeed. Usually, the turnaround managers are brought in too late when the companies are already terminally ill. In some cases, the turnaround managers are not given the full autonomy to act. Hence the first lesson that the turnaround managers have to learn is humility. For, they should expect failures as one of the possible outcomes. They must be courageous and humble enough to accept and learn from them.

Principle No. 95

The empires of the global market are the empires of the mind. (Proverbs chapter 23: 7, "As a man thinketh in his heart, so he is.")

The state of the mind is increasingly important in the modern corporate world. If you conquer the customers' minds, you conquer their loyalty and business. To conquer the customers' minds, you need to win the perception game. Perception is reality.

In this very competitive era, we are inundated by numerous brands for every product. What has changed in business over the years is the rapid proliferation of product choices and competition in every industry. It has been estimated that there are 1 million SKUs (standard stocking units) in United States. An average supermarket has 40,000 SKUs. An average family gets 80 to 85 percent of its needs from 150 SKUs. Many SKUs will be ignored. What used to be national markets with local companies competing for business has become a global market with everyone competing for the same pie. It is really the battle of the mindset to position your brand as Number 1 or 2 in the customers' minds. For most customers, they do not bother or cannot remember too many brands.

Conquering the mindsets of the staff is equally important. Hence, the emphasis is on building a strong corporate culture that can foster a unity in the mindset for all the staff.

The Bible says: "Whatever a man thinketh, so is he." If you can change your thinking, you can change your life. You will land up where you think you will be. The mind is the "taxi" of your life. It literally takes you to where you want to get to. If you want to go on the expressway of excellence, you think excellence. You want to go to the valley of depression, you think of depressing things. Everything starts with what you think. What you put in your mind, will lead you to the direction that you eventually head towards. The difference between a successful and unsuccessful person is the way he thinks. So what you think determines who you are and who you are determines what you think. People say that they cannot control their thinking. This is not true. It is possible to change your thinking. The first thing is to change yourself.

The globalizing economy has had a tremendous influence on firms, forcing them to adopt new mindsets. Firms have to face global competition even from countries which are far away. Firms need to pursue new realities and cannot continue to cope with competition using the managerial philosophy of the past. The mindset of reliance on domestic markets tend to limit one's view in the global market. The embrace of a global mindset is competitive in understanding challenges of the new millennium.

An example of global mindset is Coca-Cola. Before Goizueta took over Coca-Cola, it only dominated 35 percent of the US soft-drink market. The market was perceived as mature and seeing incremental market share was very expensive. In the 1980s, Goizueta did not accept this. He told his senior management that the average per-capita daily consumption of drinks by the world's 4.4 billion people was 64 ounces and the Coca-Cola's share of this was only 2 ounces. Coca-Cola's enemy was not PepsiCo but plain water, coffee, tea and other alternative beverages. Goizueta redefined the market to be bigger than his managers' mindset. He subsequently led Coca-Cola from a defensive market leader to be the greatest market value creator.

The new global mindset requires the managers to master dynamics not only of key markets, ranging from the background of a country to its current economic situation. They must also have global and proactive thinking across multiple markets.

Many corporations haven't learned that the boundaries of their market have grown and they are being left behind. For example, the US automotive industry cannot compete as they cannot move past the US border, because they have tied themselves too closely to the high costs of unions, limiting them to the US. Even when the US automakers are near-death, the union insisted on high wages – dramatically high when compared to Japanese manufacturers in US. The lesson is if you want to go global and compete against global competitors, you need to have the right mindset. You conquer the staff's and customers' minds, you conquer the market in the future.

Principle No. 96

Good attitudes are the nutrients of corporate success. (Philippians 2:4-11 – "Your attitude should be the same as that of Christ Jesus")

It is often said that "the difference between heaven and hell is not the altitude but the attitude." Throughout the corporate turnaround process, small changes in the staff's attitude are imperative.

Attitude makes a difference in the success and failure of countries. Why are countries with limited land and natural resources such as Singapore, Japan and Switzerland so successful whereas some with huge land and natural resources such as Indonesia, Eastern Europe remain poor? It is not even the age. The present success of a country has little co-relation with its vintage of long history. For example, countries like China, Egypt and India have more than 2,000 years in history and yet they are considered poor. Countries such as United States, Australia, and Singapore have less than 200 years in history but have attained one of the highest per capita in the world. Neither is success attributed to the intellectual capabilities of the country's population. Vietnam, which has one of the highest tertiary-educated population bases, is one of the world's poorest countries.

One significant difference is in the attitude. Successful countries tend to have an attitude characterised by high integrity, excellent leadership, good work ethics, respect for law and order and a willingness to work hard. It is not that nature is especially tough on the poor countries, but what is important is the nurturing of right attitudes for success.

People's attitudes toward their companies can mean the difference between the organisation's success and failure. Highly motivated and performance oriented people can be very constructive and beneficial for the company. On the other hand, the presence of poor and negative attitude will certainly lead to failure. Individual values and attitudes can be observed by watching how employees treat their customers, peers and company.

An individual's attitude will affect his behaviour and performance. When shared, his feelings such manifestations, whatever positive or negative in turn "rub off' and affect the behaviour and performance of others around him. Productivity suffers when negative attitudes are perpetuated over a long period of time.

Likewise, in serving Jesus or basically, in living our lives, we must have a good, positive attitude; an attitude pleasing to the Lord – of true heart, love, compassion and humility. We must have an attitude like Jesus. Philippians chapter 2 lists what having an attitude like Jesus is like and how we should follow his example. The verses read: "Your attitude should be the same as that of Christ Jesus: Who, being in very nature God, did not consider equality with God something to be grasped, but made himself nothing, taking the very nature of a servant, being made in human likeness. And being found in appearance as a man, he humbled himself and became obedient to death— even death on a cross!" Jesus had the best attitude, even in the face of death.

Because of Jesus' great attitude, God gave him the rewards that he deserved. "God exalted him to the highest place and gave him the name that is above every name, that at the name of Jesus every knee should bow, in heaven and on earth and under the earth, and every tongue confess that Jesus Christ is Lord, to the glory of God the Father." Surely we too will be rewarded if we would imitate Christ with the right motives and the right heart.

Southwest Airlines' Herb Kelleher would rank good attitude above other skills. If he is given a choice between a person who has more experience, more education or more expertise, and someone who has the right attitude, he will give preference to the latter. He does not want to have people who have lousy attitude. He notes that attitude is the one thing you will find difficult to change. On the other hand, skills you can be taught later.

Cultivating a positive attitude toward change is critical because of the impending danger of complacency ignoring, external warning signs and the risk of resistance. As the saying does, "Nothing kills like success." Employees come to realise that change is no longer a temporary phenomenon but a permanent aspect of their organisation. Consequently, they are less likely to resist change. Indeed, the first two major challenges for a company in the process of change are motivating people to function effectively in an unpredictable environment and managing the opposing dynamics of resistance. As Barnevik pointed out: "It is rather traumatic to make this sort of move (the merger of ASEA and BBC). It takes a lot of determination, a lot of perseverance, because it is always easier to be against something than to be for something. We are conservative animals, we like the past, we like the historical."

A good attitude is clearly noticeable and easily observed. It is visible in the manner employees treat the customers and staff. The choice of words used in communication can convey the level of attitudinal maturity. Attitude determines how the companies cope with crisis. When the staff adopt attitude when things get tough, the tough gets the going, the company is one likely to succeed in overcoming its hard times. However, if the staff's attitude is that the company's business is none of their business, then chances are that such company will find it difficult to work out its difficulties. This is because the staff is concern about their own self-interests.

Medical science has already confirmed that the state of attitude of cancer patients can make a big difference in the survival rate among these patients. Attitudes can cause emotional reaction, which can affect our immune, nervous and circulatory system. They can impact our risk of sustaining accidents and injuries. A strong positive attitude will create corporate successes more than any other turnaround.

Boost corporate health by embracing positive mindset. (Matthew 12:33 – "Make a tree good and its fruit will be good, or make a tree bad and its fruit will be bad.")

Wayne Dyer an American psychotherapist and author said, "You can set yourself up to be sick or you can choose to stay well." In medical science, it is called psychosomatic. The mental health of the person can affect his physical health too. This is why doctors use placebo on some patients. Placebo is a medicine, which has no physiological functions but may benefit the patient psychologically. Hypnosis is also used extensively in the medical fields and is a trance-like mental state induced in a cooperative subject by suggestions.

Medical science has generally found that in psychosomatic ailments, a person's mental attitude, mindset and psyche can have a tremendous impact on his physical health. When your mindset is negative, you may feel chronically depressed and hopeless, which will drive the immune system into a "self-destructive" mode where viruses can easily establish a foothold. You are what you think. We are primarily mental rather than physical beings.

Likewise, whatever we make of something, that is what's going to come out. We should set the tone. "Make a tree good and its fruit will be good, or make a tree bad and its fruit will be bad…" If we encourage, motivate the staff and treat them well, just like the good tree mentioned in the book of Matthew, the outcome of their work and attitude in the workplace will be good too. However, if we fill them with pessimism, and bad, negative attitudes, it will reflect in their output and attitude in the workplace as well.

This is the problem. Sick companies have negative mindsets. It may be a case of bad attitude, negativism and pessimism towards something? These negative mindsets can be easily detected when you communicate with the staff.

Particularly, in a sick company, the staff tends to wallow in self-pity, licking their own wounds or playing the game of shame and blame. They may place blame on everything conceivable – the competition is too intense, the customers are too demanding, the former bosses did not do a good job and so on. A suitable description would be: "We have met the enemies and they are us."

To combat negative mindset, one must be aware of its existence, to eradicate this, it is best to keep busy, to channel the staff's energy into something positive. Small changes in the staff's mindset can go a long way in building a healthy corporate culture. You should recognise, commend and celebrate every little success. Once people start to achieve success, it spurs them on to attain greater success. Credit should be accorded to staff when due, through public announcements, awarding certificates of appreciation and plaques, etc. Such little gestures and encouragement produce the glue that cements the fabric of corporate culture.

The wisdom of avoiding a negative mindset was clearly illustrated by the graceful exit from the 2008 American Presidential race by John McCain. That the American economy was already suffering was obvious by November 2008, when the election was held. When making the humble and self-sacrificing decision to gracefully admit defeat to his opponent, Barak Obama, Senator John McCain was careful to address the fact that he wanted no dissent and only unity between his supporters and the new administration in the coming years. His eloquent words and graceful defeat set a conciliatory tone for the rest of the country to follow. However, if he had stirred resentment, it is possible that the new administration would be facing much more opposition coming into the office in January. And that would have been dysfunctional for all concerned.

Companies have a tendency to pursue programmes for updating their staff's skills and knowledge without spending much effort in developing their mental attitudes. Investments in changing people's mental attitude are also crucial.

Perhaps, we have searched at the wrong places for the answers. Sometimes, there is a high probability that the disease is not caused by the external viruses and pathogens, but from within us through our thoughts and feelings. Similarly for corporations, their greatest enemies could be their enormous mindset.

Principle No. 98

Without discipline, the company will perish. (Job 5:17, Proverbs 3:11-12, Proverbs 5:23 – "He will die for lack of discipline, led astray by his own great folly.")

Discipline is an important attribute for a company to bounce back to the pink of health. Discipline in the corporate context refers to the knowledge of what needs to be done and that it is done timely, efficiently and effectively. It is about obtaining results through dealing tenaciously with heartaches and pains posed by the various challenges during its corporate lifespan. It means getting the job done without being bogged down by bureaucracy.

We have to realize that discipline is not a bad thing. On the contrary, it is the lack of discipline that can actually be detrimental, to the individual and to the whole company as well. God takes discipline seriously. As a father disciplines his child, so does God discipline us. We must think of it first as; it is a blessing to be corrected by God. "Blessed is the man whom God corrects; so do not despise the discipline of the Almighty." Secondly, we should think that God disciplines those he loves: "My son, do not despise the Lord's discipline and do not resent his rebuke, because the Lord disciplines those he loves, as a father the son he delights in." Third, lacking discipline is dangerous: "He will die for lack of discipline, led astray by his own great folly."

Of course, management who drives corporate discipline must be disciplined themselves. He has to walk the talk. Employees do not mind working in a disciplined manner but they will take the cues from their bosses.

Jim Collins, the author of *Good to Great, Why Some Companies Make the Leap...and Others Don't* (New York: HarperCollins, 2001) concluded that there was no magic formula to a company's success. He found that successful companies were the result of disciplined employees who acted in a disciplined manner. Successful companies do not need high-profile and charismatic leaders, state-of-the-art technology or even great strategies.

Lou Gerstner of IBM and Larry Bossidy of AlliedSignal stand as models of disciplinarian and self-discipline. Lou Gerstner took over the helm of IBM in 1993 and saved it from financial collapse. When Gerstner retired in 2002, IBM had become a service-oriented company, the envy of the industry. The key to Gerstner's success was that he imposed discipline at all levels of the organisation. Gerstner travelled frequently to understand the customers' needs and prided himself on being personally disciplined. He said IBM had great products, people and reputation but blamed it on the absence of discipline to get things done.

Larry Bossidy was credited with turning around ailing AlliedSignal in 1991, transforming it into one of the world's most admired companies a decade later.

Like Lou Gerstner, Larry Bossidy was shocked at the lack of discipline to execute at AlliedSignal. Being a former employee of GE, he was used to get things done expediently. He was vigilant to drive productivity, operation and talent management. When he retired in 1999, he had steered the AlliedSignal to 31 consecutive quarters of earnings-per share growth of 13 percent or more.

Lee Iaccoca imposed discipline by taking the union head-on. He saved Chrysler then by giving the ultimatum that that if they did not go back to work, he would close down the plants and everybody would be out of job. It worked and Chrysler turnaround in the early 1980s. Unfortunately, by the mid 1980s, Lee lost his discipline in focus and bought into an aviation business creating a financial disaster for Chrysler.

The oldest merchant banking company in England founded in 1762, Barings Bank, would still have survived today if not for the lack of discipline in controlling its overseas' subsidiaries. In February 1995, Barings collapsed because the rogue trader Nick Leeson, a Barings Bank staff based in Singapore lost 1.4 billion US dollars by gambling on the SIMEX with primarily derivative securities. There was no financial limit and discipline imposed on the amount of Nick's trading volumes. Nick Leeson, a young executive, thousands of miles away from the London head office was allowed to gamble away the fortunes of Barings. This was actually the second time Barings had faced bankruptcy, the first case happened in 1890 when a significant amount of investment was lost in South America following the Argentinean revolution. However, Barings was then bailed out by the Bank of England and other London banks. Barings should have learnt from the South American experience and imposed more discipline from its overseas subsidiaries but it did not.

Even in more recent situations, it is clearly evident that undisciplined choices can lead a corporation to failure. Morgan Stanley's collapse is a good example. This major corporation had invested in risky opportunities throughout the boom of the early 2000's – all for the sake of making big returns. However, when the market began its downward spiral, Morgan Stanley found that these risky investments had been very poorly played and discipline in decision making regarding the investment in risky opportunities was mediocre at best. As a result, during a global economic crisis, Morgan Stanley is on the verge of becoming a near-worthless stock and risky investment in its own right.

It is easy to do what is right in the eyes of the market such as maximizing shareholders' returns. Discipline is all it counts when one has to make decisions unpopular which are contrary to conventional market's wisdom. Often times, the company has to be bold and disciplined to invest in the future. It entails taking a few steps back in order to forgo short term growth for future benefits. It is not popular and it takes discipline to do so.

On the other hand, balance is required. The preoccupation with discipline can unwittingly build layers of bureaucracy into the organisation, stifling creativity and entrepreneurial. A culture of discipline, coupled with the right dosages of autonomy and entrepreneurship will create an alchemy for superior performance.

Principle No. 99

Training and development generate endorphins and provide for corporate well-being. (Luke 6:40 – "A student is not above his teacher, but everyone who is fully trained will be like his teacher.")

Training and development are like physical exercises that enable the body to generate endorphins. These are substances produced by the brain that have a similar effect as morphine. Endorphins give a sense of well-being, helping the body to cope with stress and onslaught of other ailments.

Employees need to be motivated so that they can effectively accomplish to their formal job descriptions. Fostering such synergistic behaviour requires not only the existence of the right culture of trust but also training and development. Everyone has untapped potential that can be nurtured under the right environment with appropriate training and development, this is the corporate equivalent of the release of endorphins, creating beneficial and protective elements in the organisation.

Undergoing the right training and development, a company can easily produce a workforce of highly-skilled, fully developed and well-trained professionals. In the Bible, Jesus trained 12 men to be his disciples; letting them work under him and as a result, releasing their full potential. Like Jesus' disciples, employees can become so much more if they go under training as well. Jesus said so himself, that training is of essence and reason: "A student is not above his teacher, but everyone who is fully trained will be like his teacher."

Some managers have the notion that training and development are expensive as trained staff may eventually resign. However, there is a fallacy in such an argument as companies really cannot afford not to train their staff. If you think training is expensive, then try ignorance, which will definitely be more costly. Training and development are not welfare activities. This is why it is said that you need to spend money to make money.

Time is another excuse whenever training and development is mentioned. People do not have the time to attend the training. However, you may actually gain more time through training and development. The timesaving techniques, procedures, ideas, short cuts and skills can save you both time and money in the long run.

Some managers may say that it is empowerment that will unleash the potential of their employees. However, empowerment without proper training is not good enough. You may want to empower the medical students to do a heart surgery. However, it may or may not work. But would you bet your heart on it that it will.

Many corporations have found success in the proper training and empowerment of their employees. Even countries have realized the significance of this combination. In the late 2000's, the Singapore government pumped 600 million dollars into training and development during the global recession. They did this to encourage employers not to fire the staff, but rather take the opportunity during the lull period in business to send staff for training.

Training can help in identifying hidden talents. It can result in consistent quality, provide sharper focus, produce greater efficiency, foster teamwork and increase productivity. Training and development offer more than mere incremental knowledge and learning from the 'expert' instructor. It offers the added advantage of networking and drawing from the experiences gains. When you attend a seminar or event with others of similar interests, you have the added benefit of sharing life experiences with other attendees. The seminar notes or the conference leader may not give you the golden nugget to implement in the workplace. Your best advice may actually come from somebody sitting next to you.

For the training programmes to be effective, it needs to include practical applications and follow-up techniques that will internalise into a habit. Furthermore, it is necessary to build a corporate culture that encourages training and development. This will reap both tangible and intangible rewards

Some companies will invest millions on machinery and equipment and yet fail to invest in their most important assets, their people. For many years, CEOs have been preaching that their people are the key assets but they have given lip service to training and development to boost the value of these key assets. It is timely that they actually practise what they preached and recognise that it is a fact that investment in people will pay dividends. Companies that encourage training and development are providing the best bets for the future because they bet on people.

Principle No. 100

An information system is the backbone and the nervous system of the company. (Job 12:22 - "He reveals the deep things of darkness and brings deep shadows into the light.")

Many senior managers are still ignorant and show little interest in the development of information technology. Unfortunately, this attitude can adversely affect the company's future competitive edge as electronic systems are the platforms for corporate virtual prowess and dominance in the new millenniums.

Today's computer systems are vulnerable to threats such as computer viruses, natural disasters and even terrorists' attacks. The loss of vital data or failure in its computer system can cripple the entire operation of a company. Therefore, management needs to take cognizance of the computer security policies and disaster recovery systems. Poor advice and ignorance may inhibit the management from investing and upgrading of both the company's hardware and software.

Access to worldwide information, organisational data, security and confidentiality are issues, which require comprehensive planning by managers. Failure to understand them will seriously hamper the efficiency of their future decision making.

Information technology is power. It leads to new ways to managing people, communication and competing in the marketplace. The advent of the Internet has accentuated the power of information technology. New industries such as online auction, online trading has mushroomed. The Internet allows for small companies, the "Davids" to compete against the big boys, the "Goliaths". This is something, which was impossible years ago before. The Internet allows direct access to markets which were previously unavailable to smaller players, this has enabled them to compete against the large corporations and multi-nationals. Hence the emergence and birth of the companies such as Amazon.com, AOL, CISCO and Dell Computers, which were unheard of less than twenty years ago.

In the Bible, since there exists no information technology, we can say that information for them is power, especially information from the Lord. Because the people of God relied on the Lord so much, seeking to heed his instructions. This information allows the people to know what they should do, how they should act, or even where they should go.

This information, like IT nowadays, brought people out of darkness. He gives us new insights, new knowledge, bringing us to understanding, to light. "He reveals the deep things of darkness and brings deep shadows into the light." Through this revealing of information also came the revelation of our salvation. How great information that was!

Today, there are many industries such as the banking and the airline industries which would literally collapse if their computerised systems break down. This was the reason for the big scare of the Y2K bug. Fortunately, because of a rapid response and changes in the system, it turned out to be a non-issue.

The use of the computer and the subsequent advent of the internet significantly changed the modes and channels of communication. Distance is no longer a determent. Telecommuting is possible without having to step into the office. Teleworking across the time zones is steadily increasing. The working day no longer has any meaning when communication via e-mail, voice mail, video-conferencing and facsimile transmissions can be sent or received at any time of the day or night, 24 hours per day, 7 days per week, etc.

Information technology has expedited the elimination of the middleman roles. Customers can now easily access the principals and manufacturers directly vice versa, the companies and service providers can source for their customer directly. Therefore, companies in the trading and agency businesses are finding it increasingly difficult to survive in the new technology era..

Your internal company information in the computerised system is like the cream of jewels of your business. So lock them up at all times while you are not using them or they maybe stolen though unauthorized accesses.

Principle No. 101

Be innovative or be in a coma. (Genesis 1:1-31, Isaiah 65:17 – "Behold, I will create new heavens and a new earth. The former things will not be remembered, nor will they come to mind.")

Peter Drucker once said, "Business has only two functions: Marketing and innovation. Marketing and innovation produce results, the rest are cost." Your competitors can fight you on almost every front especially on pricing. Try marketing and innovation as they are the best avenues for differentiating yourselves vis-à-vis your competitors. Management of innovation is probably the most critical and pervasive task facing business and industry today.

God is a fan of innovation, or creating something, even someone new. For each day that he was creating the whole world, each one was innovative. Every day he had a new creation. "And God said, "Let there be light," and there was light... And there was evening, and there was morning—the first day." "And God said, "Let there be an expanse between the waters to separate water from water. So God made the expanse and separated the water under the expanse from the water above it. And it was so God called the expanse "sky." And there was evening, and there was morning—the second day." Up until the 6th day, God was creating new things for us. As a matter of fact, God is still creating up until this very day, and the next, and the next. Imagine if God didn't innovate, how dull and plain our life would be! ""Behold, I will create new heavens and a new earth. The former things will not be remembered, nor will they come to mind."

There is a fundamental contradiction between developing innovation vis-à-vis the path to operational efficiency and strategy to minimize risks. Innovation can be disruptive and is not acceptable for corporations, which promote control and optimization, discourage surprises and do not tolerate experimentations and failures.

The bicycle industry went through a metamorphosis of innovation to survive. In the mid nineteen century, bicycle was the great new innovation. The manufacturers were small, flexible and able to make changes. By 1899, more than 300 manufacturers were listed in the United States alone. Six years later, only twelve remained because of the invention of automobile. After several years, new innovation came into the scene for bicycle – improved in the design, accessories that made it far easier and more comfortable to handle. In the war and the great depression years in the 1930s, bicycle became popular again as bicycle did not use fuel and was much cheaper to run and buy than automobile. As the world got back to normal, the sale of bicycle fell again until 1970s when the oil crisis hit and fuel prices were high. Bicycle had a new lease of life. Then again back to normal in the 1980s and the bicycle sales plummeted again. Then the innovators of the bicycle never gave up. In the 1990s, mountain bicycle became the rage and a major draw for young cyclists and sports enthusiasts. The bicycle became fashionable again.

Yet, an upstart with an innovation that disrupts existing business models can oust out existing market leaders nearly every time – be it Intel Corp, with the microprocessor in the 1970s or steel mill Nucor Corp, with a way to reuse scrap in the 1990s. The lowly transistor, for example killed the vacuum tube, while PCs, once derided as toys, snuffed out minicomputers and currently threaten servers from the likes of Sun Microsystems Inc.

Instead of just turning a new idea or technology into better mousetrap, one way is to transform it into a product that completely changes the game, capturing brand-new customers and thus producing much higher growth. Procter & Gamble Co., for instance, does more than simply offer "new and improved" toothpaste. In 2001, it launched Crest Whitestrips, a home tooth-whitening product that created a new market of 10 million users with nearly $300 million in sales. Hewlett-Packard Co introduced the highly successful inkjet printers, Johnson & Johnson with its angioplasty instruments and portable blood-glucose meters that it acquired.

3M expects 30% of its business to come from new areas and allow its people to spend 15% of their time to do other things apart from their job in order to innovate. 3M was the company that created memo pad patented Post-It which was a major winner.

Unlike the other tech companies, Steve Jobs of Apple Computer has not cut R&D spending despite the slowdown in the tech industry. Apple has invented the iPod (digital music player) and has built on that success with the recent release of the iPhone. Apple has had early success working with the music industry to create its online music store iTunes. Steve believed that there is limited effectiveness for legal actions by the music industry against piracy of music over the Internet. The music industry is based on selling unprotected CDs that can be read on CD players that cannot detect pirated music. The right solution is to compete with the Kazaas (music sharing services) of the world and to beat them. This is what Apple is trying to make happen.

Dell Computers plans to boost sales by turning its focus to screens that can be used both as televisions and computer monitors. This multi-function display is a new emerging category and different from existing television. Dell Computer sells 17-inch, 23-inch, 30-inch and bigger liquid-crystal-display (LCD) screens in the United States and Japan.

To be innovative, one must also be quick. It remains to be seen if Microsoft will win in the year-long bid and retract cycle of a potential Yahoo! purchase. Microsoft may miss their opportunity to add a very lucrative line of business to their portfolio. That the bid price has risen to astronomical heights and that the deal is repeatedly brought back to the table shows that Microsoft is committed to the purchase – to a point. But if they do not make a decision, we may find in 2009 that another corporation is able to snatch Yahoo away from Microsoft simply because they are taking too long to complete the deal.

Innovation is not just about chips and technology. New behaviour and attitudes can be just as effective in innovation for the marketplace. Bill Gates did not discover the software for personal computer nor does Michael Dell invent the personal computer. But both were quick to pick up what others have missed out or done before.

Therefore innovate or be in coma, not making progress and in a state of stupor and near death.

Summary of Process and Issues in Corporate Wellness

The corporate world is a very complex one and issues are not cut and dried. Many issues relate and intermingle with one another and may pervade across the five stages. However, in this book, the issues are pigeon holed to help the readers understand their underlying concepts and principles. Thus the summary of the five-stage to corporate wellness and their related issues is tabled below:

Matrix of the five-stage process and the related issues in corporate wellness

	Preliminary issues	Hard issues	Soft issues
Prevention	Direction Planning	Financial Control	People Talent Management
Diagnosis	Acknowledgement Detection Root cause	Pricing Process Competition	Communication Leadership
Treatment	Execution Focus Cost-cutting	Restructuring Rightsizing Exit	Dysfunction Techniques
Recovery	Timing Customer Inspiration	Marketing Energy Renewal	Ethics Positioning
Strengthening	Foresight Transformation Ego	Reserves Corporate culture Mindset	Development Innovation

The treatment or cure stage emphasises on the hard issues, whereas the healing stages namely, recovery and strengthening stages stress a lot more on the soft issues. Doctors have also found that there is a difference between curing and healing process. Both curing and healing processes are needed in enhancing the corporate wellness. In addition it is noticed that soft issues are primarily human resource-related.

Because of the critical health of the patient-institution, in turnaround situations, making the right decision can be the difference between life and death. You do not have time to refer to text books, seek help or speak to your staff for a variety of reasons such as sensitivity, not knowing where to seek for help etc. At the end of the day, we make decisions based on our intuition and past experiences. For many of us, we may not have encountered crisis before and thus have no past experiences to turn to. However, we can make decisions based on simple secular and spiritual principles. Thus the relevance of this book during this turbulent and tumultuous time, rife with ill corporations and subsequent economic failures.

God created man thus there are spiritual and medical principles to follow. We created companies. Thus running companies require certain spiritual and secular tenets. We can use these principles to guide us in managing companies, particularly in crisis when you have little time to make decisions.

Our companies shall need treatment as far as corporate sickness goes. We ourselves need medication when we fall ill. However, what God had established is never-failing. May the principles in this book help you to find your spot and stand under the mighty foundation of our Lord. God will always be our ultimate turnaround doctor. We can be sure that he'll always be readily available for us, whether it's the ailment of our companies, or our own, we can be sure that we can call on him and ask him to fix us.

In anything and everything, God will be there. His laws stand whether at the heavens or here on earth. Ultimately, we need his truths and decrees to run the best company we can ever run, the best company the world has never seen. As the author and manager of the whole universe, we must trust his written word, the Bible – the best management book we can ever find, ever. "To the Lord your God belong the heavens, even the highest heavens, the earth and everything in it." (Deuteronomy 10:14) To Him be all the glory.

There you are – basic principles in corporate wellness from the spiritual and secular points of views. Keep well.

References:

Advertising Age: Al Ries Your Company Depends on It

Agence France Presse (March 30, 2004), High-tech outsourcing led to 90,000 US jobs in 2003: study

Andrew Gibbons (1996*): The Loyalty Effect: Mentoring, Team Leader Development. Management Development Programmes, Customer Service Development*, United States: Harvard Business School Press

Backman, Michael and Butler, Charlotte (2003): *Big in Asia: 25 Strategies for Business Success,* New York: Palgrave Macmillan.

Baldock, Robert (2000): *The Last Days of the Giants? A Route Map for Big Business Survival*, England: John Wiley & Sons Ltd.

Boulton, Richard E.S; Libert, Barry D and Samek, Steve M. (2000): *Cracking the Value Code: How Successful Businesses Are Creating Wealth in the New Economy*, United States: Harper Business/HarperCollins

CFO Magazine (April 1996), Bureau of Business Research at American International College

Charan, Ram and Tichy, Noel M. (1998): *Every Business Is A Growth Business,* England: John Wiley & Sons Ltd

Dash, Eric and Creswell, Julie (November 2008): Citigroup Pays for a Rush to Risk, New York: New York Times

Davidson, Mike (1995): *The Transformation of Management*, London: Macmillan Press Ltd

Dive, Brian (2002): *The Healthy Organization: A Revolutionary Approach to People and Management,* United States: Kogan Page.

Dive, Brian (2002): The Healthy Organisation, United Kingdom: Kogan Page Ltd.

Dunlap, Albert J. (1996): *Mean Business: How I Save Bad Companies and Make Good Companies Great,* New York: Random House, Inc.

Ehrlich, Henry (1998): *The Wiley Book of Business Quotations,* Canada: John Wiley & Sons, Inc

Ellswort, Richard, R (2002*): Leading With Purpose: The New Corporate Realities,* United States of America: Stanford University Press

Foster, Richard N and Kaplan, Sarah (2001): *Creative Destruction: Why Companies That Are Built To Last Underperform The Market – And How To Successfully Transform Them,* New York: Currency

Gaplin and Henron (1999): The complete Guide to Mergers and Acquisitions

Geus, Arie de (1997): *The Living Company,* United States of America: Longview Publishing Limited

Geus, de Arie and Peter Senge (1997): *The Living Company,* United States: Harvard Business School Press

Gerstner, Louis V (2002), *Who says Elephants Can't Dance? Inside IBM's Historic Turnaround,* United States, HarperBusiness

Gibson, Rowan (1997): *Rethinking the Future: Rethinking Business, Principles, Competition, Control & Complexity, Leadership, Markets and the World.* United States: Nicholas Brealey Publishing Limited

Haigh, Gideon (2003) *Bad Company: The Strange Cult of the CEO,* Australia, Aurum Press

Hamel, Gary (2000*), Leading The Revolution*, United States, Harvard Business School Press

Handy, Charles and Bennis, G, Warren (1990): *The Age of the Unreason,* United States, Harvard Business School Press

Hartman, Amir (2004*): Ruthless Execution: What Business Leaders Do When Their Companies Hit The Wall,* United States of America: Prentice Hall

Harvey-Jones, John (1992): *Trouble Shooter,* London: BBC Books.

Herb Greenberg, "Against the Grain: The Buy-'Em-Up Boondoggle," Fortune (July 22, 2002)

Hiebeler, Robert; Kelly, Thomas, B.; Ketteman, Charles (1998): *Best Practices: Building Your Business With Customer-Focused Solutions,* New York: Simon Schuster

Ingebretsen, Mark (2003): *Why Companies Fail: The 10 Big Reasons Businesses Crumble, and How to Keep Yours Strong and Solid,* New York: Crown Business

Jeannet, Jean-Pierre (2000): *Managing With A Global Mindset,* Great Britain: Pearson Education Limited

Jeffrey A Krames (2003): *What the best CEOs Know: 7 Exceptional Leaders and their Lessons for Transforming any Business.* McGraw-Hill Trade

Kennedy, C. (1992): ABB: Model Merger for the New Europe." Long Range Planning 25(5), 14

Kets de Vries, Manfried F.R. and Florent-Treacy, Elizabeth (1999): *The New Global Leaders*: *Richard Branson, Percy Barnevik and David Simon*, San Francisco, California: Jossey-Bass Inc.

Kramer, Marc (2000): *Small Business Turnaround: Revitalize Your Struggling or Stagnant Enterprise*, United States: Adams Media Corporation.

Krames, Jeffrey A. (2002): *The Jack Welch Lexicon of Leadership*, United States: McGraw-Hill Companies, Inc.

Kouzes, James M. (2003): *Business Leadership: A Jossey-Bass Reader*, San Francisco, California: John Wiley and Sons, Inc.

Kunde, Jesper (2000): *Corporate Religion*, Great Britain: Pearson Education Limited

Morgan, Gareth (1998*): Images of Organisation: Executive Edition,* San Franscisco: Berrett-Koehler Publishers, Inc

Obeng, Eddie (1998): *New Rules for the New World: Cautionary Tales for the New World Manager,* United Kingdom: Capstone Publishing Limited.

Pascale, Richard T.;Millemann, Mark and Gioja, Linda (2000), *Surfing the Edge of Chaos: The Laws of Nature and the New Laws of Business*, New York: Crown Business, Member of the Crown Publishing Group.

Page 285

Reichheld, Frederick F (1996): *The Loyalty Effect: The Hidden Force Behind Growth, Profits, and Lasting Value*, United States of America: Harvard Business School Press
.

Rich Karlgaard, Purpose Driven, Forbes Magazine Feb 9, 2004. 50 Tech is back www.forbes.com/karlgaard

Ries, Al (1996): Focus: *The Future of Your Company Depends on It*, New York: HarperCollins Publisher, Inc

Ross, Elisabeth Kubler (1997): On Death and Dying: What the Dying Have to Teach Doctors, Nurses, Clergy and Their Own Families. Scribner

Scott, C. Mark (2000), *Reinspiring the Corporation: The Seven Seminal Paths to Corporate Greatness,* England: John Wiley & Sons, Ltd.

Scott, Kelvin and Grand, Greg, AMR Research, (December 12, 2000): Failed Dot-Com Fell Victim to Their Own Lack of Focus, Outlook

Sherman, Andrew J. (2001): *Fast-track Business Growth: Smart Strategies to Grow Without Getting Derailed*, Washington, DC: The Kiplinger Washington Editors, Inc

Sobel, Andrew (2003): *Making Rain: The Secrets of Building Lifelong Client Loyalty*, Canada: John Wiley & Sons, Inc.

Stevenson, H. Howard (1998): Do Lunch or Be Lunch: The Power of Predictability in Creating Your Future, United States of America, Harvard Business School, Press

Stevenson, Howard H (1998*): Do Lunch Or Be Lunch*, United States of America: Harvard Business School Press

Street Wise by Michael Arndt (January 7, 2004), BusinessWeek online

Sutton, Gary (2002): *The Six-Month Fix: Adventures in Rescuing Failing Companies*, New York: John Wiley & Sons, Inc.

Sull, N. Donald (2003), *Revival of the Fittest: Why Good Companies Go Bad and How Great Managers Remake Them*, Massachusetts, United States: Harvard Business School Publishing.

Sull, Donald (2003): *Revival Of The Fittest: Why Good Companies Go Bad and How Great Managers Remake Them,* United States of America: Harvard Business School Press

Tan, Victor S.L.(2002): *Changing Your Corporate Culture: The Key to Surviving Tough Times,* Singapore: Times Books International.

Teng, Michael (2002): *Corporate Turnaround: Nursing a Sick Company back to Health,* Singapore: Prentice Hall

The Economist (January 1999): "After the Deal".

The Great Internet Money Game: How America's Top Financial Firms Reaped Billions from the Net Boom, While Investors Got Burned," by Peter Elstrom, Business Week (April 16, 2001): EB16

Trout, Jack (2000): *Differentiate or Die,* Canada: John Wiley & Sons, Inc

Trout, Jack (2000): *The Power of Simplicity,* United States, McGraw-Hill Education

Unlocking the Real Value of Marketing by PA Consulting with the Marketing Forum
and Cranfield School of Management

Wiersema, Fred (2001): *The New Market Leaders: Who's Winning and How in the Battle for Customers,* New York: The Free Press

Woodward, Bob (2003), *Bush at War,* United States: Simon & Schuster

Zoltners, Andris; Sinha, Prabhakant; Murphy, Stuart (1997): *The Fat Firm: The Transformation Of A Firm From Fat To Fit,* United States of America: McGraw-Hill

www.ingramcontent.com/pod-product-compliance
Lightning Source LLC
Chambersburg PA
CBHW070248200326
41518CB00010B/1738